Food in the Air and Space

The Food on the Go Series

as part of the Rowman & Littlefield Studies in Food and Gastronomy

General Editor: Ken Albala, Professor of History, University of the Pacific (kalbala@pacific.edu)

Rowman & Littlefield Executive Editor: Suzanne Staszak-Silva (sstaszak-silva@rowman.com)

The volumes in the Food on the Go series explore the fascinating ways people eat while getting from one place to another and the adaptations they make in terms of food choices, cutlery and even manners. Whether it be crossing the Atlantic in grand style on a luxury steamship, wedged into an airplane seat with a tiny tray, or driving in your car with a Big Mac in hand and soda in the cup holder, food has adapted in remarkable ways to accommodate our peripatetic habits. Eating on the go may be elegant or fast, but it differs significantly from everyday eating and these books explain why in various cultures across the globe and through history. This is the first series to systematically examine how and why mobility influences our eating habits, for better and worse.

Food on the Rails: The Golden Era of Railroad Dining, by Jeri Quinzio (2014)

Food at Sea: Shipboard Cuisine from Ancient to Modern Times, by Simon Spalding (2014)

Food in the Air and Space: The Surprising History of Food and Drink in the Skies, by Richard Foss (2014)

Food in the Air and Space

The Surprising History of
Food and Drink in the Skies

RICHARD FOSS

ROWMAN & LITTLEFIELD
Lanham • Boulder • New York • London

Published by Rowman & Littlefield
A wholly owned subsidiary of The Rowman & Littlefield Publishing Group, Inc.
4501 Forbes Boulevard, Suite 200, Lanham, Maryland 20706
www.rowman.com

Unit A, Whitacre Mews, 26-34 Stannary Street, London SE11 4AB

British Library Cataloguing in Publication Information Available

Library of Congress Cataloging-in-Publication Data

The hardback edition of this book was previously cataloged by the Library of Congress as follows:

Foss, Richard (Food historian)
  Food in the air and space : the surprising history of food and drink in the skies /
  Richard Foss.
    pages cm.
  Includes index.
  1. Food habits—History. 2. Drinking customs—History. 3. Flight—History. I. Title.
  GT2850.F69 2014
  394.1'209—dc23   2014025113

ISBN 978-1-4422-2728-6 (cloth : alk. paper)
ISBN 978-1-4422-7239-2 (pbk. : alk. paper)
ISBN 978-1-4422-2729-3 (electronic)

∞™ The paper used in this publication meets the minimum requirements of American National Standard for Information Sciences—Permanence of Paper for Printed Library Materials, ANSI/NISO Z39.48-1992.

Printed in the United States of America

Contents

Food on the Go,
Series Foreword

How familiar is the lament? "No one sits down to eat any more! People just grab something on the street or at the drive through. That's not a proper meal, it's just noshing on the way from one place to another." Food on the move is nothing new. There has always been street food and fast food. People have always eaten in transit. Our tendency to dismiss such meals as quick and convenient but never of any real gastronomic distinction does injustice to the wide variety of foods available to people traveling, and sometimes these meals could be quite elegant indeed. Think of the great caravans trekking across the steppes of Western Asia, parking their camels and setting up tents for a sumptuous feast of dried fruits, nuts, flatbreads, and freshly roasted kebabs. Or think of the great age of early air travel when airlines had their own specially designed dishware and served elegant, if seat-tray-sized, meals prepared by trained chefs. Meals served on trains in the nineteenth century were among the most celebrated of their day and of course luxury cruises pride themselves on fine dining as an indispensable feature of the entire experience. Food truck fare, offered to pedestrians, has now become the cutting edge in hip cuisine.

Traveling food need not be grand though. Sometimes it merely supplies sustenance—the hikers' trail mix or high protein pemmican to sustain the intrepid hunter on the great plains. It can also be pretty rough if we think of the wartime C-Rations or hard tack and rum given to sailors in the colonial era. It seems as if some modes of transport have their own repertoire of foods, without which the trip would not be complete. What's a road trip without chips and junk food? Is there anyone who doesn't miss the little packs of salty peanuts on domestic flights? Traveling food also poses its own unique set of challenges, both for food preparation and consumption. Imagine stoking a fire on a wooden ship! Or flipping an omelet while the train rumbles violently over the tracks. Handheld food, perhaps the way of the future, is the quintessential traveling format, but so too are special Styrofoam containers and sporks, not to mention the leather bota, aluminum canteen, or plastic water bottle. Traveling food has its own etiquette as well, looser than the dining table, but interestingly quite private, perhaps intentionally in considering the public setting.

When I first thought of this series, I don't think I had ever thought through how many foods are specially designed for travel, or how complex and very culturally bound food eaten on trains, planes, cars, bikes, horseback can be. I will never forget a long train ride I took from Rome to the Tyrolean Alps. A young family sat across from me and they were well stocked with goods. Out came a salami, a loaf of bread, a hunk of cheese, a bottle of wine. They were making a mess, gesticulating wildly, chattering in Italian. It all looked delicious, and they savored every morsel. By the time we approached the German-speaking region, they had neatened themselves up, tidied the area, switched languages, and every trace of their Italian repast was gone, and would have been completely unseemly, I think, that far north. That is, people do have explicit gastronomic traditions for travel that are as bound up with nationhood, class, gender, and self as any other eating habit. So it is about time we thought of these kinds of meals as a separate genre, and this series I hope will fill the gap in our understanding of why we eat what we do on the move.

Ken Albala
University of the Pacific

Acknowledgments

The long evolution of dining in the skies has received little scrutiny from historians; this is the first book to chart the worldwide development of skills, technologies, and organizations that took aerial dining to great heights before an obsession with cost cutting brought it low, and to show how many of the same elements were taken into the space age. It is a fascinating story, and collecting and assembling over a hundred years of data has only been possible with the assistance of many people. Some stories are untold despite my best efforts: the chronicles of airlines that went bankrupt long ago, that did not maintain their archives, or that simply refused to cooperate with any project that did not guarantee them a financial return. A few carriers may not have wanted to chart the decline of their service from prior standards, and one major catering service refused to answer any questions about the past or present logistics of their operation, citing national security. The deficit has been at least partly remedied by retired airline personnel who reminisced about the old days, collectors who saved old menus and other data from obscurity, and air museums that kept original or digital copies of fragile menus and other ephemera.

I am indebted to many people who searched through dusty archives at airlines and museums to find material that was used in this book. I do not have room for all of them, but wish to particularly thank Marie Force of the Delta Airlines museum in Atlanta, Bob DuBert and Bruce Kitt of the Northwest Airlines Museum, Jon Little of the Seattle Museum of Flight, Dra. Adelina Arezes of the TAP Museum in Portugal, historian Lennart

Andersson for information about Scandinavian airlines, Robin Cookson of the National Archives, Mike Lombardi and Tom Lubbesmeyer of the Boeing Corporation Archives, Julie Takata of the SFO Museum, Graham Simons for sharing information about early British airlines, Doug Miller of the Pan Am Historical Foundation, M. Kelly Cusack of Everything Pan Am, Misuzu Ohta of the Imperial Hotel in Tokyo, Chris Sloan of Airchive, Peter Elliott of the Royal Air Force Museum, Margaret O'Shaughnessy of the Foynes Flying Boat Museum, Thore Erik Winderen of the SAS Museum in Oslo, George Banks for permission to quote his book, Rob Mulder for permission to quote his book, Professor Gordon Pirie, Sandra Olson of the Waynoka Historical Society, Caroline Foster-Atkins of the Museum of Travel and Transport in Auckland, David Crotty of the Qantas Heritage Museum, Dan Grossman of airships.net for maintaining a magnificent site, Beth Schuster of Marriott for much assistance, Matthew Exline for help dating old images, and Polina Kurovskaya for help with Aeroflot's history.

Jane Levi provided invaluable help with information about the history of food in space; anyone who is interested in the subject should read her writings.

Most importantly, I would like to thank editor Ken Albala for getting me involved in this project in the first place, the long-suffering staff at Rowman & Littlefield for putting up with endless revisions and questions, Sharon Sheffield for assistance with proofreading, indexing, and points of style, and my beloved wife Jace for her comments, suggestions, critiques, and love.

There was much material that I found while researching this book that had to be cut due to space limitations, wouldn't reproduce well, or was in video form, so I created a website to display it. That material can be found at AirFoodHistory.com. You can also send questions and comments to me via the e-mail tab on that site.

Richard Foss
April 2014

INTRODUCTION

‒‒‒‒‿‿‿‿‒‒‒‒

The First Toast

On the morning of December 1, 1783, the weather in Paris was sunny and fair, with a light breeze from the east. A giant crowd stared in fascination at a strange contraption—a hydrogen balloon with a wicker basket beneath it. The upper classes watched from the gardens of the Tuileries Palace, while the king, his courtiers, and guests such as Benjamin Franklin enjoyed better views from the upper floors, and the lower classes thronged nearby rooftops.

A hot air balloon designed by brothers Joseph-Michel and Jacques-Etienne Montgolfier had made the first manned balloon ascent a week before, but the need to have the brazier under the center of the balloon meant that in order to balance the craft, the scientist and the aristocrat who were the first passengers had to stand at opposite sides of the gondola. They were unable to see each other except through a porthole and had to communicate by shouting. The use of hydrogen on this second flight allowed the pilots to share a space where they could consult the scientific instruments they had brought, and write in their journals about the view. They were able to share natural conversations, and more to the point of this book, a beverage.

Just before the ropes that held the balloon were released, physicist Jacques Charles handed an empty glass to his fellow aeronaut, Nicholas-Louis Robert. At the moment that the balloon was set free, Charles theatrically popped the cork on a bottle of Champagne, filled both glasses, and toasted the crowd. It was the world's first inflight beverage, and it celebrated a journey that would last two and a half hours but cover only thirty-six kilometers.

A contemporary engraving of the first hydrogen balloon flight in 1783. It's hard to tell from this image, but they are drinking Champagne up there.
Image courtesy of Victoria & Albert Museum

That Champagne toast set a precedent that continues to this day—it was the first of millions of corks to be popped as balloons ascend. That flight was brief, but to Frenchmen of that era it was inconceivable that it not be celebrated with sparkling wine. Later flights would be longer and require sustenance for more than ceremonial reasons, as long-distance records were set and flights of several days became commonplace. Balloons drifted across Europe and vast expanses of America, and one doomed expedition even tried to use one to reach the North Pole.

Once motive power was added to the mix and long trips aboard dirigibles and zeppelins became possible, questions of how meals might be served aloft became more urgent. Technologies were developed for cooking safely in an enclosed cabin, lightweight dinnerware and utensils were invented, and infrastructure was created to deal with the unique logistics of the situation. All of these would be put to more extensive use in the era of heavier-than-air craft, and it is no great extension to see the leap to space as a continuous development of those technologies.

This book will examine food in the air in times of war and peace, including some promotional ideas that were brilliant and others that were almost unparalleled for silliness. It will cover the era when zeppelins loaded provisions from gourmet restaurants, when stewards in flying boats cooked steaks in cramped cabins, and when food scientists worked to bring the taste of home to astronauts and cosmonauts who would dine in zero gravity. It's a long and fascinating story, and it all started with a bag of gas, two brave men, and a cork that flew from the sky to the earth.

CHAPTER 1

〜〜〜〜〜〜

The Forerunners
Lessons from the Balloon Era

The first people to fly were not doing so for transportation—they were aristocrats, thrill-seekers, and scientists whose sole commonality was that they were from the upper classes. They dressed for flights as they might for an afternoon of riding or walking on their estates, and expected to dine as well aloft as they did at a picnic on the ground. In the early days this sometimes had comical results; when the Italian adventurer Vincenzo Lunardi took off for the first balloon flight in England in 1785, he brought with him cold chicken, wine, and a selection of salads and cheeses. He also, for reasons that have never been explained, brought a cat. Unfortunately his cargo had not been well packed, and the sand that was brought for ballast got mixed with the food. He managed to rescue a leg from the chicken, gave the rest of the bird to the cat, and drank several glasses of wine. Thus sated, he sailed for an hour and a half until he noticed that the cat appeared uncomfortably cold, so he went to a very low altitude to toss the cat to the ground, where it landed safely. He also tossed the corkscrew and empty wine bottle, the sand ballast and spoiled food, and the full set of dinnerware he had brought to eat his lunch, then floated away for another serene half-hour of watching the countryside.

On Lunardi's next flight he had booked passengers Colonel George Biggin and Mrs. Letitia Sage, but the balloon turned out not to have enough lifting power for everyone. Faced with the embarrassment of denying his important guests a space, Lunardi let the passengers go without him after giving them brief instructions on how to ascend and descend. Colonel Biggin and Mrs. Sage dined on chicken, ham, and several bottles of Florence wine, throwing

1

the empty bottles over the side without looking to see whether they might injure those below. History has not recorded whether anybody was hurt by these missiles from above, but one gets the distinct impression that the aeronauts didn't care either way.[1]

This was an era of gentlemen-adventurers who dabbled in advancing the frontiers of knowledge. The earliest balloon flights were flown by a mix of daredevils and scientists, and manned flight retained that demographic for some time. Standards needed to be maintained, and even high-altitude research flights were lavishly provisioned. The desire for familiar luxuries eventually led to the first device ever invented to facilitate creating hot meals in an aerial environment.

In 1835, inventor William Maugham demonstrated a remarkable item to an audience at the London Gallery of Science: a method of heating food without open flame. As the *Literary Gazette* reported in their January edition,

> The most novel matter was a lecture by Mr. Maugham, on an apparatus for cooking without fire. The experiment was shewn with a tin box, in the centre of which was a drawer, where beefsteaks and eggs were deposited. In the compartments, above and below, lime was placed, and slaked with water. The usual process took place, heat was disengaged, and the victuals were perfectly dressed, without receiving any peculiar flavour or taste from the means employed. . . . The operation took about half an hour.

Quicklime, otherwise known as calcium oxide, produces heat by a chemical reaction when combined with water, a fact known for centuries. Anglo-Norman travelers developed a method of cooking in clay pots while on religious pilgrimages as early as the 1200s,[2] but the idea seemed to be forgotten until Maugham displayed his apparatus. While not without risk because calcium oxide can explode if not correctly handled, the ability to generate heat without flame was the obvious answer to the problem of cooking directly beneath a highly explosive hydrogen balloon.

The first recorded usage of a quicklime stove in flight was the next year, when the balloon Royal Vauxhall set sail on September 9, 1836. Captained by Charles Green, the gigantic balloon set records both for nonstop flying and for quality of food aboard when it set off from southeast London and floated across the English Channel. The balloon traveled overnight, and at dinner that evening there were many puns about the high flavor of the food. Nine people dined on forty pounds of ham, beef, and tongue; forty-five pounds of fowls and preserves; forty pounds of sugar, bread, and biscuits; and two gallons each of sherry, port, and brandy. They also had hot coffee, thanks to a quicklime coffeemaker developed just for the purpose.

Popping a Champagne cork on launching a balloon was such a tradition by 1885 that this ginger ale company tried to suggest that their beverage would work just as well. Image from Library of Congress, public domain

Unfortunately this pioneering invention is not in any museum—as the balloon passed over Belgium in the middle of the night, Captain Green accidentally dropped the coffeemaker overboard. (Perhaps he had been indulging in the brandy.) Since the loss of the coffeemaker meant they wouldn't need the volatile quicklime any more, he tossed that overboard too. He did attach it to a parachute for the consideration of those below. One wonders what might have happened to this—quicklime can be an explosive if suddenly put in contact with water, and this canister was dropped in the dark and could easily have landed in a lake or river. Any sadness at the loss of coffeemaker and fuel was forgotten the next morning; they landed in Weilburg, Germany, having covered 480 miles in eighteen hours.[3]

The limitations of balloons as passenger craft were obvious, since they could not be steered in any meaningful way, but they continued to be used for both pleasure flights and scientific research. The Swedish explorer S. A. Andree took advantage of modern food storage techniques for his ill-fated attempt to reach the North Pole by balloon, taking with him canned pemmican, sausages, hams, and condensed milk. They also brought cases of Champagne, port, and beer, and their food and beverage weighed 767 kilos in all (1,690 pounds), enough for three people to last through the winter if necessary. The balloon launched from the Swedish island of Svalbard in July 1897 for a trip projected to last thirty days; it crashed on an ice floe on the third day. Most of the canned food was abandoned at the crash site, but the trio of explorers took some with them on sleds as they headed south in an attempt to get to a place where they could be rescued. They still had plenty of food left when they died, and many unopened cans were found with their bodies over thirty years later on the island of Kvitoya. It has been suggested that the lead with which the cans were soldered could have contributed to their death by poisoning, but a more probable explanation is that they died from eating contaminated meat from the polar bears they were shooting to extend their food supply.

Andree's expedition was the last attempt to use unpowered balloons for serious exploration, but ballooning continued to be a popular pastime among the wealthy. Among those who developed a passion for aerial excursions was an eccentric Brazilian millionaire who was destined to prove the utility of powered flight. When he made his first flight in 1897, Alberto Santos-Dumont enjoyed a lunch of roast beef, chicken, ice cream, cakes, Champagne, and Chartreuse. On his return he amused aristocrats at the Jockey Club by saying "No other dining room is so well decorated."

Santos-Dumont made many more balloon journeys and became obsessed with creating a steerable craft, called a dirigible balloon after the French word for "directable." He achieved that goal in 1901 with a craft known only as "Number 6" that was thirty-three meters long and carried only the inventor himself. The airship covered eleven kilometers within thirty minutes on a course that used the Eiffel Tower as a pylon, winning fifty thousand francs in the process. The inventor won the hearts of Parisians by dividing the reward money between his ground crew and the poor of Paris, then lost interest in lighter-than-air craft and devoted the rest of his career to inventing an airplane.

Santos-Dumont did not seriously consider the possibility of expanding his airship design to transport passengers, but the person who would was already testing his designs at a lake in the Alps. Count Ferdinand von Zeppelin would take Dumont's interesting toy and make it a reliable form of long-distance transportation, creating the need for food service vastly more sophisticated than anything previously attempted.

CHAPTER 2

〰〰〜〰〰

Luxury in the Skies

The Zeppelin Era

Count Ferdinand von Zeppelin was that rarity, an innovative inventor who was also a shrewd businessman. Alberto Santos-Dumont designed seven airships but apparently never considered the idea of carrying passengers. Zeppelin's earliest designs were for commercial craft, including an aerial version of a train complete with linked freight cars. This entrepreneurial attitude is more surprising because the Count had a military rather than business background. Though he had been involved in the engineering corps of the Prussian army, he finished his career as a general commanding a regiment of cavalry. By most accounts he was inept as a commander of horsemen, but he proved superb at assembling a team of engineers and raising interest and money to build airships.

Zeppelin's first design, the LZ-1, was described in detail in the *International Year Book* of 1901, which noted that the 420-foot-long gasbag "corresponds with a fair-sized steamer. . . . The accommodations for crew and passengers are provided by two aluminum cars, suspended fore and aft below the body of the shell." After noting that the airship had taken off, maneuvered accurately, and landed "with perfect safety," the article concluded that

> there are many high authorities in aerostatics who look upon mechanical flight as the future of navigating in the air, if it is ever navigated successfully in any such sense as water is now navigated. Contrivances of this sort are altogether too unwieldy and offer too much surface to the attack of the wind to be practicable for navigating the air except under the most favorable conditions.[1]

Only nine years after that was written, Zeppelin's airships were offering scheduled sightseeing flights from their base at Friedrichshafen, with the first long-distance transportation test flights following shortly afterward. The twenty passengers in the zeppelins Schwaben and Viktoria Luise dined in a mahogany cabin inlaid with mother-of-pearl, with a steward serving meals and pouring Champagne. The gourmet delicacies they enjoyed in flight were catered by restaurants and loaded immediately before departure, and they were served in classic style at tables with white linen and china. Hot coffee and tea were available despite the lack of onboard heaters thanks to the thermos bottles that had recently become available, so passengers in the unheated cabins could enjoy a warming cup on cold mornings.

The company that ran these sightseeing flights, called DELAG, has been called the first airline, and they did make the first international passenger flight in 1912. That trip from Hamburg to Copenhagen was made with Count von Zeppelin at the controls, and the 375-mile round-trip took just under twelve hours. The Count and his twelve passengers welcomed Danish officials aboard to dine on turtle bouillon, lamb chops a la Jardinière, bread, cheese, butter, red wine, Champagne, and sherry.[2] The feat was covered by newspapers as far away as the Sydney Morning Herald, which noted that the zeppelin had "inspected the British squadron which is on a visit here before alighting at the airdrome" and mentioned that journalists "remarked on the ease with which it could fly to England."[3]

If any officers in that British fleet felt uneasy about the giant airship hovering above them and found the ease of flights to England ominous, they might have been reassured by a response from the British Army's fledgling Royal Air Force. A day after the flight, the Press Association reported that "aeroplanists at Hendon state that the Hansa's flight was merely spectacular, and that a single aeroplane was able to destroy several zeppelins."[4]

As a former military man, Count von Zeppelin certainly understood the potential of airpower in warfare, and he courted business from the German military at the same time as he worked to increase passenger traffic. The improved design of the Sachsen, which operated scheduled flights between Baden-Baden and Vienna in eight hours beginning in 1913, inspired other companies to compete with DELAG, and money was raised to build several competing airships. By the time any of these were complete, Germany was at war and civilian traffic ceased. When World War I began in July 1914, the German military had already taken delivery of ten zeppelins, and the ones under construction and already in civilian use were requisitioned.

As the journalists had suggested, zeppelins could indeed reach England, and as the RAF strategists suggested, they could be destroyed by aircraft.

Neither the navigation from Germany to often-foggy England nor shooting down of the zeppelins that made the journey was as easy as had been predicted, and the armed zeppelins bombed London, hampered minelaying operations, and performed reconnaissance duties for the German army and navy.[5] A total of 103 airships were delivered to the German military, and though dozens were shot down in all theaters of war, they demonstrated their effective range even when dodging enemies, and ranged as far as Malta, Greece, and Norway. One zeppelin headed for Africa to resupply troops there set a distance record, traveling 4,225 miles in 95 hours—a distance greater than that from Berlin to New York.

The crews of those military zeppelins did not enjoy the standard of food that civilians had experienced, but in the early part of the war they ate well. A crewman on the L-22 named August Seim reminisced after the war that on his ship the crew ate much better than the soldiers in the trenches below, dining on

> sausages, good butter, thermos flasks containing an extra strong brew of coffee, plenty of bread and chocolate, and fifty grammes of rum or brandy per man. We were forbidden to open the alcohol flasks until we reached a height of 3,000 metres, but of course we often did so. Then if the ship never went above 3,000 metres for the whole voyage there was trouble ahead, for when we were in port again the commander made us hand over full flasks. Thank heavens he never tasted the contents, which were mostly water.[6]

The quicklime heaters used in the ballooning age made another appearance, as Seim mentioned that

> We had several peculiar and very practical kinds of tinned foods, which might be described as chemical and gastronomical miracles. These were tins containing hashes and stews which were heated up by a certain chemical process as soon as you opened them. We were not allowed to cook anything on board on account of the danger from inflammable gas, and for the same reason I was forbidden to fire my machine gun on the platform just when and where I pleased.

This standard apparently declined over the course of the war, and when British soldiers examined the wreckage of the L-32 which crashed near Great Burstead in Essex in September of 1916, they found that the crew had breakfasted on "greasy war bread, bacon and delicately sliced potatoes."[7]

Count von Zeppelin died in 1917, having spent much of the war working on plans for a commercial fleet to be built when peace was restored. The improvements in engine technology and airship design almost doubled the top speed of the airships, from forty-six to eighty-seven miles per hour, and they became much more reliable. When peace was finally at hand, the Zeppelin Company was ready to supply the world with fast, reliable airships.

The first of the improved designs was named the Bodensee and flew for the first time on August 20, 1919. It could carry twenty-four passengers in a luxurious saloon, and unlike every airship previously built, there was a kitchen for creating inflight meals. It wasn't particularly fancy, a single oven with two compartments and a stovetop with two electric heaters, but it was the world's first all-electric kitchen using all-aluminum utensils. Electric stoves had been invented in 1896 and proved their value in wartime submarines, another environment where open flame could not be used.[8] Since the electric thermostat had just been invented and was not yet commercially available, heat control was approximate—there were several electric heating elements, and the cook switched on as many as he judged necessary. The expensive and hard-to-shape aluminum utensils were used not only because they were lighter, but from fear of sparks that might be struck from iron pans with thousands of cubic feet of flammable hydrogen directly overhead.

The Bodensee began commercial service between Berlin and Friedrichshafen, a distance of about 375 miles, with the intention of extending the route to Switzerland, Italy, and Spain in the south and Sweden in the north. Between August and December 1919 the Bodensee made eighty trips, having to cancel only three scheduled flights due to heavy winds. In 1919 a sister ship called the Nordstern was built, and several more were on the drawing boards. They were not to be built, at least not immediately, because the treaty that ended the First World War forbade further production of any craft that might have the slightest military value. Production ceased, and existing zeppelins were confiscated and turned over to Russia, England, and France, all of which used them exclusively for military purposes. The Zeppelin Company was reduced to making replacement parts for their existing stock, and to projects building industrial motors, cars, and other machinery.

Though British, Italian, and American companies had been formed to build airships using the plans from captured zeppelins, they had no experience in the business. Harry Vissering, who was the chairman of the Goodyear Company and an enthusiast of lighter-than-air flight, lamented in 1920 that the most competent company in the business had been shut down.

The Zeppelin organization today is prepared to build, deliver and operate rigid airships for any purpose. It has under contract virtually all the competent airship personnel in Germany. Practically all the engineering staffs and workmen employed in developing Zeppelins have been retained, one way or another, that they may be prepared to guarantee satisfactory performance of any Zeppelin turned out.[9]

The sorry performance of the Zeppelin Company's competitors is well known, and the inexperience of the French and British crews who took over existing zeppelins doomed most of them to early destruction. Only Russia succeeded in building and operating a fleet of rigid airships, which they used until at least 1942. Though no detailed records of these flights have survived, we might surmise that the food and accommodations were spartan compared to the glamorous zeppelins.

So there was a great deal of pent-up demand when the Treaty of Locarno in 1925 loosened the restrictions on German industries, and the Zeppelin Company was ready for the challenge. The airship that became the marvel of the world, the Graf Zeppelin, was launched in 1928 and set new standards for luxury. Twenty-four passengers could fly the Atlantic in comfort in a craft that boasted showers, a lounge and dining room, and a full-time chef and steward. A *New York Times* article about preparations for the flight noted that along with attention to the quality of the meal, weight was a factor.

> In order not to overload the dirigible and yet serve the passengers adequate meals, it was decided after careful calculation to allow seven and a half pounds of victuals per capita daily, including food and drink, with an additional meal for the night watch. Breakfast between 8:30 and 9:30 will consist of coffee, tea, bread, butter, eggs or sausage. For dinner, from 1 to 2 P.M., there will be soup, vegetables, roast, compote, or dessert, and for supper, from 7:30 to 8:30 P.M., coffee, tea, cold meats, bread and butter. The passengers are privileged to order drinks between meals. The drinking water is shipped in the form of ice which is chopped off and melted as it is needed.[10]

An incident aboard the Graf Zeppelin in 1928 shows one of the problems with dining aboard early airships—the vast amount of surface area to catch the turbulent winds over the Atlantic. The passengers were just finishing breakfast when a sudden gust buffeted the ship, and famed British journalist Lady Margaret Drummond-Hay was covered with coffee that fortunately had been poured some time before and was no longer scalding. Luckily she and the other journalists on the flight found the mishap amusing. A redesign of the control surfaces of the airship and a change in the shape of the hull reduced the wind resistance, and the final generation of airships was much more stable.

In an article published in the *Milwaukee Sentinel* on October 6, 1928, Lady Drummond-Hay noted that despite the elegance of the surroundings, there was a drawback to zeppelin travel—the lack of heating. "We had fostered visions of course dinners, with snowy napery and gleaming silver . . . , but it is very certain that if the Graf Zeppelin pursues the northern course, leather coats, woollies, and furs will be our evening dress. Hot soup and steaming stew will be more welcome than cold caviar and chicken salad. There are sure to be quantities of German sausages, ham, dark bread and butter, cheese and eggs, with good Rhine wine."

In 1929 the Graf Zeppelin embarked on a voyage that was designed to show off the luxury and comfort of flight. Hugo Eckener, who headed the Zeppelin Company after the founder's death, invited influential industrialists and party bosses on a flight from Friedrichshafen to Egypt. The embarkation was at midnight on March 21, the first day of spring after a winter that was the coldest in many years, and the passengers were impressed that they were able to shed their winter coats as the ship neared the Mediterranean. As Hugo Eckener recorded it later, after flying over the Straits of Messina at sunset, the passengers "seated themselves around the candle's friendly flame at the attractively decorated tables. We had turtle soup, ham with asparagus, roast beef with vegetables and salad, celery with Roquefort cheese, and an excellent nut cake from Friedrichshafen, together with wine in abundance."[11] The reference to gathering around the candle's friendly flame is remarkable, as it is the only instance I have been able to find to a deliberate open flame aboard a hydrogen-filled zeppelin. If it helped set the mood, it was worth the risk, because after an aerial cruise that included sightseeing over Jerusalem, Athens, and Vienna and a return to icy German weather through the Alps, the politicians and industrialists were sold on the idea of contributing money toward the construction of an even more spectacular craft: a craft bearing the designation LZ-129, to be called the Hindenburg.

While that great ocean liner of the skies was under construction, the Graf Zeppelin continued commercial service and was an effective ambassador for German industry and culture. The chef aboard the craft, Otto Manz, also intended it to showcase Germany's cuisine, and in an article published in the New York Times in August of 1929, he called attention to the storage methods for his food.

Manz proudly showed his commissary department to visitors. Large, small and middle-size cans lined the rooms of his shop and house. Into them all sorts of delicacies have been placed and hermetically sealed, then labeled by his sister. The Zeppelin chef is greatly chagrinned because newspapers say only canned goods are eaten aboard the dirigible. "Naturally people think only of canned meats and vegetables from factories," said Manz. "As a matter of fact every-thing is fresh and is being put into cans now because of course, the food would not keep throughout the voyage unless hermetically sealed. I do all my own canning and my sisters affix the labels. My father was purveyor to the King of Wurttemberg, so we are used to supplying only the best."[12]

Both his culinary skills and those of local chefs were shown during the famous round-the-world flight in which passengers traveled in unparalleled luxury, as meals were catered and supplies boarded at the finest hotels along the way. The luncheon loaded aboard on the fourth day was supplied by the chefs at the Sherry-Netherland Hotel in New York and was unusually multi-cultural; it included Indian Mulligatawny soup along with Veal Bourgeoise,

THE GRAF ZEPPELIN
OVER TOKYO
THE IMPERIAL HOTEL.

The only thing Japanese about this menu for the Graf Zeppelin's flight to Tokyo was the cover, which mimics the classic eighteenth-century ukiyo-e graphic style used in traditional woodblock prints.

a recipe dating from Mrs. Beeton's English cookbook of 1861. (There were also canapés, fresh vegetables, and fruit compote.) When the zeppelin visited Japan, the dinner catered by the Imperial Hotel in Tokyo included anchovy fillets, pâte de foie gras, dill pickles, beef tea, asparagus tips vinaigrette, and a sand cake. The only item to be in any way identified with Japan, a "cold Kamakura ham with jelly," was not remotely Japanese, and it seems that the whole meal was designed to show that the Japanese could cater to European diners without compromise.

In the course of its round-the-world flight, the Graf Zeppelin inspired songs in Trinidad and Tennessee,[13] started a craze for zeppelin-themed toys, and had at least one food named after it. Contrary to some reports, the *zeppole*, a deep-fried filled doughnut, was not. Though the name is similar, the pastry was invented in the middle ages, though it became more popular when the giants of the air started flying. The airship-themed food is from much further north; in Lithuania fat potato flour dumplings stuffed with meat came to be called *cepelinai* (singular is *cepelinas*). The dumplings are often served with cream sauce and bacon and are also popular in northeastern Poland. They are time-consuming to make and are regarded as a special-occasion dish. It certainly makes sense that a food named after zeppelins was a luxury item, because that was the signature of the travel experience aboard.

Another culinary reference to zeppelins is less glamorous—the book *Soldier and Sailor Words*, published in 1925, lists "zeppelin in a cloud" as slang for a sausage covered in mashed potatoes. Similarly, Margery Allingham's novel *Look to Lady* has a passage in which a host proclaims "I'll bring yer a spot o' coffee and a couple o' Zepps in a smoke screen."

There were no food items and little glamour associated with the airship operations of other nations and companies. It is worth noting just how far behind other nations were in airship technology, particularly with regard to passenger comfort. America's navy embarked on an ambitious construction program that seemed successful at first. In 1924, the USS Shenandoah traveled nine thousand miles from New Jersey to San Diego and back. The sole member of the culinary staff was a Filipino messboy who made sandwiches and served hot soup. That journey was the high point of American airship flights—a year later, the ship was torn to pieces by high winds. Two other airships, the Akron and Macon, suffered the same fate within a year of their launch, and as a result the program was canceled.

Italian explorer Umberto Nobile had a vision of piloting an airship to the North Pole. Errors by his crew resulted in the loss of the ship in a crash, but he decided to build a bigger and better airship. The Norge reached its goal in 1926 and eventually made a forced landing in Alaska, where it was

LZ

SIXTH DAY

DINNER

❦

Fillet of Anchovies,   Pate de foie gras,   Dill Pickles

Beef Tea
———o———
Cold "Kamakura" Ham with Jelly
———o———
Asparagus Tips Vinaigrette
———o———
Cheese and Crackers
———o———
Sand Cake
———o———
Coffee

Imperial Hotel

TOKYO

AUGUST 1929

Image provided by Imperial Hotel, Tokyo

destroyed. It was not a comfortable trip; despite the fact that the ship was built for an Arctic expedition, there were no facilities for heating food. The crew had hot coffee and soup in thermos bottles, but after these ran out the rest of their food was cold. The trip from Svalbard Island to Alaska took three days, and the crew in the unheated ship with cold food was cranky and irritable.

The British were Zeppelin's sole competitors when it came to passenger airships, and they did manage to turn out one magnificent and airworthy craft, the R-100. That ship could carry one hundred passengers on three decks and had a well-appointed galley, and it had the largest passenger capacity and most spacious quarters ever provided in an airship. In 1929 a journalist for *Flight Magazine* who had taken a ride wrote that "there was nothing to suggest that we were in an aircraft and actually in the air. We might have been in some well-appointed restaurant." His only complaint was that "some passengers may find that in the saloon of the R-100 there is too much of a smell of cooking before and after meals."[14]

The *Los Angeles Times* published an article about the R-100's flight from London to Toronto that was lyrical when it came to the dining experience.

> The British dirigible R-100 tonight is sailing over the tossing Atlantic. . . . Those aboard are enjoying the flight. When the breakfast of ham and eggs with coffee was served this morning, quite in hotel fashion, hardly a movement of the ship could be felt. . . . As darkness fell tonight the electric lights were switched on and a bell summoned the hungry passengers to dinner. Plates of hot soup awaited them in the dining room. . . . The printed menu cards, the glittering silverware and spotless linen made the scene resemble Piccadilly or Fifth Avenue rather than mid-Atlantic.[15]

The R-100 might have been a serious competitor for the Zeppelin Company, but in 1929 the spectacular crash of another British airship, the R-101, soured the government on commercial lighter-than-air travel. After one round-trip to Canada in 1931, the R-100 was grounded for political reasons and never flew again. Britain had the technical skills to build an airship, but not the commercial acumen to fly one profitably. In contrast the Zeppelin Company was a viable commercial concern.

Though aircraft were becoming more reliable by 1930 and could travel much faster than airships, they were seen as too uncomfortable to compete for luxury passenger traffic. In an editorial in *Flight Magazine* on September 26, 1930, Stanley Spooner stated,

Most travelers still prefer a fortnight in a P&O steamer to a week in an aeroplane, even though the aeroplane lands for meals and for the night. It may well be in the future most passengers will prefer traveling in a 70 or even 60 mile an hour airship to remaining day and night in a 100 or 90 mile an hour aeroplane. It is technically impossible to provide ample comfort in an aeroplane without an extravagant loss of payload per horsepower.

Airships were seen as the equivalent of ocean liners of the air, and the designers of the R-100 and the zeppelins did their best to deliver on that promise. The Hindenburg (official registration number LZ-129) carried a team of fifteen cooks and servers under the watchful eye of Heinrich Kubis, who had begun his career aboard Zeppelin airships as the first steward aboard the Schwaben in 1912. Passengers dined in a bright modern room adorned with murals painted on each panel of the cream-colored walls, seated on aluminum-framed chairs that were light but comfortable.

Douglas Robinson, in his book about the Hindenburg, described the dining room and service in detail:

The dining room aboard the Graf Zeppelin could be mistaken for any fine restaurant of the era. Steward Heinrich Kubis, the first professional to serve food in flight, is on the right in the dark jacket. Historic photo used by permission from Airships.net

To port, occupying an area measuring 15 x 50 feet, was the dining room. Here, with all the luxury and refinement of a small restaurant, were seats for 34 passengers—at four small tables for 2 persons along the inboard wall, and at six larger tables outboard. The tables—and chairs likewise—were of a special lightweight tubular aluminum design—'as light as possible, as stable as possible'—created for the "Hindenburg" by Professor Breuhaus. . . . the colorful paintings in the dining room represented "Graf Zeppelin" on a South American journey. . . . Meals in these surroundings were an unforgettable experience. Passengers were assigned seats by the chief steward. . . . The tables were laid with white linen napkins and tablecloths, fresh-cut flowers, fine silver, and the special china service created for the "Hindenburg." . . . the chief steward and three waiters served meals prepared in German style. Breakfast appears to have been a standard affair of rolls freshly baked in the ship's ovens, with butter, preserves or honey; eggs (served boiled in the shell for German passengers, fried or poached for Americans); Frankfurt sausage, ham, salami, cheese, fruit, coffee, tea, milk or cocoa. On Monday, August 17, 1936, "Hindenburg's" passengers ate for luncheon: Strong Broth Theodor, Fattened Duckling, Bavarian Style with Champagne Cabbage, Savory Potatoes and Madiera (sic) Gravy, Pears Convent Style, Mocha. For dinner there was: Cream Soup Hamilton, Grilled Sole With Parsley Butter, Venison Cutlets Beauval with Berny Potatoes, Mushrooms and Cream Sauce, Mixed Cheese Plate. All this was served with tall bottles of Rhine and Moselle wines . . . as well as a few French red wines and an assortment of German champagnes . . . (some 250 bottles of wine were carried on each crossing).[16]

The Hindenburg made its first flight in March 1936, carrying fifty passengers in lavish comfort to Rio de Janeiro. On that first transatlantic commercial flight, there was at least an attempt to reflect the destination in the cuisine. Morning poached eggs on toast were served with "Sauce Brasilienne," probably a mix of peppers, rum, vinegar, and parsley. In case that was too exotic, passengers could also request porridge a la crème, coffee, fruits, and butter (presumably bread too, unless the butter was for the porridge). After meals, passengers could adjourn to the bar, where bartender Max Schulze served LZ-129 cocktails of gin and orange juice and a cocktail called the Maybach 12 after the zeppelin's engines. (The recipe, alas, is unknown.) The trip from Germany to Brazil was completed in four days, a vast savings in time compared to the fastest ship, and passengers remarked wistfully that they wished it had taken longer.

The Hindenburg made a round-trip from Germany to Lakehurst, New Jersey, in early 1936 that was very well documented since most of the passengers were journalists. United Press International journalist Webb Miller mentioned in his report that the dining room was forty-six feet long and had two tables seating twenty-five people. He also mentioned that at breakfast "the tables bore vases of fresh flowers and exquisite blue and white china."[17]

After meals passengers could adjourn to a salon to enjoy music from the world's first aluminum piano and sip wine from one of the 250 bottles carried aboard. The piano was removed after the second flight so that more cabins could be added, bringing the airship's capacity up to seventy-two people.

The stability of the giant ship compared to all that had gone before was remarkable, and journalist Miller remarked that even as the airship flew through a severe storm in the Atlantic, the vases of carnations and sweet peas on his dining table did not fall over. Diners' comfort was explicitly referenced in standing instructions to the pilots to never let the ship's inclination exceed five degrees, since wine would spill at ten.[18] It was an order that no officer aboard the zeppelin's competitors, the luxury cruise ships, could ever give.

The Hindenburg made seventeen commercial round-trips between Germany and the Americas in 1936, alternating between New Jersey and Brazil. She carried 2,798 passengers and transported 160 tons of freight and mail, and became the global standard for luxury and speed. In the popular 1937 film *Charlie Chan at the Olympics*, a criminal takes a fast steamship to Europe, but the Chinese detective and a pair of witnesses beat him there by taking the Hindenburg. The film was released on May 21, 1937—two weeks after the Hindenburg met a fiery end in Lakehurst, New Jersey. The investigating team that looked into the disaster did not have the freedom to investigate crimes that was granted to the fictional detective. They were told specifically not to consider sabotage as a possibility, so the true reason will never be known.

Even this disaster did not eliminate the demand for zeppelin flights, and a sister ship, the Graf Zeppelin II, flew for the first time in 1938. Though it made thirty flights, none carried paying passengers; the Nazis had always had a hostile relationship with the Zeppelin Company, especially after the company's director Dr. Eckener announced his intention to run against Hitler in the next election, and the government responded by nationalizing the airship. In an ironic twist, the great airship named after the pioneer of commercial flight was used only for propaganda and espionage. In April 1940, with World War II already in progress, Hermann Goering ordered the airship scrapped and the metal used to build warplanes. The era of airship travel was over, and it would be decades before anything resembling luxurious food was served aloft again.

CHAPTER 3

≈≈≈⋙⋘≈≈≈

The Early Days of
the Airplane Age
(1920–1930)

Unlike the hydrogen balloon or zeppelin, it isn't easy to pinpoint the first meal eaten or served aboard an aircraft. It's hard to imagine what food might have tempted even a starving man in an open-cockpit aircraft, enveloped in the stink of exhaust and lubricating oil and concentrating on keeping a fragile wood and canvas machine aloft. Inflight refreshment before World War I was probably limited to sips of water from a canteen, if even that was available.

The war spurred aircraft development, and by the end of the conflict the Germans, Russians, British, and Italians were all operating multiengine aircraft with closed cabins. The British built more of these than anyone else, and the Royal Flying Corps, predecessor of the RAF, set a global standard for reliable long-distance operations. Huge bombers like the Handley-Page O-series aircraft had a one-hundred-foot wingspan, a crew of five, and could stay in the air for eight hours. In the course of flights of up to seven hundred miles the crew drank soup or tea from thermos bottles and ate military rations that had been packed in wicker hampers.[1] These were probably the first full meals eaten in a fixed-wing aircraft, but history does not record what was supplied or where it came from. Details of these missions were classified at the time, and the British public learned very little about these aircraft beyond the mere fact of their existence before one of the big bombers fell intact into German hands after a forced landing.

The war was nearly over when the Royal Air Corps first flew the Handley-Page V/1500, a twin-engine biplane behemoth that carried a crew of up to nine and could stay aloft for seventeen hours. That was intended to allow a round-trip from England to Berlin with up to two thousand pounds of bombs going only one way. The first sortie by three aircraft was actually taxiing down the runway when word arrived that an armistice had been signed. Only two months later, one of the aircraft that had been in that aborted bombing run made the first flight from England to India, covering almost five thousand miles with only four stops. Others had already been converted to passenger service and carried as many as forty passengers for flights between Croydon, near London, and Paris. The French Compagnie des Grands Express Aériens began scheduled service between Paris and London's Croydon airfield in 1920, using fourteen-passenger Farman Goliaths. The flight typically took just over two hours.

At the end of the war the British had both the largest fleet of multiengine transport aircraft and the most experienced aircrew; the only large American aircraft manufacturer, the Curtiss-Wright Corporation, built fighter aircraft and small seaplanes, but had never designed an aircraft that would carry more than three people. The Wright Brothers had suppressed domestic competition by aggressive lawsuits to protect their very broad patents, so Curtiss-Wright had no serious competition until 1917 when a court ruled the patents invalid.

The lack of appropriate aircraft and trained pilots stunted the growth of airlines in the United States, and those that did come into existence were mostly air taxis that crossed narrow bodies of water to provide an alternative to ferryboats. An example was America's first successful airline, Chalk's International Airline, founded in 1919. Despite the grand name, they only flew one route, the fifty-three miles from Fort Lauderdale to Bimini, The Bahamas, carrying three passengers per trip.

The dense network of rail lines in the United States promised fast, efficient transportation in almost any weather, while the English Channel was a barrier to rail travel that would not be conquered until the opening of the channel tunnel in 1994. Given the commercial ties across the channel and economies that were reawakening after years of war, the potential for passenger air travel in Europe was obvious. The armistice with Germany was signed on November 11, 1918, and only one week later, Reuters carried an article predicting imminent cross-channel service with "cabins which will be electrically heated and lighted, and will be as comfortable as Pullman cars." The very same week the *Sydney Morning Herald* carried an article predicting flights from London to New York in twenty-four hours and Australia to London in five days, an audacious estimate given the long sea and desert crossings along the route.

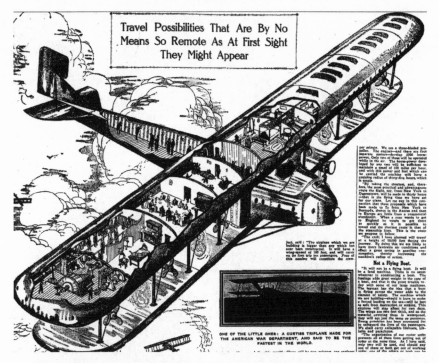

In 1919 anything seemed possible, including this "flying hotel"—a biplane with a thousand-foot wingspan and multiple dining rooms. Apparently nobody considered what might happen to dishes, glasses, and passengers in one of those wingtip restaurants when the aircraft banked to make a turn.
Image from TROVE Australia, Australian National Library

The first barrier to cross-channel commercial air service was neither technical nor financial, but bureaucratic. The British government had prohibited all civilian flights over its territory in 1914, and the ban was not officially rescinded until 1919. The world's first scheduled daily air service began between London and Paris on August 25 of that year aboard twelve-passenger Handley-Page W-8 airliners operated by Air Transport and Travel. These services were followed almost immediately by French competitors Messageries Aeriennes and others. Those early flights took about two and a half hours, and "lunch baskets" were offered at one shilling, three pence each. These were made by local hotels and contained "luxury sandwiches" and other cold items.[2]

Air Transport and Travel was taken over by Daimler Airways in 1920, and that company hired the first inflight staff—a "cabin boy" named Jack Sanderson, who was chosen mainly because he was lighter than an adult. Sanderson greeted passengers with glasses of fruit juice as they boarded, though apparently no food was offered at this time.

According to the Reuters Aeronautical News column on July 22, 1922,

Excellent provision is made for the carriage of goods and the comfort of passengers has also received careful attention. In this latter respect it may be stated that a small folding table fitted in front of each seat in the passengers' cabin so that the uniformed Daimler stewards are enabled to serve light refreshments during the air journey while sporting passengers with a gambling propensity indulge in the latest fascinating game known as "put and take."[3]

Food storage was not well thought out in the early days; when KLM designed a wooden cupboard to contain the alcohol and glasses served aboard

There are only two known pictures of Jack Sanderson, the man who served the first inflight meals aboard Daimler Airways. In this 1920 shot he greets passengers who are about to board a De Havilland 34 with glasses of juice.
Image provided by Graham Simons

their Fokker2 aircraft in 1921, they used screws to hold it to the bulkhead. The vibration of the aircraft shook the screws loose after only about fifteen minutes of flight, and the box fell into the lap of a surprised passenger.[4]

Passengers apparently didn't entirely trust the airline to provide sufficient food and drink, as the Aeronautical News column carried by Reuters in October of 1923 refers to passengers on a flight to Cologne boarding a flight carrying their coats and flasks.[5] The contemporary references to service of light refreshments onboard might be taken in more than one way, since there was great attention to the weight of everything. Passengers were allowed only ten pounds of baggage, and wicker was used for seats, meal hampers, and baggage racks to save weight. On one early transatlantic flight, from Ireland to New York in 1928, a newspaper account noted, "An indication of the care in loading at the last minute was the decision to reduce (pilot) Huehnefeld's dozen oranges by half. The remainder of the food consisted of bananas, coffee, water, and chocolate."[6] There was a particular obsession with saving weight on long over-water flights; when Spanish aviators Ignacio Jiménez

This undated Imperial Airways beverage menu is probably from about 1926 and shows the towns passengers might be expected to see out the window during the flight. It is interesting to note that of all the brands named on the menu, only Perrier managed to get their logo included.
Image provided by Graham Simons

and Francisco Iglesias flew the 2,400 miles from Seville to Rio de Janeiro in 1929, they carried only a chocolate bar and water as refreshments.

The amenities weren't the point on the first European air services—speed of travel trumped other considerations, and passengers put up with whatever they were offered. It didn't take long, however, for the airlines that flew sophisticated travelers on business trips to start competing on the basis of service. A wave of consolidations had created four large carriers in Western Europe by 1925, when the British company Imperial Airways and the French Air Union decided to launch upscale services. Imperial used the "Silver Wing" name for those flights that featured a steward and included food and beverage, while Air Union called theirs "Rayon d'Or" (Golden Ray). Air Union's advertisements referred to the plane as a "flying restaurant," a bit of hyperbole that would surface many times in airline ads. It was a piece of marketing genius, because newspapers all over the world picked up the term. A 1925 article in the *Daily Record* of Morris County, New Jersey, gushed, "The first aerial restaurant car in the world is now engaged on the regular London-Paris airway service. A uniformed steward, the first aerial waiter, is in attendance, and passengers on the aeroplane can obtain hot and cold meals while flying thousands of feet in the air."[7]

The meal was described as consisting of hors d'oeuvres, lobster salad, cold chicken and ham, nicoise salad, ice cream, and cheese and fruit. Beverages were also offered with the meal and consisted of Champagne, wine, whiskey, mineral water, and coffee. Both services involved fine china set on linen-clad tables. This was problematic because nobody had thought to put raised edges on the tables, so plates and cups slid off in turbulent weather.

In April 1928 Lufthansa upped the ante, offering both the first hot meals and the first culinary professional, as opposed to someone who also helped passengers board and carried their luggage. The meals were loaded warm in sealed thermos bottles and served by Arthur Hofe, who had been a waiter at upscale German hotels. He was allowed to focus on food service while a "luftboy" took care of nonculinary duties.

Elsewhere in Europe, the Czech airline CSA and Belgian SABENA were flying international flights using French Farman Goliaths. KLM was flying once a week to what is now Indonesia in three-engined Fokker monoplanes, but little food was served aboard. All meals on the six-day trip were taken on the ground, probably because of the obsession with saving weight on a flight that traversed oceans and deserts. The aircraft had been fitted with extra fuel tanks, but still could only hold five passengers in a passenger compartment designed for twelve. Dutch airline historian Paul van Weezepoel stated that "the flight engineers in the early days also had the role of 'steward.' In the

Fokker's cabin was a closet or cupboard in the front which could be opened, containing tea, refreshments and some bread."[8]

This was the typical pattern worldwide, for the aircraft to stop for meals whenever possible, with all passengers deplaning to dine while the aircraft was refueled and serviced. Inflight meals were available on short services as an option, and only included on long journeys over water, mountains, and other inhospitable territory.

In Europe, a densely populated continent with cities within short reach almost anywhere, this was easily accomplished. Pioneer air services in the United States and Canada were not so lucky, and some routes took detours in order to make meal stops at airports where no passengers were expected to board or depart. The unreliability of early aircraft and lack of weather forecasting technology meant that some flights ended in cornfields or on country roads, and until the mid-1930s airline personnel always carried railroad timetables so that if an aircraft was disabled the passengers could keep traveling.

Though meal service came later to the United States than it did to Europe, flying there received a boost with the introduction of the first American-designed passenger aircraft, the Ford Trimotor. The aircraft was advanced for its time and could carry nine passengers along with a pilot and copilot (sometimes called a first officer). The aircraft's range of 550 miles made long journeys conceivable, and its speed of 150 miles an hour was fast for its day. Articles praising the Trimotor's all-metal construction and high reliability whetted the public appetite for air travel, and an airline called Transcontinental Air Transport (later to become TWA) was formed as a response. When the carrier started flying in 1926, the first officers were required to serve meals when not engaged in helping to navigate the airplane. As they had flying experience but had never served drinks before, they were taught to kneel in the aisle rather than bending over while pouring to minimize the risk of dousing passengers.

Though the airline had the word Transcontinental in its name, less than half of the mileage across the country was actually flown. Passengers took a night train from New York to Columbus, Ohio; flew to Waynoka, Oklahoma, during daylight; traveled overnight by rail to Clovis, New Mexico; and then took another aircraft to Los Angeles.

Stout Air Services, which started flying in 1926 with a much less ambitious route between Grand Rapids, Detroit, and Cleveland, was the first American airline to hire a cabin attendant, who was called an "air courier." TAT followed shortly, calling their cabin attendants "couriers"—most were the children of the investors who financed the airline. Their duties included picking up the food from the local caterer, delivering it to the airport, and

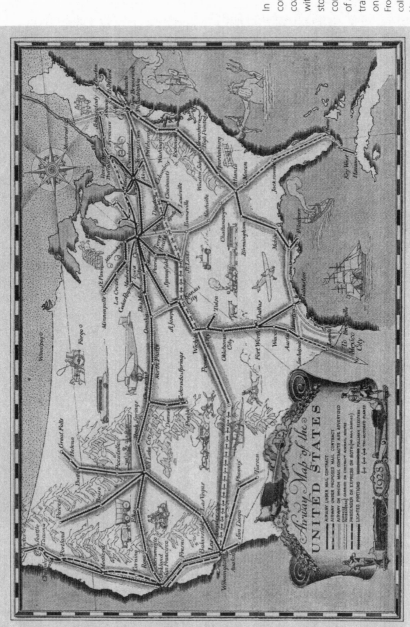

In 1929 you could fly from coast to coast with fourteen stops or take a combination of aircraft and trains with only six. From the collections of Henry Ford

stowing it aboard the aircraft. Service was advanced for the era—hot bullion was served at breakfast with bread and butter sandwiches, and at lunch passengers were offered boiled chicken that had been kept hot in Thermos containers. The chicken was served with salad, fruit, coffee, and milk. In the afternoon, tea was served along with cold sliced meats and fancy sandwiches; there were no evening meals because all flights were on the ground by dusk even during winter.

According to the book *Howard Hughes' Airline: An Informal History of TWA*, aboard a 1926 flight that left Columbus at 8:15 a.m., lunch consisted of cold meats, sandwiches, and coffee between St. Louis and Kansas City. Both that book and Frank Taylor's *High Horizons*, a history of United Airlines, mentioned that aboard some of TAT's early flights lunches were served on gold plates with lavender tablecloths and napkins.[9]

TAT boasted that food service was catered by the Fred Harvey Company, a chain of restaurants that provided meals at railroad stations in the western United States. The Fred Harvey Company's experience with catering for the railroads, which required attractive meals that were made en masse for passengers based on a train schedule, gave them unique experience in catering, and their locations in train stations were ideal for services in which trains made connections to aircraft. Since there were railheads next to airports across the country, the company already had facilities where they were needed and were ready for an expansion of air service. According to the *Harvey House Cookbook*, the venture with Transcontinental Air Transport was so successful and profitable that the restaurant chain was inspired to become the first airline catering specialist.[10] They don't quite deserve the name, since the company never made any special meals with inflight service in mind and didn't open any locations in airports as opposed to railroad stations, but they did cater at other locations where there was both a train station and an airport.

The managers of TAT understood the value of articles about their service, and frequently carried journalists who turned in glowing reports. In 1929, *New York Times* writer T. J. C. Martin wrote about service between Los Angeles and Clovis, New Mexico.

The plane is fitted with ten comfortable chairs with adjustable reclining backs. Walls are decorated in gray and burnt orange with gay curtains at the windows. . . . Two hours after starting a steward served lemonade and cookies while the plane was flying high above the sweltering desert. At 1 o'clock small tables were fitted over the passengers' knees and luncheon was served. The tables were draped with mauve linen. The food consisted of cold bits, salad, piping hot coffee, dessert and fruit. A packet of chewing gum rounded off the repast. In mid-afternoon tea and cookies were served. The company provides each passenger with a narrow map of the course on one side of which is a signed certificate that the passenger has made a transcontinental flight.[11]

Similar service was offered aboard Western Air Express, which began flying between Los Angeles and San Francisco in 1928. Northbound flights were catered by the Pig & Whistle restaurant in Hollywood and were served by steward Miles Davis (not the trumpeter). Unfortunately no known photographs of inflight meals survive, and the service folded after two years of operation.

One of TAT's main rivals was Boeing Air Transport, an airline owned by the aircraft manufacturer that flew routes from Chicago to the west. They used Boeing 80-A Trimotor biplanes, which were slower and had a shorter range than the Ford Trimotors but could carry up to eighteen passengers. These aircraft originally were supplied with a table with one supporting leg that fit into a hole on the floor with two clips to attach it to the side of the cabin. This worked very poorly, because plates routinely vibrated off the tables. Once the airlines started hiring stewardesses in 1930, a solution was found for this problem. The first women hired were all former nurses; they knew an old trick from hospitals, putting a pillow in passengers' laps and serving the food there instead of setting up the tables.

Boeing Air Transport developed a reputation for decent but monotonous food; pioneer stewardess Inez Keller Fuite, who flew the multistop run from Oakland to Cheyenne, Wyoming, recalled that "Regardless of the time of day, we served the same meal of coffee or tea, fruit cocktail, fried chicken, and rolls."[12] Boeing's meals from Chicago were loaded by the famous Palmer House hotel and were generally regarded as the best food in the air on any American airline. Boeing's management showed a high level of practicality compared to other carriers—they began with modernistic china and glasses, but so much of it was broken during turbulent flights that they eventually substituted paper plates, the first carrier to do so.

All carriers flying inside the United States during this era had to deal with the laws regarding Prohibition. Alcohol was never officially served, but a cat-and-mouse game developed with nervous passengers who needed a little liquid courage and brought flasks and bottles in their coats. In stewardess Harriet Gleeson's article in the excellent anthology *Footsteps in the Sky*, she recalled that Boeing aircrew had to watch for passengers who carried cough syrup bottles that had been refilled with whiskey.[13]

Though early flights were oriented toward businessmen, organized air tourism was in flower by 1928, when London travel company Thomas Cook operated the first "air cruise," a pioneering development in group travel. The *Daily News* of Perth, Australia, covered the announcement in their Overseas Aviation column as follows:

> The announcement, of the first air pleasure cruise organised by the Imperial Airways, Ltd., and Messrs. Thos. Cook and Son, Ltd., marks another step in the development of luxurious and rapid travel. For this pioneer air pleasure cruise, which will leave London on January 31, 1928, the Imperial Airways, Limited, will use one of the largest types of the famous "Silver-Wing" triple-engined aeroplanes. It has accommodation for 20 passengers, but the members of the cruise will be limited to 12. The crew will consist of the pilot, the pilot-engineer, and a steward, the latter in charge of a plentiful supply of refreshments, which will be obtainable at all times. Luncheon will be served 'in the air' on several of the long "hops."[14]

It is a measure of how much the technology of aviation and the expectations of passengers had changed that within a decade of the introduction of commercial air service aboard converted bombers, the word *luxury* could be used in connection with an inflight meal. It was a trend that would peak in the next decade with what is sometimes regarded as the most romantic era of travel, when a network of piston airliners and flying boats linked the world in a way that had never been done before.

CHAPTER 4

~~~~~~~~~~~~~~~

The Technology of Heat
in Flight before 1940

The earliest food in the air was served cold, and though it was an improvement over eating nothing at all, the hot coffee that accompanied it was
certainly welcome. Aircraft in those days were unheated, and even bundling
up in overcoats and furs wasn't enough to completely banish the chill. Passengers relished warm beverages, even if they had been made hours before
and brought aboard in a thermos.

As flights became longer, aeronautical engineers started to work on the problem of how to heat things in flight. Two technologies were obvious contenders,
but each had their drawback. Zeppelins had electric stoves in their kitchens,
but those flying passenger liners had a much more plentiful supply of electricity.
The giant Maybach twelve-cylinder engines that pushed the zeppelin through
the sky had plenty of spare horsepower to run generators; with the gas providing
the lift, there was leftover energy for lighting and heating. Fixed-wing aircraft
were in an entirely different situation, and there was great concern about
diverting power away from propellers for passenger comfort. As a result, even
though electric heating was a proven technology, it was rarely used.

The alternative to electricity was to use some kind of fuel in a stove, and
according to *History of Flight Catering*, by Peter Jones, at one time experiments were made using charcoal in an inflight oven. We can guess how
successful that was by the fact that all subsequent methods involved liquid
fuel. Though there were obvious safety concerns about any flaming liquids
in an aircraft, the first food heating systems in aircraft used this method.
The British Supermarine Southampton flying boat, built in 1929, was first

to have a built-in stove that burned "methylated spirit"—otherwise known as denatured alcohol.[1] (Flying boats were more likely than other aircraft to have a stove aboard, because they flew some very long routes and occasionally landed on lakes and bays far from civilization.) The Southampton was a military aircraft, and the first definite evidence of the use of an alcohol stove while in flight on a civilian aircraft was not until 1934.

Alcohol was chosen over other fuels such as butane or kerosene because it is the most lightweight fuel, the least explosive, and creates no strong odor when cooking. It has the disadvantage of giving off about half the heat output per ounce compared to those fuels, and alcohol stoves are slightly harder to light in a cold environment.[2] As a result, those stoves were primarily used for warming premade foods rather than doing serious cooking. The danger of any open flame aboard an aircraft was obvious, and the stove must have been used for the briefest period possible. In later aircraft this type of heating would be less practical due to the buildup of exhaust gases in an enclosed cabin, but on these early craft the windows could be opened and there were adjustable vents in the kitchen area.

Aircraft manufacturers who were constantly trying to eke out better performance experimented with various other ways of heating food. Engineers at both De Havilland and the Boeing Company considered running the hot exhaust pipes from the engines inside the aircraft and channeling the heat around an oven. When this was tried, the disadvantages immediately became apparent; along with the heat, this design brought in deafening engine noise. There was the additional danger that after the pipes heated and cooled repeatedly they might crack, which could fill the cabin of the aircraft with exhaust. Another idea—bringing the high-temperature propylene glycol liquid engine coolant into the cabin instead of the engine exhaust—was tried on the Boeing 314 and at least one De Havilland variant and found to be no more practical.

In 1933, a pair of American inventors filed a patent for a new innovation that they called a "steam cooker and food warming device."[3] This was similar to the chafing dishes still used by modern caterers, in which hot liquid or steam is passed under a series of enclosed trays. It was an improvement in that the alcohol flame was enclosed and less likely to come into contact with clothing or other flammables. The disadvantage was that it was only capable of relatively low temperatures, better for reheating than cooking. This system, called a "steam chest," was installed in some airliners in the late 1930s.

During the era of unpressurized aircraft with relatively weak engines that flew at low altitudes, liquid fuel stoves and steam chests worked well enough. It was not until the eve of the Second World War that high-flying aircraft with robust engines enabled a return to electric cooking.

CHAPTER 5

═══〰〰〰〰〰═══

From 1930 to the
Second World War

Flying Boats

As the volume of air travel increased, markedly different patterns in service evolved in response to different circumstances. Aircraft designed to operate over land established regular and increasingly reliable operations, and most flights made stops that were timed to allow travelers to dine on the ground. When they didn't, passengers were usually served a cold meal at their seats. Usually a single steward or stewardess distributed prepackaged meals that were made on the ground, served beverages, and took care of all passenger needs. The first airline caterers went into business to deliver food to aircraft that typically held between twelve and thirty people.

Things were different on long over-water flights, where gigantic flying boats carried as many as seventy-four passengers, requiring as many as seven service staff. Full meals were cooked on board using increasingly sophisticated equipment, and the logistics of arranging for food to be available at every stop became part of the job of running an airline.

To anyone considering the future of global travel in the late 1920s, it was obvious that the great potential for flight would be over water. Though aircraft could travel at twice the speed of railroads, that was four times the speed of the fastest ocean liners, and aircraft could take a more or less direct route rather than navigating around islands and unsafe waters. The savings of time for businesspeople made it well worth the additional cost.

Given the concern about possible failure of the less-than-reliable engines of that day while over the ocean, aircraft that could land on water seemed to offer the best option for safety. As Frank Taylor remarked in his book *High*

Horizons, "Nobody even considered flying the ocean in land planes at that time, and flying boats seemed to be the answer to transatlantic and trans-pacific air travel."[1] Once radio communication between aircraft and ships became standard procedure, passengers could take comfort in the knowledge that if an aircraft ran out of fuel or had engine trouble they could set down on the water and radio for help. The airline companies also were aware that flying boats did not require as much airport construction in order to start serving a route.

As in so many other aspects of early commercial aviation the British were first, with Imperial Airways using flying boats to operate the portion of their London to Cairo service that went over the Mediterranean. It was a relatively short section of a very long flight—by 1927 connections with land-based aircraft went the rest of the way to India—but the services over oceans, jungles, and deserts operated without mishap for years. The route extended south and east with startling speed, and by 1934 it was possible to fly from London to Australia using Imperial Airways and Qantas in twelve and a half days. The 12,754-mile journey involved several overnight stops, four changes of aircraft, and one short rail journey to get from a seaplane base in Alexandria to an airport in Cairo, but it compared favorably with the forty-four days that would be involved in taking the same trip by sea. Most meals on the long chain of flights were eaten on the ground, but when this was not practical, hot meals were served from containers called hay boxes, after the insulating material that helped minimize heat loss.[2]

Though the meals may have been loaded in places as different and exotic as Athens, Karachi, Bangkok, and Batavia, the airline staff strove to keep the experience as British as possible. One of the rare exceptions was on the final section from Singapore to Melbourne operated by Qantas, which often served "Potage du Kangarou" along with otherwise typically English roasts with potatoes and vegetables. Contemporary reports of Qantas's inflight ser-vice were complimentary; a glass manufacturer's representative named W. H. Pilkington who flew from London to Brisbane in 1937 reported that the food aboard was superior to that served at some of the isolated waystations that were used for night stops. Pilkington described a "bumper lunch" loaded on board at Rambang, Indonesia, as "omelette, macaroni, peas, salmon, tinned fruit, mineral water and milk," and called it "very enjoyable."[3] Given that many of the stops on Qantas's routes were at places with no reliable refriger-ation and primitive ground transportation, it is not surprising that no local products were used. Qantas was able to provide the standard of service that travelers of the day expected, and their flying boat services were integrated into their network of internal flights operated by land-based aircraft.

NURS'AIRY RHYMES

This King Cole is a modern old soul
He wanted the wide world to see,
    He likes good food
    And he likes good wine
So he travels by flying boat, see!

. . . *Bar and Buffet Service on every Flying Boat* . . .

QANTAS EMPIRE AIRWAYS

SYDNEY — BRISBANE — TOWNSVILLE — DARWIN — JAVA — SINGAPORE — INDIA — EGYPT — LONDON

Qantas Empire Airways presented possibly the most whimsical ad of the prewar era in a 1939 Australian magazine. Since smoking was allowed on these aircraft, King Cole could have called for his pipe along with the three fiddlers.
Image provided by Qantas

Seaplanes were regarded as so advantageous for long-distance travel that in June 1937 Imperial Airways replaced the land aircraft that had been operating between Southampton and Cape Town with Empire-class flying boats. The route included landings on the Nile River in Khartoum and on Lake Albert in Uganda before a series of stops at ocean ports along the coast of East Africa. Again the airline strove to avoid serving anything remotely resembling African food on the eight-day journey. When asked if any indigenous foods were featured on these flights, Professor Gordon Pirie, author of two books on British Imperial flying, responded, "You can be sure that it was all very period British: white gloves, silver service, and huge efforts into mimicking home."[4]

Imperial Airways sourced fresh produce from Croydon market on the outbound flight and made it last as long as possible, switching to canned food when necessary. They must have used some local suppliers, because Pirie noted that he had seen references to sherbet and lobster being served in East Africa, and the airline set up a rudimentary logistics operation to make sure that appropriate meals were supplied.[5]

All food was loaded in giant baskets and served at room temperature or from insulated boxes, but an initiative to improve onboard service in 1936 raised the standard considerably. As George Banks noted in his excellent book *Gourmet and Glamour in the Air*, at that time "A typical menu on the flying boat *Corsair* included Foie Gras or grapefruit, roast chicken, ox tongue and York ham with Russian or green Salad, completed by peaches with Melba Sauce, Cheshire, Camembert and Kraft Cheeses offered with a good wine list and an interesting 'Airways Cocktail.'"[6]

In 1938 Imperial became the first European airline to set up a rudimentary catering service that standardized the meals aboard their Empire-class flying boats. Though heating and refrigeration were still not available on board, the meals developed a reputation as the highest-class picnic in the air. Since most nights were spent on shore at stops along the way, passengers were given the option of selecting their meals the night before, so they could be cooked just before departure and put on board.

Imperial was able to spend lavishly on passenger comfort because they didn't need to make a profit, since the airline had a subsidy of a million pounds sterling when it was founded in 1923. The airline was periodically resubsidized until 1939, when the government merged it with other carriers to form BOAC.[7]

Imperial eventually operated services most of the way around the world, from Bermuda and New York to Singapore, but they never crossed the Pacific or ventured to South America. That entire quadrant of the world was ruled by Pan Am, which eventually developed a sophisticated onboard experience, high-tech logistics, and the most advanced cooking techniques in the sky.

Pan Am was different from all other American carriers in having no domestic land routes, but the carrier's founder and president, Juan Trippe, used his political connections to make sure that his airline had no international competition. It became a de facto flag carrier for the United States, and Trippe exploited his monopoly for decades.

In 1929, Pan Am introduced their first stewards; the original hiring instructions called for "alert and good looking youngsters" for Sikorsky flying boat service between Miami and the Caribbean. They would have had to also be limber, since in the Sikorsky flying boats the galley was in the tail and could only be reached on hands and knees—stewards had to crawl back balancing a tray.

Following Lufthansa's lead, Pan Am became the second airline to require culinary expertise among cabin staff. Candidates had to have experience preparing and serving food in "first class restaurants." According to the excellent book *Footsteps in the Sky*, a compendium of reminiscences by airline employees, an early Pan Am steward named Joey Carrera was quoted as saying that Pan Am carried several days' worth of food outbound on Caribbean and South American flights, as "nothing edible could be found at their destination."[8]

The decision to source all the food from Miami may not have entirely been due to this sort of snobbery, as Pan Am had rocky relations with local people at many of the places the airline served. As detailed in the book *An American Saga: Juan Trippe and His Pan Am Empire*," at many South American stops there were violent clashes between Pan Am employees and those of local carriers, and some Pan Am airports were like armed camps. In any case the travelers on Pan Am were overwhelmingly Americans and Europeans, most of whom presumably preferred the cuisines they knew.

Pan Am was the first commercial airline to actually heat food inflight,[9] which was done beginning in 1934 while crossing the Caribbean on four-engine Sikorsky S-42 flying boats.[10] In a novel use of technology, stewards would take orders from passengers on one leg of a flight and radio ahead to the next station, where the requested meals would be prepared. At the next stop the stewards picked up the desired meals, which would eventually be reheated and served in a dining area separate from the main passenger cabin.

Pan Am proved adept at marketing their services based on the quality of the food on board. Among the innovations they came up with was what they called "The 160 Mile Dinner," which was explained in glowing terms by a *Washington Post* correspondent.

Food by the mile! That's the result of the advancement of transportation. Fifteen miles for tomato bisque, 100 miles for fried chicken, 15 miles for the salad, 20 miles for the dessert, and 10 miles for your coffee. That is the way a 160-mile dinner in the air may be eaten.

It hasn't been so many years since cheese and ham sandwiches were served for breakfast, lunch and dinner to air passengers by the co-pilot. But that type of service disappeared along with the single-motored transports—now delicious, nutritious meals, "just like mother cooks," are regularly a part of air service. It's fun to watch the stewardesses serve 21 dinners from her (sic) kitchenette in less than an hour, as you skim past gorgeous scenery, and soft, billowy clouds.

The dinners that are served in the air are complete from soup to nuts, including a large variety of food. The menus are carefully chosen—balanced and

nutritious—with the idea of pleasing most of the people most of the time. . . .
On every ship's departure from the airport along goes some kind of food, all the
way from hot coffee, light and heavy breakfasts to full dinners. Then there is the
snack box for the in-betweeners. The stewardess can soon assemble a delightful
lunch from it—cold chicken, fancy cheese, olives, crackers, cookies—anything
to hit the spot, with milk, hot chocolate and coffee.[11]

Unlike other American carriers that served the same meal of fried chicken
and salad on every flight, Pan Am varied their meals on a daily basis. Pioneering steward and purser Ovilio "Bill" Moreno recalled that one of his
duties before every flight was to type up as many copies of the menu as there
were passengers.[12]

The apex of flying boat luxury was reached in 1939 when Pan Am started
operating Boeing 314 aircraft, which flew on the Pacific routes only. These
were equipped with sleeping berths for forty, separate dressing rooms for men
and women, and well-stocked bars. A lounge and dining room was separate
from the passenger seating or sleeping quarters, and a deluxe cabin in the tail
section could be converted into a bridal suite. The 109-foot-long fuselage
was divided into two levels connected by a spiral staircase.

The Boeing 314 galley had an icebox, ample cooking and preparation
space, and a variety of heating methods that hadn't been in existence since
the Hindenburg made its last flight. A crewman named Sam Toaramina
gave a reminiscence for an oral history project[13] and was interviewed for this
book, and he described the experience of cooking in that galley on flights to
Honolulu and the South Pacific.

> The food was put on in San Francisco, and we cooked it on the airplane—we
> had steam tables and pressure cookers. Coffee was made in 4 or 5 gallon urns.
> We had electric ovens with big fans in them, and that cooked the meat. Ev-
> erything was built so if we had a bumpy flight, it wouldn't go flying around.
>
> We didn't (serve meals) for an hour and a half to two hours (after take-
> off).[14] It took us that long to prepare the food. If I had a roast beef, the meat
> was put on raw. We had electric ovens that we put that in, a little larger than
> a microwave. It would hold a five or 6 pound roast. . . . That food was put on
> there according to how many passengers I had. So if I was going to have 30 or
> 40 passengers, maybe I needed two or three of those roasts. . . . We had to peel
> the potatoes and put them in pressure cookers, and the steam tables took care
> of that, the carrots and the other items you put in there. When that food was
> ready, then we decide, OK, maybe another half hour, we want to get the pas-
> sengers ready for dinner. We did all the slicing and preparation in the galley.
> We didn't do any carving in the cabin, in those days.

Since there was only room for twelve people at the table and the aircraft held more than that, passengers dined in shifts. Toaramina remembered that "people were quite surprised to see the table set with sterling silver and Irish linen, silver water pitchers and flower arrangements on the table. It was like a first-class restaurant."

Those aircraft left San Francisco and Honolulu with fresh food, but fruit and vegetables were less reliably available on stopovers on sparsely inhabited Pacific islands. Cans of beets, carrots, ham, and chicken à la king formed the main courses, and at every stop the purser on the aircraft went shopping for whatever was available in the local market. The pursers carried receipt books and took the paperwork back to the airline to be reimbursed at the end of each flight.

They had time to do some shopping because there were multiple overnight stops to refuel the aircraft, service the huge radial engines, and allow the passengers some time to relax. The "China Clipper" flights from San Francisco to Manila were scheduled with just under sixty hours of actual flying time, but took almost six and a half days to complete if everything ran on schedule. Frequently the flights ran off schedule; the seaplane might not be able to take off for days if the ocean was particularly rough, and it was not unusual for the aircraft to arrive a week late.

To provide passenger and crew comfort, Pan Am constructed hotels on all the islands, along with fuel storage tanks, caches of canned food, spare parts depots, and lodgings for the workers who remained on the islands. The airline personnel stayed in the same hotel as paying customers, and passengers and crew mingled during the days of enforced idleness. On the average it took the aircrew between a month and six weeks to make the round trip to San Francisco.

On the return to Hawaii and the Mainland, the aircrew had to perform a ritual they did nowhere else—the United States had strict health regulations about importing food, and that included the waste scraps on the aircraft. At Hawaii it was unloaded from the aircraft, inspected, and incinerated close to the dock. There was a much more hazardous procedure for San Francisco arrivals. When the Farallon Islands, which are thirty miles offshore from San Francisco, were sighted, a steward was tasked with opening a rear door and throwing bags of trash out of the aircraft. The Northern California weather made this task more difficult; as Toaramina remembers, "There were times when it was fogged in, and we didn't know where the Farallon Islands were because we couldn't see them. I'm sure sometimes we might have thrown it over San Francisco Bay, or over San Francisco as a matter of fact." It would be decades before concern about environmental regulations and recycling forced a reevaluation of the problem of how to dispose of airline trash.

Pan Am, Qantas, and Imperial weren't the only airlines to have flying boat operations prior to World War II; Tasman Empire Airways, the predecessor to Air New Zealand, started flying to Australia in 1940, and the South American airlines SCADTA and Varig operated a network of services around the continent using Junkers seaplanes.[15] None pioneered innovations in service or passenger comfort, so their operations in that era have no place in this book.

Seaplane service worldwide was interrupted when the war broke out, with all flying boats nationalized and pressed into government service. The flying boats that survived would carry passengers again, and a few new ones would be built, but it would be in a changed world.

CHAPTER 6

<center>~~~WWW~~~</center>

Land-Based Craft from 1930 to the Outbreak of War

In Europe in 1930, most airlines were state owned or directed, and there was very little competition between carriers. Many routes were flown between capitals like London or Paris and current or former colonies as an instrument of government policy rather than commercial necessity. Passenger comfort aboard such flights was a matter of prestige rather than profit.

Similarly, at that time almost all American airlines were making more money carrying mail than passengers, and many flights made stops far out of their way to take advantage of these subsidies. Though all US airlines were under private ownership, the federal government had created a system that forced them to make route and schedule decisions based on where mail needed to go. Payments were based on pounds carried per mile and were very generous; Pan Am employees in Miami were actually assigned to mail bricks to their counterparts in the US-administered Panama Canal Zone, who mailed them right back as soon as they were received. Other airlines also found ways of gaming the system, and in early December 1929 United Airlines distributed thousands of Christmas cards weighing exactly one ounce for their employees and investors to mail to anyone along their routes.

Passengers were unimportant in this situation, and sometimes were made to fly with bags of mail in their laps. Occasionally people were actually bumped from flights so aircraft could carry more of the heavily subsidized cargo. At a time when European carriers were flying large numbers of passengers on fast aircraft between major cities, most US airline flights carried fewer than six people on flights with many detours.

That changed in 1930, when the incoming Hoover administration named Walter Brown as new postmaster general, the official responsible for administration of mail services. Brown took the job with very little knowledge of airlines or aircraft but learned quickly, and he decided that the existing system was retarding the development of efficient domestic air service. (As was pointed out later, developing an efficient airline network wasn't really his job, but he decided it should be a national priority and used the power of his office to do it.) Brown and friendly Republican legislators drew up a bill called the McNary-Watres Act that passed in April 1930, which suddenly and drastically changed the rules by which airlines were paid for transporting airmail. Instead of paying by the pound for airmail no matter how it was transported, this act set a very low base rate that had substantial extra payments if the delivery aircraft flew at night, over mountains, had multiple engines, or most importantly, carried passengers. As a result, passengers became much more important, and getting people to their destination on time and in comfort spurred airlines to buy larger and better-equipped planes. Brown also created incentives for long-haul routes instead of multistop flights, saying that he thought all airlines should fly "from somewhere to somewhere."[1]

The very short timeline on implementing those rules meant that many previously profitable enterprises could not react in time and went bankrupt, and later investigations showed that Brown had acted in a way that was dictatorial. At a 1934 senatorial hearing investigating charges of collusion and arbitrary enforcement, Brown vigorously justified his actions:

> I could think of no other way to make the industry self sustaining, make it economically independent, than to come tell the airmail contractor to get some revenue from the public. Almost all of them were refusing to carry passengers and were depending almost wholly on the post office department, and we were getting nowhere in the development of airplanes. . . . I believe it was my duty to force them if I could, under the law to get revenues from non-postal sources, and the obvious one was passengers.[2]

Though the administration essentially admitted the charges that some companies had been favored over others and mergers had been forced by government coercion, the rules remained in place. The result of Brown's meddling was a drastic consolidation of the industry, as small lines that had depended on airmail subsidies were sold to carriers that owned larger aircraft, or could afford to purchase them immediately. Almost overnight the American airline industry was transformed into a pattern that held for almost forty years.

Pan Am retained an effective monopoly on international routes except to Canada, and three major domestic long-haul airlines emerged from the chaos: United, American, and TWA.

Other carriers established strong regional presences, such as Eastern Airlines, which dominated the New York to Miami and Atlanta market. As was the case with many carriers, Eastern served no inflight meals except breakfast, which consisted of Coca-Cola, tea biscuits, coffee cake, George Washington brand instant coffee, bouillon, tea bags, and boiling water. Passengers didn't always get even that, because stewardesses found making coffee and tea on turbulent flights dangerous. They often wouldn't mention that hot beverages were available unless passengers asked.[3] Eastern was evidently the first airline to serve carbonated soft drinks on board, which isn't too surprising, since the airline was then headquartered in Atlanta. This was also the home of Coca-Cola, whose executives were frequent passengers.

Eastern avoided the effort of serving lunch on board by having all flights in both directions stop at Richmond, Virginia, where a huge Southern meal was served at picnic tables while the aircraft was refueled and serviced. The meal was catered by a local restaurant and included in the ticket price. This strategy was copied by other carriers, not always successfully; United tried opening a restaurant at the airport in Cheyenne, but it was unpopular. The harsh weather in Wyoming during much of the year may have been one factor in dooming an outdoor restaurant, but according to *High Horizons*, passengers liked to watch the airplane being serviced and then wanted something when they got back on board.[4]

Among the major carriers, TWA took advantage of their investment in fast and technologically sophisticated Fokker F-10 Trimotors to do something nobody had done before: flying long-distance overnight passenger flights that also carried mail, reaping multiple subsidies in the process since they were flying overnight, over mountains, and carrying passengers. On February 2, 1931, a Trimotor took off at 8 p.m. in Pittsburgh and arrived in Los Angeles at 6 p.m. the following day. The glory the airline received for this feat was almost immediately eclipsed when an identical TWA aircraft suffered a structural failure inflight and crashed the next month. The resulting bad press doomed that airliner in the American aviation market, and canceled bookings almost caused the airline to go out of business.

American flew a tangled route system with a motley array of aircraft, the best and fastest of which was the twelve-passenger Curtiss Condor. Someone at the carrier believed in experimenting with the menus, which were different from the plates of fried chicken featured aboard almost all other flights. American's first stewardess, Velma Maul Tanzer, remembered that in 1933 she served salted nuts, consommé, sandwiches, green salad with a special American Airlines dressing, pickles, cake, coffee, and pistachio ice cream.[5]

In 1937 an American Airlines manager at Washington's Hoover Airport (now National Airport) who wanted to improve the food on board made what turned out to be a momentous decision—to ask the manager of a nearby restaurant called the Hot Shoppe to provide sweet rolls and coffee for morning flights. The manager of the restaurant was William Kahrl, and after delivering food in paper bags as was usual, Kahrl decided there had to be a better way.[6] Kahrl organized the deliveries, providing all the food and paper supplies preloaded on trays and putting it on a pushcart to roll across the street to the airport.

The operation was efficient and profitable and came to the attention of the Hot Shoppe's owners, the Marriott Corporation. The company decided to replicate the process elsewhere, and this was the foundation of the huge Marriott airline food service operations. Though American had pioneered the service on an informal basis, Eastern Air Transport was first to sign a formal contract to cater their flights, with American following a few months later. This was the beginning of a relationship between those carriers and Marriott Catering that lasted for many decades.

Marriott was the second restaurant chain (after the Harvey House) to start a substantial airline catering operation, and the first to deliberately situate catering operations in or near airports. Marriott innovated on the delivery of food service to the aircraft, but at first did not go beyond the very limited selection of sandwiches and fried chicken.

The airline that became most deeply involved in food service was United, and they focused on food because they had no choice. United was a successor to Boeing Air Transport, which was owned by the aircraft maker, and even after they became independent they used Boeing's products exclusively. In 1930 United's fastest aircraft were Type 80-A biplanes that held twelve passengers and averaged 120 miles an hour. At this speed, flights from New York to San Francisco took thirty-two hours of flying time under the best conditions and involved fourteen refueling stops en route. A United Airlines manual of the time read, "Remember to carry on board picnic hampers containing cold fried chicken, apples, rolls, cake, and vacuum flasks of hot coffee for passenger meals."[7] It's a measure of how monotonous the meals were that the exact menu was written in the airline's manual. The food may have been predictable, but schedules weren't; stewardesses were told to carry a railroad timetable in the event the flight was grounded somewhere, and to accompany stranded passengers to the railroad station.

The change in airmail contracts spurred Boeing to rush a new aircraft into production in 1933. The Boeing 247 was a monoplane that was forty miles an hour faster than the Type 80s and flew twice as far, though usually carrying only ten passengers. Armed with a new, faster aircraft that had public confidence, United's management congratulated themselves on achieving lasting technical superiority. Less than a year later, American and TWA flew their first flights with DC-3s, which could fly over two hundred miles an hour and carried twenty-four passengers.

United struggled to find ways to entice the public aboard not only their 247s, but the even less competitive 80-A Trimotors that they still flew on some routes. Stuck with smaller, slower aircraft that they hadn't paid off yet, United decided to improve their meals and promote their service. On the Trimotors, which were eventually relegated to the shortest routes, they started offering a choice of different types of sandwiches. Stewardess Mary

This picture of the galley of a DC-3 shows the peak of prewar technology aboard American aircraft. Note the space-saving stainless steel compartments and beverage dispensers. Because this is a Delta Airlines publicity shot, the bottle of Coca-Cola is prominently displayed—that Atlanta-based company gave Delta a lot of business.
Image provided by Delta Airlines museum.

O'Connor remembers that when she started flying aboard these aircraft in 1933, "We served fruit cocktail and three kinds of sandwiches: chicken, Canadian bacon, and cheese. The first passengers offered the tray always got the chicken and the last, the cheese."[8]

United kept tinkering with ways to improve inflight service, including introducing dry ice to keep meals cool and fresh in 1935. (This made sense because dry ice has twice the cooling energy per pound, and as it warms it creates no puddles of water to slosh around the airplane.)[9] United also broadened the available beverages beyond coffee and tea to include cocoa, though the water to make these was still kept in thermos bottles rather than heated on board. United also apparently installed chafing dish–type "steam chests" on some 247s,[10] but if so only aboard a few of them. None of the memoirs I have been able to find that were written by stewardesses mention any experience with these, and such a significant departure from normal operations would seem to be worth noting.[11]

In 1936 United hired an engineer named Henry Dreyfus to design a combination lunchbox and serving tray that was made of papier-mâché and used lightweight cups and plates made from an early form of plastic called beetleware. The lunchboxes could be packed attractively in advance and saved stewardesses the effort of plating the meals before serving them. The food at that time was still the usual fried chicken, but that wasn't the case for long. That same year United's management made what turned out to be a momentous decision—they hired a Swiss chef named Don Magarell to make a complete break with the tradition of chicken and sandwiches purchased from local restaurants. Magarell had originally been brought in from Cornell University as a food consultant to help design galleys for future aircraft, but he became so interested in the question of how to improve airline food that he quit the company he had been working for to join United as an employee.

Magarell's first initiative was to convince the airline to set up their own flight kitchens at major airports to prepare meals just before flight time, instead of contracting with restaurants that could be as much as an hour away by car. United's management let him try out the idea at Oakland Airport, which was then the busiest hub on their system. Magarell's kitchen opened in December 1936 and paid for itself in three months with the savings in food cost. Passengers sent enthusiastic letters about the food served aboard the planes, the first positive comments the airline had received in a long time. United's management was delighted and told Magarell to set up kitchens at all of their principal airports.

Even before Magarell had his facilities built, he hired a team of Swiss, French, and Austrian chefs to transform the meals at United. Sensing that passengers would prefer light, varied meals, Magarell came up with ways to serve less food but arrange it beautifully, and he introduced menus printed with the names of the dishes in English and French. Choices expanded at every meal, and milk started being offered to passengers alongside coffee and tea, originally as a promotion with the Borden Company.[12]

Though Magarell's improved and varied meals received rave reviews, nothing that United did could attract time-sensitive business passengers to their older and slower aircraft. The airline lost market share wherever they had competitors. United's former owners and longtime partners at Boeing didn't have a new land-based aircraft ready because all their efforts were going to designing a new seaplane, and the aircraft then available from Holland's Fokker and Germany's Junkers were no great improvement on the 247. Another American aircraft, the Lockheed Electra, was very fast but held only ten passengers and was apparently never seriously considered. United finally broke their long relationship with Boeing and ordered DC-3s from competitor McDonnell-Douglas in 1937. The logic was inescapable; it was the fastest and most cost-effective aircraft in the skies. It has been estimated that by 1940 eighty percent of air passenger traffic worldwide was in DC-3s, which were also built overseas by companies that licensed the design. Among the many novel features of this workhorse aircraft was the first galley with work tables and insulated food storage in latched drawers, plus built-in thermos jugs with spigot handles for storage of hot beverages. It was a major step forward for the cabin crew, who no longer had to unpack wicker hampers of premade meals in flight and repack them with dirty dishes when lunch was over.

When United finally got DC-3s, they again experimented with inflight service to try to obtain a competitive advantage. Their first idea was a concept called the Skylounge, featuring extra legroom and swivel chairs, but passengers grumbled at the two-dollar extra cost, and the idea was scrapped. The next idea was to outfit an aircraft on the overnight San Francisco–Chicago run as a sleeper similar to a Pullman rail car, with full beds for all passengers. The stewardesses awakened passengers in the morning with rolls, coffee, and scrambled eggs.[13] These were loaded at a refueling stop in Omaha, Nebraska, just before dawn, and served as soon as possible so they wouldn't deteriorate.

United's daytime flights on DC-3s offered luxurious appointments, with Haviland china and damask linen with fresh flowers at every table. Don Magarell's efforts at improving the taste and style of food aloft were the subject of a major PR campaign by United. The response from the press and public was overwhelmingly positive. In an unattributed article headed "Tasty Menus Now Offered by Air Line," printed in the *Oakland Tribune* on March 5, 1937, the writer gushed,

Some three months ago United decided they wanted to have actual control of the kind of meals served passengers aloft. Knowing the tremendous advantages and conveniences of the new Douglas planes, they figured there was no good reason why piping hot meals could not be offered and service given comparable to a fine club lounge. And so this progressive concern set about to do a job. First in their planning came the setting up of the commissary at the Oakland Airport—the only one of its kind at present, but forerunner of nine others to be situated at strategic points throughout the country. A well known chef, with an equally well known pastry chef selected a group of assistants and under Maître Magarell's direction started giving the passengers something besides a picnic lunch. Variety, as well as tasty and eye-appealing foods will be the aim and from now on passengers will never know until the menu is presented what the selection will be. This will be a boon to the folks who fly frequently. Dainty linens, attractive china, a glassware of special make, and gleaming silver will make the estimated 415,000 meals served aloft by United Air Lines a true epicurean delight—a finished service for perfect foods. Would you feel that you had luncheoned well if you were served a Crabmeat Cocktail, Half Avocado and Grapefruit Salad, Relish, Buttered Bun, Cheese on Rye Bread, Ham and Turkey on White Bread, Royal Hawaiian Pudding Cake, Cookies, Nuts, Coffee, Tea or Chocolate? That's what the noontime passengers had yesterday. Or how about this dinner: Shrimp Cocktail, Lettuce, Tomato and Egg Salad, Relish, Fried Chicken, Buttered Buns, Almond Blanc Mange, Cake and Cookies, (with) Mints, Coffee, Tea or Chocolate.[14]

Among other innovations, Magarell's chefs created special meals for holidays; a St. Patrick's day menu from 1940 was printed in green and listed a minted fruit cocktail, "Dublin style" leg of lamb stew, and "St. Patrick's Ice Cream and Cakes." The mint in the salad was presumably there to give a hint of green, and we can guess the color of the cake icing.[15]

Don Magarell turned out to be a showman as well as a chef—he did dozens of interviews that went so well he was eventually invited to radio host Fred Allen's popular *Hour of Smiles* show. His banter with the host about the technology of cooking was by all accounts a highlight of the program.[16] He had a long career with United Airlines and never lost his flair for publicity. When he was a vice president of the company in the 1960s, Magarell formed a jazz band composed of United Airlines executives, in which he played upright bass.[17]

After years of having superior service aboard inferior aircraft, United suddenly had an unbeatable product, and revenues soared. Other carriers scurried to catch up, not by establishing their own kitchens but by contracting with outside caterers and demanding that they expand their offerings. They did so at high speed—in 1938 Grace Turner of the *Los Angeles Times*

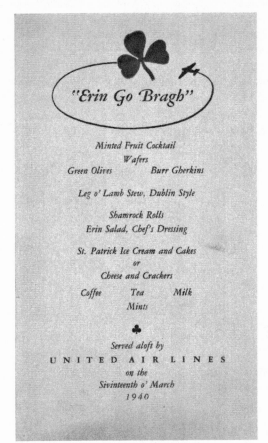

"Erin Go Bragh"

Minted Fruit Cocktail
Wafers
Green Olives   Burr Gherkins

Leg o' Lamb Stew, Dublin Style

Shamrock Rolls
Erin Salad, Chef's Dressing

St. Patrick Ice Cream and Cakes
or
Cheese and Crackers

Coffee   Tea   Milk
Mints

♣

Served aloft by
UNITED AIR LINES
on the
Sivinteenth o' March
1940

Don Magarell's sophisticated kitchens allowed varied meals, including special selections for holidays. We can only wish a color photo of this St. Patrick's meal had survived—every item but the lamb stew and crackers was almost certainly green.
Image from NYPL online menu collection

interviewed Mrs. G. Thomas French about the extensive food service opera-tion that had recently opened at Newark Airport.[18]

It takes rather a large staff and a very efficiently directed kitchen to supply food for several meals a day, to four airlines, each with its own timetable. Mrs. French's husband and her mother both have an active part in the business. There are ten girls in the kitchen (including two cooks), and six boys who help with the commissary work. There is also a baker who takes possession of the kitchen after the day-force leaves, and works there alone all night. "Except for the sandwich bread, we do all our own baking—pies, tarts, pastries, creamroll desserts, breads, and muffins." She pointed to the day's supply—orange bread, date-and-nut bread, and rolled cinnamon bread, all very delicious. . . . Our airplane service special features . . . are particularly important. "And we also make a great deal of our salads," . . . "They "constitute a part of the meal that you can dress up to look particularly attractive."

. . . Mrs. French is guided by the commuters. "We get to know them," she explains, "and to expect them regularly on the same days. So we are careful not to plan the same dish for successive Mondays—or whatever the day may be." Yet the fact that the food must be cooked in advance and kept palatable until it is served makes a real problem. This is a difficulty, however, that Mrs. French considers a challenge. The roast meats—turkey, beef, or lamb, for example— are the simplest to plan. Beef-steak-and-mushroom pie is also good. . . . Baked stuffed lamb chops are also very delicious and they bear up well under delay."[19]

Marriott expanded both the number of airports they served and the variety of their offerings, but some people were still critical about airline food, one person so much so that he started a catering operation to compete with the established entrants. In 1941 entrepreneur William K. Dobbs took several flights around the country to check the operations of his Toddle House restaurants. Annoyed by the low standard of food inflight, he started Dobbs International Services to open catering operations inside airports. His principal innovation was to completely standardize the recipes from location to location, which gave the airlines a more consistent product.[20]

The meals all these enterprises planned for their customers offered variety and beautiful presentation when service elsewhere in the world was still stuck in the late 1920s. Even on long flights within Europe and South America, inflight food was generally monotonous, and most airlines still stopped to allow passengers to deplane for meals. This lack of progress may probably be attributed to the fact that most non-US airlines were money-losing monopolies; there was no economic reason to compete. As budgets tightened in the deepening Depression, and as nations prepared for war, neither airlines nor aircraft designers were thinking very much about how to deliver enticing meals to every seat.

The exception as regards aircraft design was in Russia, where Soviet ideology demanded that state industries do everything that their Western counterparts did, if possible on a larger scale. The Tupolev ANT-20 aircraft certainly fit that description; when it flew for the first time in 1934 it was twice the size and capacity of any other land-based aircraft in the world. The gigantic and luxurious airliner had the wingspan of a modern 747, carried seventy-five passengers, and had the first dedicated galley on a land-based craft at which flight attendants had space to prepare and plate meals and clean used dishes. They needed the space, since those flight attendants boarded carrying cases of cutlery that were only sufficient to serve seven or eight people at a time. Since the aircraft had insufficient water to wash everything, all items were cleaned with a cloth soaked in water between each use.[21] On short flights, meals were loaded already packed in cardboard boxes; usually these consisted of cheese, sausage, bread, an apple or orange, pastry, and chocolate. Tea was served in traditional-style glass cups held in metal frames called "podstakanniki," an almost comically inconvenient method for airline service, and in this case too there were never enough for all passengers to be served at once.

The quality of food on board was fairly high even though the serving staff were tasked with buying food just before each flight from restaurants in or near the airports. Since anybody who was flying inside Russia in that era was a party member or other important person, airports had a priority and got luxury items even in these times of severe food shortages.

That first ANT-20 crashed after only a year of use when a fighter pilot's unauthorized stunt at a Moscow airshow caused a midair collision. A sister aircraft served until 1942, when another instance of pilot error doomed that plane. Several others were under construction when the outbreak of war caused the Soviet aircraft industry to switch to building fighters and bombers.

Most flights within Europe were flown aboard Fokker, Farman, or Junkers aircraft that were distinctly more modest in ambition. The sole exception was the Focke-Wulf 200 Condor, an aircraft that was designed with flights over water in mind. The four reliable engines could take twenty-six passengers to ten thousand feet, as high as a nonpressurized aircraft could ascend, and it was the first to fly between Berlin and New York nonstop. The power of those engines was so ample and the new generators so efficient that electricity could be diverted to boil water for coffee and soup, though apparently it was not used to heat solid meals. For a brief time, this was the fastest, longest-range, and technologically most advanced passenger aircraft in the world.

A memoir of service aboard the Condors was captured by historian Rob Mulder, who interviewed two stewardesses who served before the war. In 1938, DDL Airways of Denmark (later merged with other carriers to become SAS) hired stewardess Doris Jensen, who remembered,

> There were spacious tables, very nice in stainless steel and the top was also crème-coloured in the same colour as the walls. They were easy to clean, when somebody spilled a drink. On the back of the single seats a table could be pulled down, while the smoking cabin and the first four seats in the non-smoking cabin had a table between the seats. There was sufficient space for cutlery and glasses. Once in the air and above the clouds and the sun shining through the cabin windows, it became really cosy and the stewardess had enough space to walk around, serve and help or converse with the passengers. The galley was situated in front of the aircraft right behind the cockpit, and here too we had plenty of space. There was a sink, and practically designed

It's cocktail time aboard AB Aero's Fokker F12 trimotor above Scandinavia in 1936. Modern airline passengers will envy the headroom and legroom as much as they do the white-coated cabin attendant.
Image provided by historian Lennart Andersson

cabinets for glass, china and drinks. On board, sandwiches from the Kastrup Airport's Restaurant Hammers were offered, served in nice boxes.[22]

Fellow stewardess Hanne Hansen recalled,

There was also a cabinet with cups and glasses, an electric water boiler and a small sink. Also a small cabinet with duty free product like cigarettes and whisky, gin and beer could be found here. It was nothing compared with to-day's pantries in modern aircraft, but at that time the challenges were not as big either. If one could get a sandwich with ham or cheese, a glass of beer or a cup of coffee and a Danish pastry, the passenger was content. We had more time to look after the passengers, and that was needed as well.

The British and French aircraft industries, which had led the way with large aircraft in the 1920s, fell behind in the 1930s and produced no successful large, land-based transports. With most European aircraft manufacturers moving toward war production even before hostilities broke out, it was once again an American company that made a technological leap in passenger aircraft.

Boeing had no aircraft to compete with the DC-3 for years because they had put all their effort into the model 314 flying boat, but when they reentered the land-based airliner market they did so with an aircraft that had major technological advances. The four-engined Boeing model 307 Stratoliner began service in 1940 as the first pressurized passenger aircraft. It was able to fly to 20,000 feet, twice as high as the Focke-Wulf Condor, and though it couldn't fly quite as far, it could carry thirty-eight passengers while doing so, compared to the Condor's twenty-six. At that height the Stratoliner could fly high above weather systems that other aircraft had to fly through. The fact that Pan Am, an airline that flew almost exclusively over water, had ordered them meant that the flying boat's days were numbered. Like the seaplanes that Boeing had so much experience building, the Stratoliner had a large galley with electrical burners and water boilers—the first land-based aircraft built outside Russia to do so.[23] The galley had an ample work space that was well laid out so that stewardesses could plate and serve food faster.

Boeing actively collaborated with several airlines in the design of the Stratoliner, and at least once they sent senior engineers to fly aboard DC-3s and Stratoliners to make a comparison of the food and service. While researching this book, I found the handwritten notes from three flights taken in 1941 in Boeing's archives and transcribed them. They make both amusing and instructive reading and are included after this chapter.

The Stratoliners were in service for less than a year before the outbreak of war forced the cancellation of passenger service first to Europe, then to South America. The Stratoliner was the civilian version of an aircraft that became much better known in its military role—the B-17 bomber. Once the United States entered World War II, the passenger aircraft that were under construction were converted into C-75 military transports or B-17s. When the war was over, new aircraft that could fly higher and farther had the technological edge, and now that pioneering airliner is nearly forgotten. In its brief heyday it had previewed the technologies that would bring new sophistication to every aspect of flight, including aerial dining.

CHAPTER 7

A Window into
the Design Process

People who use many products sometimes wonder if the designers ever had actually tried using them to see how they work in practice. This is true in aviation just as it is elsewhere. In most of the world, the people who designed aircraft and the crews who worked in them did indeed have little contact with each other. In the United States, however, longstanding relationships developed between aircraft manufacturing companies and airlines.

The earliest was between Boeing and United, logical because the Seattle-based company started an airline as a market for their products, only selling it when a law made it illegal for manufacturers to own carriers. There was still a close tie between the two, and Boeing executives occasionally took flights to study how their designs worked in practice and try to come up with ways that things could be improved.

The notes from one very important journey have been preserved in Boeing's archives, and they show the way that the engineers pondered every aspect of the experience. On November 22, 1941, engineers John A. Herlihy, William W. Davies, and William C. Mentzer departed Seattle on an overnight flight that made six stops on the way to Chicago. The three men spent part of one day there before taking a TWA flight to Los Angeles, and then immediately hopped a flight back to Seattle. The first flight was on a United DC-3 configured as a sleeper flight, the second on a TWA Stratoliner, and the third on a DC-3 in daytime configuration. The engineers made notes about minute details of the experience, all writing in the same notebook. Since I can't tell whose handwriting should be associated with which person, it is impossible to attribute any given comment, but all three studied every detail from the seat comfort to the way that trays fitted into the armrests. They estimated the relative weight of the luggage carried by women as compared with men, timed the steward who made up their sleeping berths, and compared the legroom of window and aisle seats. The first to make notes jotted terse comments about their meals aboard the overnight DC-3:

Dinner beetleware cup—saucer—plate—food served in pottery (retain warmth) Juice cocktl. turkey-dress, asparagus, coffee.

(severe vibration of coffee & table for two brief periods)

Salad—small bowl, small cream cheese and crackers.

Table not hard to set up, 2-spring pin attachments @ wall, Single leg inboard set in recess disk in floor.

Two napkins for cloth clipped to table edge. Light silverware.

Drink water tastes slightly & is a bit warm

Before landing dressed for breakfast. This meal loaded at Omaha consisted of coffee, sweet roll, fruit juice, scrambled eggs, small piece ham and two l.p. sausages. Service was on table in compt. next to galley.

On the second flight, someone who had a more chatty style of writing took over, with occasional interjections by someone whose spelling was decidedly eccentric:

The appointments are very convenient except the TWA drinking cup is jigger-size which may be to avoid possibility of encouraging air sickness from drinking too much water. It tastes better than UAL.

Breakfast: Seated in left hand reclining chair #7. A stewardess took my order and within 5 minutes returned with a pressed plywood tray (no attachments) which rested with ½" upset border bearing on inside edges of armrests. It had sufficient spare width to compensate for corner compression of arm rest & still not slip.

Back to the subject of breakfast: this service consisted of fruit juice, toast, sweet roll, jelley [sic] and cream in jigger-size wax cups, 2 patties [sic] butter, coffee in tall cup with silver loop-frame bangle (Beetleware cup insert type), silverware in celophane [sic] envelope, scrambled eggs and two l.p. sausages. Others had breakfast foods. Very tastey [sic].

Two different hands were also involved in writing about the flight back to Seattle:

Lunch service is in a deep tray with removable lid. The depth for the purpose of bring [sic] the food close to the table level. Tables are also available. The tray lid is provided with openings in which are inserted coffee cup, salad, dessert, juice cocktail, salt & pepper in cardbd capsuls [sic], cream, jelley [sic], butter, roll, main serving beef & corn in pottery dish, silverware, candy mints, sugar cubes, & napkins. Galley isn't quite convenient, similar but better than DST while stewardess remarks the 247 type is very different from which to serve.

Though the engineers had a typically analytical attitude toward the service, they were not entirely immune to the mystique of flight. Just after an observation about the design of the armrests, a note reads, "On the prairie below a passenger train energetically scuttles along at a snail's pace," and after observing the outside temperature, there is an aggrieved interjection about the fact that the pilot has pointed out the famous meteor crater, but it can't be seen from the writer's seat.

Two of the three men, Herlihy and Mentzer, would have long and successful careers with United, rising to senior management positions and influencing the design of aircraft for decades. They can't have suspected that their little notebook full of analysis and unguarded thoughts would survive to be read over seventy years later. That document gives a valuable look at the spirit of collaboration that was to bring the world the finest passenger aircraft ever built.

CHAPTER 8

〰〰〰

World War II and
the Postwar Bonanza
(1941–1950)

As the skies of the world became battlefields, civilian aviation around the world shut down and aircraft designed for luxury were repurposed for bombers and troop transports. Commercial flights in Europe and Asia ceased, and though they continued inside the United States, soldiers with orders could bump civilian passengers from flights. Business travelers with confirmed reservations were stranded across America, and most resorted to train travel even though it was much slower. The only continent that was relatively unaffected was South America, but even here the war had consequences—most airlines there used Junkers aircraft, and as spare parts became unobtainable due to the blockade of Germany, the reliability of flights suffered.

Since the United States' principal theater of action was in the Pacific, the government requisitioned all aircraft capable of flying there, most of which belonged to Pan Am. That airline was involved in the war almost as soon as it started; on December 8, 1941, only one day after the attack on Pearl Harbor, the Japanese bombed the Pan Am flying boat base at Wake Island. Operations manager John B. Cooke hid in a shallow ditch with two other staff members as Japanese aircraft roared overhead, bombing and strafing the island. When he emerged, he saw that the training the staff received had stayed with them even in this most unexpected of emergencies—Pan Am personnel were rushing into the flaming hotel to get the airline's precious dishes to safety.[1]

Pan Am's staff were the most experienced in the Pacific, and they were put into service not only on Pan Am's own craft, but on PBM Mariners and

59

other military flying boats. Steward Sam Toaramina remembered that the PBM's galley was nothing like the aircraft he was used to—they used paper plates and cups, and one steward served as many as thirty-five passengers. Toaramina remembers a rare moment of levity in the middle of the war, an incident that showed that even generals and admirals had no control over turbulent weather.

> Admiral Nimitz was on my plane when we had a downdraft, just when I was serving him coffee. That coffee went up to the ceiling, like a black ball, and it hung there for a minute and then all came down on his nice clean white uniform. He laughed like hell, like that was the funniest thing he'd seen in his life.[2]

Qantas performed the same function, transporting military personnel both in flying boats and in converted Liberator bombers. The latter were used to fly the longest unbroken passenger flights in history—twenty-seven hours from Colombo, Sri Lanka, to Perth, Australia. No stewards were on board to pamper them—passengers prepared their own meals and coffee while in the air for over a day. On arrival they were presented with a certificate enrolling them in the "Order of the Double Sunrise"—an attempt by the crew to celebrate flight even in the midst of the war.[3]

The crews aboard bombers and submarine chasers who endured flights nearly as long did so in even less luxury, though there were differences in the British and American military. Some of the long-distance bombers operated by the RAF had stoves aboard, and it became the duty of crew who were only busy during actual combat to prepare meals. Archivist Peter Elliott of the RAF Museum was once told by the commanding officer of the Operational Training Unit that "the main reason rear gunners failed the course was that they couldn't cook!"[4] Meal preparation on these aircraft was limited to heating canned food on a hot plate, so their inability to do so says a lot about the domestic skills of Englishmen during this period. Elliott noted that the British military apparently didn't think that hot and appetizing crew meals were very important, then or later, and wrote, "Bomber crews in the Second World War certainly had to rely on sandwiches and coffee. . . . Even the Vulcan, which continued in service until 1983, seemed only to have facilities for heating cans of soup or similar food."

American aircrews were pampered by comparison, motivated by studies that suggested that morale and combat readiness were enhanced by good hot meals. The US military studied the problems of inflight food for aircrews and passengers, and in 1944 produced a document called the Flight Feeding

Manual that detailed the various strategies they had tried.[5] These were the first trials of frozen food for inflight catering, so the report is a landmark in the field. The meals were created at the request of the Naval Air Transport Service by the W. L. Maxson Corporation of New York, and included either ham, veal cutlets, or beef stew along with two vegetables, all partially cooked and then quick-frozen so they could be finished in flight. They were cooked in a special appliance called the Maxson Whirlwind oven, the first convection oven that used heat circulated by fans. The whirlwind ovens didn't get very hot, only about two hundred degrees, but they cooked six meals at a time in fifteen minutes while a conventional oven would have taken thirty. The resulting meals were called "Strato-Plates" and were judged superior to canned food.[6]

The other contender for hot inflight food was the final iteration of the quicklime chemical heaters invented in the ballooning era, called "hotcans." Preparation simply involved puncturing the chemical seals on the cans, and they could be activated anywhere in a large aircraft so nobody needed to leave their duty station. The principal drawback was that they did not get very hot, a crucial flaw in the unheated aircraft at altitudes where the temperature could be below freezing. They also had to be activated and opened with two hands, and pilots complained that this couldn't be accomplished at all while wearing the flight gloves that were mandatory at high altitudes.

The other types of meals that were tested included so-called packet meals, which were cold snack packs containing "one can of meat, one of fruit, one dessert unit with cookies and confections, and one B-unit can with five round crackers." These packet meals were manufactured to a spec called "Food Packet, Individual, Combat, In-Flight (IF-2)," and were designed so they could be opened with one hand by a person wearing gloves. The effort in developing these packets was not wasted, since they were repurposed into the emergency rations that are still used today.[7] Though these studies were carried out during wartime, the technologies developed for storing, packaging, and serving frozen food had far-reaching consequences in postwar civilian flight.

Conflict always is a spur to technology, and often items developed for military use have peaceful applications. The flight characteristics of new aircraft in 1945 were vastly superior to those of 1940, but the technology of cooking and serving food aloft was right where it had been. With the exception of those studies late in the war by the US Air Force, considerations about the flavor of inflight meals had been ignored.

The first airliners to debut in 1946 did have many new features, but all had been designed before the war. The DC-4 was actually developed in 1938, in a unique collaboration between the aircraft manufacturer and several airlines. Douglas Aircraft solicited design ideas from engineers and executives from United, American, Eastern, Pan Am, and TWA while in the planning process, and the resulting craft was far easier to work in than anything that came before it. The galley had been moved to the center of the aircraft instead of being located in the tail section, which made it easier and faster to load and serve meals. United's Don Magarell is generally given credit for this innovation.[8] (Delta Airlines' chief engineer, J. F. Nycum,[9] created a variant on the design that was used on converted military aircraft.) The move sped up inflight service immensely because stewardesses had to walk only half as far over the course of the flight, and it was copied on almost all future airliners.

This change was important because the speed of the aircraft had increased and would continue to do so. Though the DC-4 could only fly at 215 miles per hour, barely better than the DC-3, other new airliners flew far faster. The Lockheed Constellation, also a prewar design but one that had been improved in light of new technology, carried 95 passengers at 320 miles an

The DC-4 set a new standard for passenger comfort, and for the first time food was served in the compartmented trays that are now standard. The passengers aboard this flight in 1947 are all enjoying Portuguese wine with their meals.
Image provided by TAP Portuguese Airways museum

hour, and when the DC-6 first went into commercial service in 1946 it was capable of carrying 102 passengers at the same speed. The result was that flight staff had to serve twice the number of people in two-thirds as much time. Instead of leisurely meals being a way to interrupt the boredom of a long flight, there was pressure to serve food and beverages before trays had to be taken away for landing. Food had become expected on every journey—an Eastern Airlines stewardess remembered that in 1946, even on a flight from Washington, DC, to Richmond, Virginia, that took only twenty minutes, sandwiches and drinks were served.[10]

In the "Cloud Club" aboard a Capital Constellation, painted especially for Capital Airlines by Ben Stahl.

Just a Meal and a Magazine away

You forget old fashioned ideas about distance when you fly Capital.
You relax in cushioned comfort amid congenial, club-like informality.
Distance dissolves delightfully . . . and all too soon, you're there!
By the map, many miles. By Capital, Just a Meal and a Magazine away.

Typical non-stop services . . . between
New York and Atlanta · Cleveland and New York
Washington and Chicago · Detroit and Washington
Chicago and Detroit · Pittsburgh and New York

Dependable service for 24 years . . . 450 flights daily serving 75 major cities

Capital AIRLINES

The speed of the Lockheed Constellation allowed airlines to boast of the brevity of flights, and Capital Airlines was one of many that boasted about the elegance of the experience on board. This ad enthused about the "Cloud Club" lounge aboard their flights. Airline bankrupt 1959

These new aircraft, as well as those that would come from other manufacturers in coming years, faced formidable competition in the American market: thousands of war surplus transports were sold very cheaply at the end of hostilities. These, along with prewar passenger planes, ended up in the hands of pilots who started new airlines to compete with the major carriers. The new entrants operated their obsolete, slow planes with few amenities on what was technically a charter basis, to avoid the regulations of the scheduled airlines. They came to be called "nonscheduled services" or "non-skeds," and were a major irritant to conventional airlines. These companies arranged flights that literally operated without any schedule—the carrier would announce a flight between two cities, and whenever enough passengers showed up, the aircraft would take off. Carriers like California Eastern Airlines, Peninsula Air Transport, and Blatz Airlines charged little more than the railroads, and their unpredictable arrivals and departures caused traffic jams at airports across America. The tie-ups harmed the scheduled carriers more than the non-skeds, since passengers who paid a fraction of the price were willing to put up with the inconvenience, but passengers booked seats on scheduled flights with an expectation that they would actually arrive on schedule.

The non-sked carriers couldn't afford flight kitchens with their shoestring budgets and had such irregular operations that major caterers weren't interested in their business. Faced with the need to provide some kind of food on their longer flights, some returned to a catering model not practiced since the early 1920s—charging for meals. This was documented in a 1948 book on the theory and practice of the industry called simply *Airline Operations*, by R. Dixon Speas.[11]

Food service in a transportation service can be administered in three ways each of which is applicable to airline service as follows:

1. Complementary (sic) (usual airline service feature). Food service prepared either by the airline or a caterer and placed on board in sufficient quantity for total passenger and crew.
2. Charge. Same as complementary except quantity placed on board for passengers according to their orders. The food is then delivered on a cash or food ticket basis. Has been practiced in the past by some airlines.
3. Concession. Food service is provided by concessionaire who gains sufficient profit in sales to passengers to pay fees to the transportation company for servicing privileges. In the instances of Airlines the concessionaire principle can reduce operating cost for low-cost service by elimination of cabin attendant expense (Concessionaire would have responsibility of providing qualified attendants), and increase revenues by concession fees.

The third option is the most surprising; this is the only instance I have found of non-airline employees serving aboard airlines as service staff while not paid by the carrier. We can only guess about how well this worked from the fact that it was never tried again.

Implementation of new traffic control technology soon improved the on-time reliability of the American airline system, and the scheduled carriers fought the non-skeds in the area they knew best: service. An article in the *Christian Science Monitor* in 1948 called "Food and Fun Are Free" (the title of which pointedly contrasts the non-skeds' pattern of charging for meals and the spartan nature of their cabins) included a paean to the new world of airline food.

> Those tasty meals you eat on flights from Boston to points around the world have become so much a part of flying—an anticipated treat by travelers taking the air route—that airline heads here see little danger of aeronauts having to bring along their own victuals for a sky hop anytime in the near future. Hundreds of meals, ranging from short snacks for "short hoppers" to full course meals for overseas and transcontinental trips, are prepared by three catering houses at Boston's big air terminal. At Sky Chefs, Boston unit of a nation-wide chain of airline caterers, cooks, salad makers and bakers work almost around-the-clock to provide meals on some 50 flights a day . . . the Sky Chefs staff starts to work at midnight to prepare meals for "breakfast flights" that leave Logan Airport between 6 and 8 a.m. . . . . Typical breakfast on an hour hop from Boston to New York offers fresh fruit, sweet rolls, hot drinks or milk, but there's more substantial fare for the morning traveler who soars off for far points. Long trip breakfasts also include scrambled eggs and ham. Dinner on a long flight like a jaunt from Boston to London includes soup, olives and celery, filet mignon, fried chicken, or pork chops, vegetables and salad, hot rolls, hot drinks or milk. . . . Sky Chefs first cook the food as short a time as possible before the flights leave; then place the cooked meals in an electric oven till plane time, when the food is rushed to the skyliner and given more electric heating at the same voltage used in the kitchen. As a result, sky meals do not suffer from being dry, mushy, lukewarm or cold. . . . The caterer works on a deadline like a newspaper man, too, for planes don't wait for tardy cooks and the caterer's men must stow their food aboard the liner 15 minutes before it leaves. . . . Faster airline speeds, incidentally, are greatly complicating the caterer's problems. Where there was formerly time to serve a meal between New York and Boston, it's about all a stewardess can do now to just hand around cookies and a beverage.[12]

As enthusiastic as this article was about the quality of inflight meals, the next phase of innovation was on the way even as it was written. TWA was the first carrier to intensively study the use of frozen food, building on the work of the Naval Air Transport Service during the war. They experimented with the degree to which meats and vegetables should be separately cooked before placing them in the trays, the percentage of water in stocks so they would be tasty at high altitude, and made the first systematic study of how spices were perceived at high altitude. The next section of this book deals with their findings in detail; suffice it to say that they set a standard for airlines worldwide.

TWA had just obtained their first international routes, and they and Pan Am both introduced frozen food to their overseas operations in 1947, with mixed results. The book *Inflight Catering Management* notes that "some catering chefs believed that frozen food was a threat to their job security"[13]—it is not hard to believe that they may have deliberately tried to sabotage the system. The same source notes that

> many of the early products that appeared on the market were of inferior quality and gave the system a bad reputation. . . . The problem was not the system, but the quality of food products being prepared for the system. . . . These concerns with meal quality caused Pan American to seriously consider eliminating this frozen meal concept in 1948. . . . However, to revert to locally prepared meals at that time would have meant the development of flight kitchens in such areas as Damascus, Syria; New Delhi and Calcutta, India; Bangkok, Thailand; and Johannesburg, South Africa. At the same time, they were in need of new aircraft to expand their fleet; so funding and development of inflight kitchens in these rather remote areas was not economically feasible.

Another reason frozen food caught on with airline management was that it eliminated a certain kind of wastage: when a fresh meal was made but a flight was canceled, the food made for that flight could not be held for later. Every frozen meal that was made was eventually used, and the savings was substantial. The only people who were unhappy with the change were the workers at the local caterers who had been taking unused airline meals home with them as a perk of their job.

Pan Am and TWA developed their own flight kitchens in New York and Paris to supply meals on their flights, and these were shipped around the world to supply their aircraft. It was the first international distribution of prepackaged airline meals, and other airlines would eventually adopt this model. Pan Am's adoption of this technology had another effect on the ground. In 1953, an American food salesman named Gerry Thomas visited Pan Am's flight kitchens in Pittsburgh and was struck by the aluminum tray that was used to hold meals. He requested a sample of the container and took it back to his company, Swanson Foods, which was at that time trying to figure out a use for 520,000 pounds of turkey that they had bought in the expectation of robust Thanksgiving sales. Thomas bent the tray into three compartments and suggested to his company that the turkey be placed in one section, mashed potatoes and peas in the other two, and it should be sold to the public rather than airlines. The world's first TV dinner had been created, and fast meals would never be the same.[14]

British Overseas Airways Corporation, the successor to Imperial Airlines, also explored using frozen food on a large scale, recognizing that their existing catering system was behind the times and delivering a substandard product. They spent two years studying the subject, but were strangely slow to implement it, so the honor went to Qantas. In his book *Wings to the World*, a history of Qantas, Sir Wilmot Hudson Fysh noted that

> Lyon's of London were the leaders in the early days of frozen food catering. In their factory outside London they erected a mockup where quick frozen meals were served to potential customers who incredulously handled solid bricks of soup which quickly turned into piping hot liquids steaming up from the plate.[15]

A letter from the Qantas archives captures their findings succinctly. Sent to the managing director from the catering superintendent (signed only "R. Edwards"), dated September 30, 1947, it reads:

> Recently I have had the opportunity of studying a concise and confidential report of BOAC on quick frozen food after they had experimented for nearly 2 years, attached is a list of facts at the conclusion of the report.

1. Only the best quality foods should be cooked for freezing.
2. Food having a highly liquid content requires a stabilizer such as pectin.
3. The use of wine in sauces is recommended.
4. Food for freezing should be slightly undercooked.
5. Packaged food must be handled with the greatest care.
6. The best temperature for freezing precooked food is -29°F.
7. Food, when cooked must be cooled as fast as possible.
8. Precooked food must not be thawed, but heated straight away.
9. Food once removed from the freezer must never be refrozen.
10. Food when heated must be served at once.
11. Piecrust should be frozen and separately treated.
12. Cream and custard should not be frozen.
13. Dishes containing salt pork will keep much better if cured pork is used instead.

The response to this letter included a warning to keep things confidential, and noted that "QEA are first in the field in the aviation sphere to adopt this new principle for the storage of food and we should use every item of publicity . . . to retain leadership in this regard."

It is possible that the person who wrote this letter did not know that the ideas had been developed by TWA and BOAC, though Qantas may have been the first to actually use this technology rather than merely research it.[16] Whoever served frozen food in the air first, these letters showed that Qantas was aggressively pursuing leadership in food quality. Some of their other attempts may seem comical to modern connoisseurs, as in this exchange of letters from 1947 between the managing director and catering superintendent.

> A high-ranking Swedish passenger on a recent Lancastrian service ex Singapore for Sydney has complained to me that the coffee was rather dreadful, while it was good at Karachi by flying boat to Singapore. These foreign people set great store by the coffee especially as Australian coffee is notoriously bad, it should be worth your while to see what you can do to buck up the coffee on our main overseas lines.

The response has a somewhat aggrieved and defensive tone:

> For your information, we make every effort to serve good coffee, but unfortunately it is not possible to obtain a standard strength of coffee throughout the routes. Just recently, I endeavored to obtain from Nestlé's Nescafe in bulk, but they would not agree to supply the company with 56-pound drums and owing to the scarcity of tin plate are unable to pack in the usual type of packing.
> To ensure good coffee, we dispatch ex Sydney to Darwin, Bowen, and Townsville, weekly, freshly ground mocha and Kenya beans mixed. With regard to Singapore, on my last visit, catering Ofc. O'Brien was having difficulty in purchasing a decent blend of coffee, but I will acquaint him with the facts of your memo, and ask him to take steps to improve this commodity.[17]

The fact that Nescafé instant coffee, delivered in fifty-six-pound drums, was admitted by Australians to be an improvement over postwar Australian coffee makes one grateful to have never tasted the latter.

Qantas had to improve their standard of service for the same reason American carriers did—an unprecedented wave of new airlines in their most lucrative markets. In their case the competition was even more severe, coming as it did from both ends of the spectrum. The same proliferation of charter airlines broke their monopoly on many routes and siphoned off the bargain-conscious, while new private and government-owned carriers competed at the high end.

Among the domestic carriers, Trans Australian Airways started flying in 1946 with DC-3s. Pioneering stewardess Audrey Bussell reminisced that she hadn't been fully trained and described the service for the book *Gourmet and Glamour in the Air*. "In the tiny DC-3 galley would be 21 plastic trays in a slot with each one containing ham or chicken, lettuce and tomatoes with tinned peaches or pears." Audrey recalled her first flight alone on the DC-3 when she unfortunately put the mayonnaise on the peaches and the custard on the salad. "Not one passenger complained and all said the meal was lovely! In those early days after the war passengers were delighted even with the tea out of the urn and a biscuit."

Things improved after the airline purchased DC-4s—a TAA advertisement in the late 1940s showed a typical menu as follows:[18]

Roast Chicken and Ham with Lemon and Parsley Seasoning
Baked Potatoes, Garden Salad
Apple Slice and Custard Dessert
Cheese and Biscuits, Fresh Fruits
Coffee and Mints

Internationally, Qantas's competition was even stiffer, including carriers from former British colonies. Once India became independent in 1948, the government immediately set up a national airline using new Lockheed Constellation aircraft. Air India's service was a landmark because they were the first airline to serve an extensive selection of non-European food, with vegetarian options on all flights. Indians were used to eating snacks from metal lunchboxes called tiffins, a style of dining that was conveniently similar to airline meals, and the airline took advantage of the tens of thousands of restaurants in the country that already made these prepacked meals. Curries, chutneys, and other traditional items were served on board, all served along with European beers, wines, and Champagne.[19]

BOAC also faced competition on many routes, including in Africa, where new carrier East African Airways and previously small South African Airways started rapid expansion. Neither made any attempt to innovate in catering or reflect their cultural roots, which was fortunate for the British carrier, as that company was in no position to improve things. The government-owned airline was under pressure to buy British aircraft, and none were ready that matched the American designs. BOAC had purchased Avro

Lancastrian aircraft that were very fast but had no heating facilities, which put their meal service a decade behind their competitors.[20] The carrier also continued to operate the slow but stately flying boats and even bought new ones like the Short Solent. These offered space and luxury but were up to a hundred miles an hour slower than their competitors. In order to not lose transatlantic business traffic the airline bought American Lockheed Constellations, their first purchase of foreign aircraft. Aboard these craft BOAC's food options improved, though they did not match the standard of their competitors until the mid-1950s.

As Europe's economy revived, some carriers tried to compete on the basis of superior food and service. Alitalia started service in 1947 with meals made by the famous Rosati Restaurant on the Via Veneto in Rome, serving lavish dinners and plenty of good Chianti wine. The service did not become popular because the airline was forced to buy Italian aircraft, and the only ones available were obsolete Savoia-Marchetti 95s, probably the last passenger aircraft built with plywood wings and fabric-covered fuselages. The aircraft were not pressurized, so when they flew over the Alps passengers had to don individual oxygen masks. Only when Alitalia bought more modern aircraft did their service become competitive.[21]

Air France was also under pressure to buy domestic aircraft but only operated those on uncompetitive routes; they wisely purchased Constellations for their Atlantic service. Ads proclaiming "The Magic Door to France" promoted their food service as a way to experience French culture the moment you started traveling. The pictures of happy people drinking Champagne in flight helped make them a popular choice, and they quickly gained a substantial share of service to Europe.

The major American carrier across the Atlantic was Pan Am, once the United States' only international carrier, and it too faced new competition. United obtained routes to Hawaii, Northwest to Alaska, TWA to Europe, and dozens of carriers to South America and Mexico. Pan Am continued to operate flying boats on some routes but also invested in what they hoped would be another game-changing aircraft—the Boeing 377 Stratocruiser. This double-decked aircraft carried 114 passengers in unparalleled luxury, with meal service called the President Special on flights from New York to Paris. This involved a staff of five serving seven-course meals after takeoff, then taking requests for morning breakfasts that would be cooked to order.[22] After dinner, passengers could relax over drinks in a lounge on the lower deck.

After decades of prohibiting alcohol on their flights, Pan Am had to copy their European rivals and serve it transatlantic, though at first they still charged for it in the Pacific. This policy caused confusion on Pan Am's round-the-world flights—eastbound passengers had free drinks as far as India and had to pay for them the rest of the way. The policy changed in 1948 when a stewardess insisted on charging Pan Am's president Juan Trippe $1.50 for a cocktail on a Pacific flight; he didn't have any change and had to borrow it from another passenger. The policy was changed almost immediately after Trippe got back to his office.[23]

Though the Stratocruiser proved too inefficient and costly to maintain for Pan Am and other airlines to operate profitably, it was a public relations coup for carriers that had it when they started flights in April 1949. The faster, higher-flying jets that would replace this aircraft were already making their test flights, and the 1950s dawned with the promise that everything would be faster and better.

CHAPTER 9

~~~~~~~~~~~

Physiology of Taste in Flight

Prior to 1935 most aircraft flew below three thousand feet, unless mountains forced the decision to go higher. Even though many airliners had the ability to fly far above this level, climbing to higher altitudes required so much fuel that pilots preferred to fly low. In an era before reliable electronic navigation, this also allowed them to keep track of landmarks on the ground.

Unfortunately for passengers, flying this low means the aircraft is usually in more turbulent air, which is why as many as a quarter of the passengers on any given flight were airsick.[1] For those passengers who had a meal of any kind on the aircraft, the experience was much the same as it would have been aboard a boat in moderate seas—tight quarters and some motion, but no change in the taste of meals.

Once airliners started routinely flying higher, airline caterers discovered something that people who live in cities like Denver or Mexico City already knew; food tastes different at high altitudes. This is partly because in conditions of very low humidity, the human sense of smell is much less acute, and scent is a major component of taste. This means that most items that are cooked at sea level and spiced accordingly will taste bland if eaten at high altitude. It is not too surprising that one of the major centers for research in this question, the Rocky Mountain Taste and Smell Center, is located in Denver at over five thousand feet altitude. Codirector Tom Finger, speaking at the 2008 International Symposium on Olfaction and Taste, said, "(When you) lose the olfactory component, you lose much of the flavor component of food,"[2] and anyone who has ever had a cold is well aware of this fact.

The dryness of the air inside an aircraft above five thousand feet is compounded by the lower air pressure at this altitude. A study by the German airline Lufthansa reviewed in the *Wall Street Journal* showed that even in a modern pressurized aircraft, the combination of the two makes human taste buds 30 percent less sensitive.[3]

The fact that recipes need to be adjusted for altitude probably didn't escape the people who usually live in these regions, who found that recipes straight from cookbooks were less appetizing. Until the era of flight there was no way of quickly going from one altitude to another without time to acclimate to the change. It is interesting to consider that the pioneering airline caterers like Dobbs, who started into the business because he was dissatisfied with airline food, did so after flights at higher altitude became commonplace. It may be, as Shakespeare might have put it, that the fault was not in their meals, but in themselves.

Passengers aboard high-altitude but unpressurized aircraft like the Condor must have endured tasteless meals, regardless of the talents of whoever made them. Most flyers probably would have been unlikely to be hungry in any case, because long periods of low pressure suppress appetites and make people slightly queasy even when they are not in motion. The era of pressurized aircraft like the Stratocruiser helped alleviate these problems, but by no means eliminated them. Pressurized aircraft do not have an artificial climate that is the same as sea level; instead an aircraft flying at twenty thousand feet has an environment akin to that of normal conditions at about eight thousand feet.[4] To pressurize the aircraft to sea level would require diversion of a huge amount of power from the engines, and would place such stress on the aircraft that it would risk blowing out the windows. To humidify high-flying aircraft to sea level conditions was not even tried until BOAC installed equipment on their 747s in the 1970s. This required huge amounts of water, which added weight, displaced paying passengers, and added to the risk of corrosion of the aircraft's fuselage.[5] Even modern aircraft have not overcome these challenges, so the problem must have been greater with the more primitive technology of early high altitude aircraft.

The problems with the way our sense of taste works were compounded by the ways that common food items react under these conditions of dryness and low pressure. These challenges were recognized as early as 1939, when United's Don Magarell gave a lecture at the St. Regis Hotel in New York that was covered in an article in the *New York Times*. That piece began,

> At 5,000 feet in the air it takes six minutes to boil a three-minute egg. Hot coffee packed in a thermos bottle for an airplane lunch is wont to expand

rapidly and blow off the cork. Milk had better be drunk quickly because it curdles almost instantaneously. Freshly baked rolls will be dry as a bone within a matter of minutes, and dire things happen to inferior fruits and vegetables in the high altitudes of airplane travel.[6]

Magarell and other prewar caterers did not have the scientific studies that would be available to later generations, and made adjustments based on their empirical studies and interviews with passengers. The early experiments with frozen food gave them valuable data, such as the advantages of using wine sauces and other fragrant preparations. Studies of human physiology in the 1960s revealed more details about the way we taste in different environments. These showed that when it comes to our taste buds, some flavors are more impacted than others. Perceptions of sweetness and saltiness are disproportionately reduced, and sauces that are tasty at ground level seem watery and insipid.

It was not until 1973 that chef Raymond Oliver of the French airline UTA started reformulating that airline's meals in light of that research. Oliver, who earned three Michelin stars at his Paris restaurant Le Grand Vefour before consulting for the airline, made drastic changes. He increased the salt, sugar, cream, and fat in recipes made in that carrier's flight kitchens, and the improvement was recognized immediately. Even carriers that were much less ambitious about meal service or flew shorter routes learned the lessons about what made passengers happy, and sugared and salted peanuts became standard items aboard commuter flights.[7]

Collaborations between scientists and chefs followed, and continue today. One sponsored by German caterer LSG in 2010 showed that while most mild European spices are much harder to perceive at high altitudes, strong flavors such as cumin and cardamom are only slightly diminished. Noting that these flavors are prominent in Indian food, LSG catering manager Ernst Derenthal was quoted in the Wall Street Journal in 2010 as saying that airline food might be better if he only offered curries inflight, "but the passengers wouldn't let us." In stating this, he might have identified why some travelers like to fly Air India transatlantic despite that carrier's dismal on-time performance.

Another study by British Airways focuses on one of the sensations less affected by altitude: umami. Chef Heston Blumenthal did a series of taste tests with researchers from the London-based Leatherhead Food Institute in 2013 and found that manipulating recipes to heighten this sense of savoriness improved the satisfaction of diners. Blumenthal's first idea about what to do to make meals more enjoyable was to issue everyone on the aircraft saline nasal spray that they could use just before meals to temporarily restore their senses, but this was vetoed by the airline. Blumenthal then devised recipes with enhanced umami so that even impaired palates could be stimulated.[8]

The taste of wine is even more affected by altitude, because humans lose the ability to taste sweet, fruity flavors and to perceive alcohol itself. Wines that are well balanced at sea level taste watery and acidic at mealtime inflight. In an interview with CNN in 2012, *Meininger's Wine Business International* editor-at-large Robert Joseph said, "Within your body you perceive less of the fruit that is in a wine and more of the acidity and more of the tannins, the hard texture, you'll get in red wines. Ironically, some of the finest wines in the world, some of the finest Bordeauxs, actually don't taste good at altitude."[9] The result is that the powerful and highly alcoholic Italian, Australian, Chilean, and Californian wines are more popular than their more subtle German and French counterparts.

The change in perceptions also explains why another beverage is one of the most enjoyed in the air. Tomato juice is salty, sweet, slightly acidic, and relatively thick, and one of the most popular and refreshing beverages inflight. (This also explains why Bloody Marys are one of the most often ordered tipples.)[10] Hot tea, with steam that helps rehydrate the mucous membranes in the nose, is more popular than iced tea, but since the conditions aboard aircraft enhance bitter flavors, only mild teas should be served. British Airways food and beverage manager Christopher Cole commissioned the Twinings tea company to come up with a special blend that would taste better at high altitude and started serving it in late 2013.[11] Unfortunately they were unable to find a blend of coffee that didn't taste significantly worse at high altitude, so the first hot beverage ever served inflight will probably continue to taste awful for the foreseeable future.

Recent studies have shown that another factor may influence our perception of food inflight—a study commissioned by the Dutch company Unilever showed that people who dine in an environment with loud white noise and vibration taste things less acutely.[12] The 2013 study by Chef Blumenthal and the Leatherhead Institute revealed another possible environmental factor—that the cool temperatures and grayish lighting typical of airline cabins also dull the sense of taste.

The people who prepared airline meals in the early days of passenger flight couldn't have known that they were combating so many different factors, which makes the fact that they managed even slightly palatable food more remarkable.

CHAPTER 10

———≋≋≋≋———

Competition, Regulation, and the Dawn of the Jet Age
(1950–1958)

The great American philosopher Frank Zappa once observed that "You can't be a real country unless you have a beer and an airline." In the postcolonial era of the 1950s national pride demanded that new countries have their own carriers, regardless of the passenger travel their home markets might support. The book *Government Birds* details how competition by government-subsidized airlines affected the once-dominant carriers, noting that between 1949 and 1957, the number of carriers flying international routes to the United States rose from twenty-two to thirty-nine. American carriers had captured 75 percent of all traffic between the United States and other nations at the beginning of this period, but this dropped to 63 percent by the end.[1]

Pan Am had lost their monopoly on international flights but continued as the dominant carrier between the United States and the rest of the world. Though they still operated some seaplane services with the last generation of flying boats, they also adopted the Stratocruiser and DC-4s. The latter had the first tray tables that folded down from the backs of the seats, and old hands who had been used to setting up elaborate contraptions aboard flying boats were pleased by the ease of working aboard these aircraft. They also liked the efficiency of frozen food—as steward Sam Toaramina remarked,

We had a little oven, about 24 inches long and 16 or 18 inches high and little shelves in it. . . . It might have held 6 to 8 meals, and you took those out, took the foil off of them, put them on a tray, and that was your meal. Just take the foil off and give it to the passenger—Oh, and add a roll to it and a salad, a little salad that was already prepared. I could carry two in one hand and one in the

In 1948 it was possible to get breakfast in bed for a "modest surcharge" on Pan Am's around-the-world flights.
Airline bankrupt, permission given by EverythingPanAm

other so I could feed three people at a time, go back and get three more, and keep doing that until we finished the whole airplane. Passengers had a little tray that folded down from the back of the seat, it was very small, I'd say 12 x 12" or so. It was an easy meal to do, you had nothing to do . . .[2]

The stewards no longer had to carry trays after Pan Am adopted an innovation pioneered by BOAC—a wheeled trolley that could carry food and drink for meal services but could be folded and stored when not needed. This was invented by an engineer named Stan Bruce, and it made service faster and more reliable because staff no longer had to balance the trays while walking down the aisle.[3]

The simpler service in these and later aircraft allowed a reduction in staff—instead of the crews of eight to ten cabin personnel, Pan Am's DC-4s could operate with as few as two service staff and a purser. The latter spent much of his time dispensing another innovation; the first airline miniature bottles, which at first sold for thirty-five cents each. There was theoretically a limit on these, but in practice passengers could usually get as many as they wanted.

Pan Am also served Champagne for free, though the carrier was plagued with employee pilferage of the expensive wine. Former Pan Am Pacific

Division chief Anthony Olanio recalled that when he was a passenger on a flight in the early '50s, the staff weren't offering refills as they were supposed to. He found out that the extra bottles were being saved for the wedding of one of the stewardesses—when Olanio looked in a closet in the crew quarters in Hawaii, he found "bottles and bottles of the bubbly stuff, enough to float a battleship."[4]

Pan Am did their best to maintain the standard of service they had pioneered in the prewar era, and they prospered despite competition from the flood of new entrants. In part this was because they had a trusted brand, in part because some of their competitors were forced to operate most services for political reasons rather than economic ones. The British, French, Dutch, and Portuguese national carriers operated a route system that connected current and former colonies with the mother country, even if there was little traffic. The finances of most of these carriers were deliberately opaque, but it is safe to say that all of them lost money on most of their worldwide operations. As a result, they became increasingly interested in attracting passengers on those routes that offered some chance of actually making a profit. In the early 1950s most of those were across the Atlantic, and since most carriers were flying identical American-built aircraft, the only way they could compete was on the basis of service. Before the introduction of frozen food, this involved a high level of individual choice that could only be achieved by onboard cooking. On the fourteen-hour flight from London to New York on BOAC, passengers could request their roast beef rare, medium, or well-done, and their breakfast eggs were cooked to order. Drinks flowed freely, and stewardesses poured fine wines for delighted passengers who had never known such luxury.

The cost of providing this type of service became ruinous even for carriers that had substantial government support, and in 1951 the trade association for the major airlines, the International Airline Transport Association (IATA), met in Nice, France, to consider what to do. They were faced with increasing competition from charter operations that only served profitable markets and siphoned off budget-conscious leisure travelers, leaving them to compete with each other for demanding business passengers. At that meeting the carriers agreed to an innovation: a separate compartment aboard their aircraft for tourist-class passengers, who would accept a lower standard of service in exchange for lower fares.[5] Originally it was decided that passengers would pay for meals, but the agreement was almost immediately amended to make them free.

In order to prevent airlines from raising standards in tourist class to poach business from competitors, the amenities that could be offered were carefully spelled out. The detailed restrictions, called "Conditions of Service," included the definition of a lunch or dinner as follows:

One glass of fruit juice or one cup of soup or one canapé.
One entrée main course with two vegetables or one vegetable and a salad.
One piece of fruit or one pastry or one piece of chocolate.
Bread, butter, biscuits and cheese.

Drinks had to be charged for in economy class, and any additional items given to passengers—even in first class—had to be shown to be "for use on board."[6]

Had all of the airlines that were signatory to these pacts actually rigorously enforced them, food in flight worldwide might have become as boring as the endless parade of cold fried chicken lunches that greeted most airline travelers in the late 1920s. However, as soon as the ink was dry on the agreement, airlines started figuring out ways of circumventing the rules without actually violating them.

As an example, in 1952 KLM started serving genever gin in specially designed Delft blue porcelain bottles made in the shape of traditional Dutch houses. The shape and style of these beautiful bottles was varied, and the ninety-three different porcelain houses quickly became collector's items. Other airlines cried foul, citing the section of the conditions of service that specified that no gifts be given to passengers. KLM's management argued straight-faced that they were allowed to give out free drinks, and nothing in the rules said they had to be served in a glass. It was later pointed out that on flights to Muslim countries where no alcohol was served, KLM gave the ceramic houses out empty, but no protests could make the Dutch stop.[7]

The British carrier BOAC, which was one of the instigators of the restrictions, was also in violation of them during 1952, the year of the coronation of Queen Elizabeth II. In that year they offered an "Elizabethan" meal service as a celebration—as a former employee wrote on the *Stewardist* website, an online forum for retired airline personnel, "if I recall correctly, they offered some *fifteen* courses, most of them meat. (Try doing *that* as a Buy-On-Board service)." It didn't last long but roast beef, presented on a trolley with all the trimmings and carved at your seat by the purser, was a staple of BOAC/British Airways catering for years.[8]

The agreement had specified the amenities in tourist class with the expectation that all carriers would continue operating their first-class service as it had been. There was nothing in the rules about offering an even more luxurious service, so in 1952 Air France debuted a premium cabin aboard the first aircraft configured for three-class service. This service had different names depending on the route—"Epicurien" on the London service, "Etoile de Dakar" on flights to Senegal, and "Parisien Special" on flights to New York. The meals were lavish, with items like truffled foie gras and trout with tarragon served on Limoges porcelain, and brandy and liqueurs served after meals.[9] Air France hauled out the old description of their London service as a "flying restaurant," boasting that their menus changed daily. In 1953 British European Airways responded with Silver Wing service on the routes where they competed, serving rare whiskies after similarly sumptuous meals that might include lobster mayonnaise, roast beef, white asparagus, petit fours, and banana splits. Despite the fact that the food wasn't quite as fancy, those flights became more popular because BEA was flying the new Vickers Viscount turboprop aircraft, which were quieter, faster, and had less vibration.

These premium services were principally offered on routes where the airlines faced competition, but on routes where the airlines had monopolies, passengers endured inferior food aboard older, slower aircraft. On many of these, inflight service was nonexistent. As late as 1954 it was estimated that 40 percent of all passenger flights still stopped for meals rather than serving them in flight. This continued for a surprisingly long time—as late as the 1980s Air Afrique flights from Dakar to Kinshasa stopped for two hours for lunch in Lomé and again for dinner in Libreville.[10]

Despite the IATA agreements, the level of competition gradually rose, as airlines that flew routes that were seasonally unpopular piled on the amenities to sell their connecting service. The prime example was SAS, whose management knew that very few tourists would want to visit freezing Scandinavia in fall and winter. They resolved to offer service so good that passengers would decide to take a connecting flight through Stockholm or Copenhagen on their trips from the United States to southern Europe, rather than a nonstop flight on an airline with a reputation for inferior service. They did this by creative interpretation of the meaning of the word "sandwich" to include an entire traditional smorgasbord as long as it was served on top of bread. Stewardesses came through the aisles with platters of shrimp, caviar, lobster, and other delicacies, all followed by shots of traditional aquavit. For several years SAS offered extraordinary service while their competitors grumbled and growled. Other carriers tried to upscale their own meals with similarly creative definitions of the term, in a comical episode that came to be known as the "sandwich wars."

It all came to a head in 1958, when someone in SAS's sales department sent an intemperately worded letter to prospective business clients, which included the line, "On our planes you won't find rubbery indigestables wrapped in cellophane." The letter got around, and eventually a copy wound up in the hands of an executive at TWA, who blew his top. That executive contacted the airlines' legal department, and in short order a lawsuit for defamation was in the works. Eventually a $20,000 fine was slapped on SAS, and an emergency meeting of IATA was convened to resolve the situation. After two full days of argument in London, it was ruled that a sandwich must be "cold, largely of bread or something similar, unadorned, self-contained, and must not include such fillings as caviar, oysters, or lobster."[11] It was a fittingly ridiculous end to one of the most absurd battles in the history of regulation.

Besides this sort of rule bending, the carriers that formed IATA had to deal with other companies that had not joined their cartel, and hence were not bound by its rules. These carriers were called non-IATA airlines, and by being outside that club those carriers lost the ability to broadly interchange tickets, sell their flights using the common ticket stock, and be a member of certain revenue-sharing deals.[12] They could, however, undercut the rates set by IATA and set their own standards of service. In the case of many airlines that faced no competition, standards and fares were both rock-bottom, but some managed to innovate. One of the most famous of these was the Icelandic carrier Loftleidir, which offered extremely low prices on one-class flights between American East Coast cities and smaller cities in Europe. All flights made a stop in Iceland, and after the sandwich wars, Loftleidir took advantage of the company's Scandinavian heritage and presented a more modest imitation of the famed SAS smorgasbord. It was a way to draw passengers to an airline that simultaneously boasted of their cheap fares and admitted their tendency to run off-schedule with a 1960s PR campaign that advertised, "Slowest But Lowest."[13]

Another carrier that sought to attract passengers based on food quality was Malayan Airways, the predecessor of Malaysian Airways. Unlike Air India, they served primarily Western food—hot tomato soup just after takeoff, followed by chicken casserole, parsley potatoes, and vegetables, then fresh fruit, coffee, and tea.[14] One of their competitors was Philippine Airways, which initiated an aggressive expansion that included flights to Europe and the USA. At various times they apparently offered a choice of European or Filipino-style food on their international flights, but their operations were chaotic due to graft-ridden and incompetent management.[15]

None of the charter lines that competed with both IATA and the non-IATA carriers made any attempt to provide interesting food, preferring to compete only on price. These carriers ceded the business and luxury market to their scheduled competitors, but the system did not change in response. The pattern of multiple-class flights had been set for long-distance international operations by major carriers, and with rare exceptions it was to remain that way.

The international initiatives to standardize multiclass travel were mirrored inside the United States, but as with the changes to the American airmail subsidy system, things were started by an aggressive federal bureaucrat. Major airlines had instituted coach service as early as 1948, but this was limited to flights at unpopular times, and all travelers experienced the same level of service on those flights. Those flights were designed to put pressure on the bane of the majors' existence: the non-skeds. Those carriers were highly unreliable but extremely cheap and threatened to reduce the public perception of air service, and the major carriers hated them. Scheduled airline operators wanted the non-skeds put out of business so that they would

Ads to attract businesspeople in the 1950s were unabashedly sexist. Comparable ads aimed at women during this era tended to emphasize visiting family members. Image from author's collection

be able to conduct orderly operations for their business-oriented clientele, and were shocked when the bureaucrat who regulated their industry said that they needed to make changes themselves. To compete with the non-skeds, he theorized, the scheduled airlines would have to offer service that was cheaper and would entice new passengers aboard their flights. They could do that by expanding a product many of them already offered: reduced fares on inconveniently timed flights. These went under the name of coach or economy service.

In a speech in 1950, Donald Nyrop, the chairman of the American Civil Aeronautics Board, noted that only one-third of scheduled airline passengers were on pleasure trips, and said "Coach service is an effort to increase public acceptance of air travel." The next year he issued a policy statement that announced that certificated (i.e., scheduled) airlines would be expected to expand their coach services.[16] Most carriers were against this idea, with United Airlines president William Patterson initially a fervent opponent, but he was persuaded that the proposed fare cut of 30 percent for the tourist-class flights would increase traffic and help drive the non-sked carriers out of existence. It is hard to establish the degree to which it did, since shortly after the regime went into practice several non-sked carriers suffered crashes or highly public failures to operate. In any case, within five years the non-sked market had collapsed, though more regular charter operations continued to thrive. Though the competition had disappeared, tourist-class flights didn't, as the airlines figured out that the same square footage of the more densely packed economy-class cabin produced the identical revenue as first class. Meals in economy were initially sold for $1.50, slightly more than they actually cost, and were not a large part of the calculation.

The CAB's actions to promote discounted travel occurred at the same time the agency was allocating routes in a way that effectively froze out the ability of new carriers to start scheduled service. As a result, the established carriers didn't have to worry about new competitors, and they were allowed to focus on building their brands. They did this with food and beverage service.

One of the first innovators was Western Airlines, which was branded as "The Champagne Airline" and started serving that beverage to all passengers in 1952.[17] This was unusual, because some carriers didn't serve alcohol of any kind on domestic flights until several years later. TWA served Champagne between Los Angeles and Chicago to compete with Western, but not on most other domestic flights until 1957.[18]

Western's decision to serve Champagne on all flights was not without its technical challenges. The first time they tried serving bubbly and a meal on flights between Los Angeles and San Francisco, they found that it took about an hour and fifty minutes to serve the whole planeload of people—fourteen minutes longer than was available. Flights services director Richard Ensign came up with various ways to speed the process, including opening one-third of the bottles before takeoff and pouring at the passengers' seats rather than pouring in the galley and serving from a tray. These and other innovations shaved off fifteen minutes, so the service could be delivered as promised.[19]

Western upgraded inflight services so they could compete with United on West Coast routes, at the time one of the few year-round competitive markets in the United States. The management instituted a choice of meals on flights, a rarity in those days, and served salad, a choice of seafood or filet mignon, vegetable, and dessert. Gifts helped seal the deal—Western-branded cigars were handed out to the men, and perfume to women. Western also introduced the oddest meal-based promotion to date: "Hunt Breakfasts," for which the stewardesses donned red coats and black hats so they would look like English fox hunters. In case the clothing didn't tip off passengers to the theme, a tape recorder hidden in the bottom of the service cart blasted the sound of bugles blowing and hounds barking. The service was wildly popular, but a decision by the FAA to outlaw the use of the tape recorder ended it.[20]

The most daring and unusual innovation in the marketing of inflight meals came from an airline that had previously served almost nothing. Northwest had a history going back to 1926, but before the war had operated a fleet of Lockheed Electras and other aircraft without galleys. During the war Northwest pilots gained considerable experience flying the North Pacific, and in 1947 the airline whose longest route had been from Chicago to Seattle started flying to Hawaii, and was also awarded a route to Tokyo and onward to Manila. They bought Stratocruisers and DC-4s, painted the tails their signature bright red, and started calling the carrier Northwest Orient.

Service on those overseas flights was apparently conventional, though Asian-style meals were loaded for flights beyond Tokyo. It was another story in the United States, where Northwest decided to promote their Asian service by decorating their aircraft with Japanese motifs. This was a daring decision less than ten years after the end of the war with Japan, when animosity toward the former enemies was still fresh in some people's minds. Nevertheless Northwest went whole-hog with the concept, calling the lower-level cocktail lounges aboard their Stratocruisers the Fujiyama Room, with a live bonsai tree by the access staircase. For passengers on flights from Minneapolis to Portland this must have been the height of exotica, a taste of the larger world to enliven a business trip or holiday jaunt.

The experience was detailed in a book called *Fujiyama Trays and Oshibori Towels* by former Northwest stewardess Ann Kerr, who served aboard these aircraft. In one passage she quotes Northwest's food service manager Al Cariveau describing the centerpiece of Northwest's service at that time, a luxuriant platter of canapés called the Fujiyama Tray.

> In the center of the large colorful tray was a pineapple cut flat on the bottom. The following items were skewered onto the pineapple with Asian type picks—shrimp, cheese, ham, cherry tomatoes, and various types of fruit cut into squares. Tray decorations included small wooden Asian dolls and other oriental trinkets, parasols and ribbons.[21]

As is obvious to anyone who knows Japanese food, this wasn't it—this arrangement has more in common with the pu-pu platters served in tiki bars, minus the flaming spareribs. Dinners that followed these appetizers were more conventional, though more opulent than served aboard most other carriers. Anne Kerr remembered meals consisting of

> chilled lobster tidbits mignonette with rye wafers; then consommé Regale and Terrace salad bowl. The main course was served from a heated serving cart: choice prime beef . . . or on Fridays beef or African lobster tail; potatoes duchesse, long cut green beans and onion rings, pumpernickel bread and oven fresh rolls with creamery butter. Wines served with a dinner included Vino Orvieto Orlando; Pommard cruise (sic) burgundy; and Imperator champagne, dry. Soon to roll down the aisle was a dessert tray featuring your choice of French pastries, cheesecake, or cheese variants and wafers. After dessert the cart rolled again—carrying silver decanters of B&B, Drambuie and crème de menthe. Mints Diane and the ever-present Marlboro cigarettes completed the service.[22]

Though the subtleties of traditional Japanese food may have eluded their chefs and passengers, Northwest's slogan at this time was direct and to the point: "You Dine The Best When You Fly Northwest."

Other carriers preferred to reflect American regional cuisine; Memphis-based Chicago & Southern Airlines called their aircraft "Dixie Liners" and boasted in 1950 that on their flights to New Orleans they served "cuisine influenced by the best traditions of famed Southern chefs." In an article in the *Memphis Commercial Appeal*, food and beverage director J. W. Meyer said that their most popular dishes included Creole salad remoulade, Mardi Gras onion consommé, black bottom pie, and a dish that modern diners would connect with the food crazes of the era more than Southern traditions, "plantation frozen tomato salad."[23] Meyer provided the recipe for these items in that article, and you will find it and others at the back of this book.

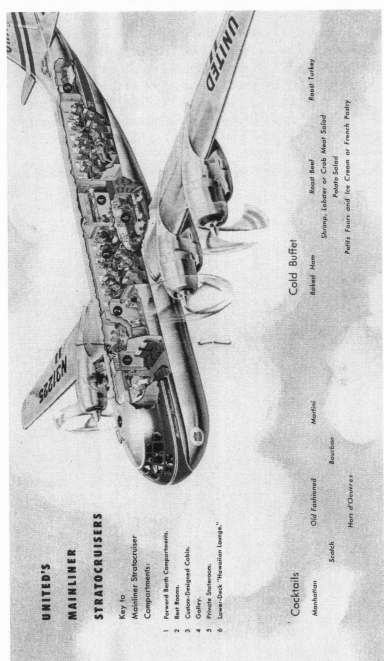

UNITED'S MAINLINER STRATOCRUISERS

Key to
Mainliner Stratocruiser
Compartments:

1 Forward Berth Compartments.
2 Rest Rooms.
3 Custom-Designed Cabin.
4 Galley.
5 Private Stateroom.
6 Lower-Deck "Hawaiian Lounge."

Cocktails

Manhattan   Old Fashioned   Martini

Scotch   Bourbon

Hors d'Oeuvres

Cold Buffet

Baked Ham   Roast Beef   Roast Turkey

Shrimp, Lobster or Crab Meat Salad

Potato Salad

Petits Fours and Ice Cream or French Pastry

This menu from United Airlines in the 1950s shows the Stratocruiser's layout, with the galley in the center and a lower-deck "Hawaiian Lounge." There was no attempt to serve Hawaiian-themed food or beverages.

Image from author's collection

Every carrier that served meals created themes that were carried through in the design of their china and glassware and the color schemes of napkins and tablecloths. Long-lasting brands were created at this time—American Airlines Flagship flights and United Airlines Red Carpet service both debuted in the early 1950s and remained those airlines' trademarks for decades.[24] These themed services and others like them showed that airlines both domestically and internationally were trying to differentiate their services and create brand identifications as never before. They continued doing so as a new generation of aircraft brought improved technologies to both cooking and flying. The jet age was dawning, and with it an era of fast mass transit in the sky.

CHAPTER 11

Airline Food in Popular Culture

The combined efforts of airlines to woo the tourist market and the regulations that forced carriers to lower their fares had the desired effect: people who had never flown before took to the air as passengers, and in the process tried airline food for the first time. If we are to believe most published reports, they did not like it. Having had no experience with the era when inflight food was not available at all, or was limited to cold picnic lunches, they measured their meals against dining experiences on the ground. Not surprisingly, it was found wanting.

Even some people who should have known better were highly critical. The eminent historian Bernard DeVoto wrote a famous account of long-distance flying for *Harper's Magazine* in 1952. He wrote lyrically about the joys of surveying rivers and farmland from above, but was more a curmudgeon when it came to his meals. Among his comments were,

> The airlines will hear no complaint from me if they go back to the box lunch they used to serve, and served well. They ran an excellent lunch counter then; they run a poor restaurant now. I have seldom even had a mediocre meal at it; most are definitely bad. Chair-bound for hours, I would rather trade the counterfeit banquet for a sandwich and a cocktail.[1]

Other commentators were even less complimentary, and in the late 1950s a comedian named Alan King started making airline food a feature in his routines. He usually began these monologues with the line, "Don't get me

Mother Goose and Grimm

Among the many cartoons that bashed airline food was this "Mother Goose and Grimm" comic by Mike Peters from October 2001. It suggested that lack of flavor might have been a problem for longer than expected.
Cartoonist Group

started about airline food," and then, though nobody had asked him to expand on the topic, he would continue with a litany of high-speed jokes and complaints. His favorite target was Eastern Airlines, and after one particularly savage appearance on *The Ed Sullivan Show* in the late 1950s the president of the airline threatened him with a lawsuit.[2] It was a measure of the popularity of air travel that King's routine was considered funny by a broad audience; a decade before, when few people had flown except elite business travelers, these references would have been obscure as jokes about playing polo or yachting.

In subsequent years jokes about airline food became staples of the comics in *Playboy*, *The New Yorker*, and other publications. The topic was even featured in a Broadway musical, the 1964 Steven Sondheim and Richard Rodgers flop "Do I Hear a Waltz?" That play included a song called "What Do We Do? We Fly." The plot involved a lonely American tourist who has a brief affair with an Italian merchant. The other tourists have a number in which they complain about the horrors of air travel, and the verse on food goes:

I hate most of all the chow.
To know what is what
Is difficult, but
I think I've discovered how.
The shiny stuff is tomatoes,

The salad lies in a group.
The curly stuff is potatoes.
The stuff that moves is soup.
Anything that's white is sweet,
Anything that's brown is meat.
Anything that's gray—don't eat!
But what do we do? We fly. Why?
What do we do? We fly![3]

Airline meals continued to be vilified; Joan Rivers got a laugh with "The average airplane is sixteen years old, and so is the average airplane meal."[4] On a more elevated plane, the British food guide author and critic Egon Ronay called airline food "premeditated gastronomic murder"[5] in the 1960s.

The steady stream of invective continued despite two decades in which the standard rose by any objective measure; it has continued into the twenty-first century and an era in which most flights don't actually feature meal service. Ellen DeGeneres is one of the modern comics who has joined the pile-in:

> It's horrible food, but we get so excited when we see that cart coming down the aisle . . . it's the tiniest food I've ever seen in my life, but it's all relative—you look out the window and then back at your tray and say, It's the size of that house down there! I can't eat all that! . . . Anything you get, chicken, steak, has grill marks on it, like we actually believe there's a grill in the front of the plane.[6]

It seems safe to say that the modern comedians who are mining this particular vein of comedy probably don't realize that there was a time when steaks were indeed cooked in flight, and there are few survivors from the flying boat era who are still alive to correct them.

CHAPTER 12

—————≈≈≈≈≈≈≈————

Jet Age Mass Transit and Luxury Competition (1958–1966)

Though it was obvious halfway through World War II that jet aircraft could fly far faster than anything with propellers, a variety of technical difficulties kept them from being widely used as passenger aircraft for over a decade. The first passenger jet to be available, the De Havilland Comet, went into service in 1952 with BOAC and Air France, offering passengers hot and cold meals from a full galley and the option of relaxing in an onboard bar. It could carry as many as 44 passengers at 460 miles per hour with very little vibration and was hailed as the future of aviation. After only two years in service, three instances of aircraft disintegrating in flight caused them to be grounded. The Comet was completely redesigned and a new generation entered service in September of 1958, but that new model was overshadowed by another aircraft that debuted less than a month later. This was the Boeing 707, which could carry 179 passengers at 570 miles per hour. Douglas had their similarly sized and slightly faster DC-8 in the air less than a year later, and it was those two aircraft that became the world leaders in commercial aviation.

The introduction of these big jets changed the aviation world and had huge repercussions for meal service. With flights almost twice as fast as previous aircraft and passenger numbers almost twice as large, the onboard crew were faced with a challenge—serve more meals in less time, follow up with beverages, clean up afterward, and keep smiling all the way through the process. For airlines that operated short flights like those between Los Angeles and San Francisco, even beverage service became difficult. Richard Ensign, the director of inflight services for Western Airlines, conducted a

Western's "Fiesta Service" to Mexico in the late 1950s had nothing resembling Mexican food, but was famous for a lavish dessert cart. This postcard is from 1956.
Image from author's collection

study just after that airline got its first jets. He found that excluding the time for takeoff, reaching altitude, descending, and landing, the average period of level flight for Western's routes was fifty minutes. This meant that if meal service started as soon as it was practical, there was less than thirty seconds per passenger. Ensign found that emptying and storing the glassware took more time than anything else, so in 1958 he tried using plastic glasses and snack trays for the airline's signature service. The disposable plastic cups cost two cents each—less than the cost of buying real glassware and sanitizing it after each use—and it saved over ten minutes on every flight.[1]

Ensign also came up with ways to motivate passengers to eat faster, eliminating any foods that had to be cut with a knife and introducing small foods that required little chewing, like precut club sandwiches and deviled eggs. His ideas were copied by other carriers, and this kind of service became the norm for commuter flights.

Innovations in loading and unloading meals on the aircraft came along with speeding the inflight service. This was necessary because there was a much higher volume of food to be transferred during what was often planned as a brief stop. This was a complex issue, because in this era aircraft did not pull up to a terminal to load and unload passengers, baggage, and cargo—at some airports forklifts were used for meal loading, and at others everything was carried

up and down stairs to the tarmac. Both Dobbs and Marriott have been given credit for the invention and first use of hydraulic scissor lift trucks to load meals aboard aircraft, and I have been unable to determine which was first.[2]

These speeded things up immensely because instead of all supplies being loaded from the kitchen to a truck or van, driven to the airport, and unloaded to be transferred to the aircraft, everything was accomplished with the same vehicle. Specialized meal trolleys were developed that were loaded at the catering kitchen and could be stowed directly into a refrigerated compartment aboard the aircraft without unloading, as well as others with electric units that could be plugged in both during the transfer and aboard the aircraft.[3] The process was faster and subjected the food trays to less vibration and jolts, so fewer meals were damaged in transit. A dining service checklist from United Airlines during the time when they were making the transition from piston aircraft to jets shows how much easier it was for the cabin crew to keep track of things using the new system—there are fourteen items to inventory on the older equipment, six on the jets.[4]

Until the invention of the hydraulic lift catering truck, aircraft had to be loaded by hand from vans like those on the left, regardless of the weather. The lift truck simplified catering, as shown in the picture on the right from the early 1960s.
Image provided by Marriott Corporation

The need to invest in this equipment in order to service the new aircraft led to a rapid consolidation in flight catering in the United States, as local airport restaurants and independent caterers could not compete with major companies. In 1957 Don Magarell of United Airlines employed over 750 chefs and catering workers at fifteen flight kitchens, a huge jump from the four facilities they had owned ten years before, and the staff almost doubled in the next decade. Airports around America were remodeled, developments that were paid for by including retail space in the design so the rents would be an ongoing income stream. Restaurants were also included in airports, many of which used the facilities of flight kitchens, but making recipes that were suited for a good experience on the ground. As a result, airports in the United States became money-making enterprises, while they were regarded as a cost of doing business everywhere else in the world.[5]

Serving different food in airport restaurants and in the air must have come more naturally to flight caterers because they were already learning to cope with making meals to more than one standard. In the United States most airlines had run coach services on entire flights at off-peak hours, but with the introduction of jets carrying twice as many passengers this was impractical. It was decided to reconfigure part of the aircraft with extra legroom and serve better meals there while having the lower-fare service on the opposite side of a curtain.[6] The new jets had at least three galleys, and in the new configuration the first-class meals were loaded into one galley, coach meals in the others. Flight crews had to get used to maintaining inventories of different qualities of meals, and of course the ones in first class were both more varied and involved a higher standard of individualized service.

The explosion of economy seats brought many more passengers but also meant that the airlines aggressively started differentiating their product to encourage business travelers not to use the cheaper service. Typical of these were ads for Delta's Royal Class Service in 1958, which showed stewardesses fawning over passengers with the text

> Not two, but three alert stewardesses assure you of every attention in the brief span of a Delta Royal Service Flight. So linger over your luncheon or dinner with its complimentary champagne and choice of entree (tenderloin steak to order, Rock Cornish hen or seafood on appropriate days). There's also music by Muzak, fast baggage handling, and beverage service for the discerning passengers who specify these luxurious flights.[7]

Rock Cornish game hen was a fad food of the era; actually an immature crossbreed of a Malayan fighting cock and a Plymouth chicken first bred in Connecticut in the 1950s, the tiny birds were tailor-made for inflight service. A whole bird was a single portion and made a pretty presentation; *Inflight Catering Management* noted that "Idle Wild farms' development of the oven-ready stuffed Rock Cornish game hen brought product consistency and a gourmet quality to the use of poultry products for inflight meals."[8]

National Airlines, based in Miami, also advertised in 1963 that they served the little hens in first class along with stuffed baked potatoes and "fancy French pastry" and boasted that they would rotate meals "for variety's sake" even though their other entrées of filet mignon and baked chicken were popular.[9] In the same article, sales manager Paul Bell announced "Cloud Dining" service in coach, making the promise that "no meals would be duplicated both eastbound and westbound, or northbound and southbound, and the schedule would be changed once a month," so that passengers would be

For unexcelled luxury aloft

FLY DELTA *Royal Service Flights*

Folks who discover Delta's Royal Service are eager to tell friends about the sparkle of a dinner that is leisurely, with complimentary champagne and three alert stewardesses in attendance . . . about the choice of entreé (*tenderloin steak to order, Rock Cornish Hen, or seafood on appropriate days*), the beverage service and music by Muzak. Such service in the royal manner is all at regular fare. It's truly *Royal Service!*

These luxurious flights serve:
NEW YORK • WASHINGTON • ATLANTA • HOUSTON • CHICAGO • MIAMI
NEW ORLEANS • DALLAS • PHILADELPHIA • BALTIMORE • MEMPHIS • DETROIT

Delta's DC-8 Jetliners are on their way!

Delta AIR LINES

So many US airlines named their first-class service some variation of the names regal or imperial that it might be suspected that Americans had a lingering fondness for monarchy. This ad ran in 1959. Image from author's collection

guaranteed variety. Three choices were guaranteed even in coach, a high standard for the era.

Some airlines that hadn't invested in jets tried the same strategy that United had used over twenty years before to attract passengers to their flights: upgraded meal service. Northwest offered what they called Regal Imperial service on their Stratocruisers between Chicago and Florida in 1959. For only three dollars over the economy price, passengers were offered a menu that reflects the faux multiculturalism of the era:

Scandinavian pastries and coffee as soon as the plane is airborne.
Hors d'oeuvres: Shrimp in Indian currie (sic) sauce, frankfurters and meat-balls in customized (sic) sauce.
Wintergreen-scented hot and cold towels.

Starter service: Lobster cocktail, salad, and consommé.

Choice prime beef, or on Fridays, choice of beef or lobster tail, duchess potatoes.

Choice of Italian white wine, French red wine, or champagne (from New York).

Dessert: French pastries or cheesecake or cheese and crackers, with coffee.

After-dinner beverage service, from magnums.

Fancy after-dinner mints.

The menu was the same out of Miami, except that a "limeade cooler frappe" replaced the coffee service at the beginning of the flight.[10] The three-dollar extra charge for this kind of service smacks of desperation; Northwest didn't get jets until 1964, six years after their competitor National Airlines, and they were willing to do almost anything to lure business away from them.

One airline had a few aircraft that were so old that they were flying museum pieces—in 1960 Mohawk Airlines still operated prewar DC-3s on flights from Buffalo to Boston, making two stops. Some marketing genius decided that since the aircraft were archaic, they might as well be decorated that way. Mohawk painted them to look like Victorian railroad cars, appointed the interiors with red velvet curtains, fake gaslamps, and brocade wallpaper, and Mohawk's gaslight service was born. Stewardesses dressed like dance hall girls solemnly requested that passengers not open the windows when the aircraft was going through tunnels and passed out pretzels, beer, and cigars. The promotion was so popular that instead of retiring the aircraft after a year as had been planned, Mohawk bought another one, painted it the same way, and expanded the service. The DC-3's last scheduled commercial flights in the United States ended on cheerful note. Mohawk's profits on the service helped make them enough money to buy jets, and they became the first regional American carrier to do so.

Small airlines on competitive routes that didn't have the genius of Mohawk's marketing department or the money to buy jets were faced with a dark choice: merge or go bankrupt. The CAB, which regulated American carriers, didn't like bankruptcies and forced several carriers into "negotiations" that could have only one outcome. Venerable names disappeared, strong carriers got stronger and extended jet service, and with it better food service, to places that had previously been underserved.

The opposite happened internationally, where government-owned or subsidized airlines were often given preferential loans to buy private competitors. Only in Britain was there much competition, as several small carriers arose to provide service within the country and to points in Europe and Africa.

The logistics of inflight meals were also different in Europe, where most air-lines operated their own catering departments or contracted piecemeal with local firms. Catering was seen as a loss-making division by most airlines and not worth investing money in, so food continued to be delivered to aircraft in a motley collection of vans, pickup trucks, and even modified bicycles with large baskets. Given that BOAC and BEA were serving over ten thousand meals a day in the air, some consisting of six or seven courses, this was a huge volume of food to be loaded using antiquated methods.[11] BEA didn't set up their own catering center at London-Heathrow until 1967, almost a decade after most American carriers had sophisticated operations on-site.

The complexity of catering was magnified by a proliferation of classes on some international aircraft. In 1959 BOAC had four different classes of ser-vice on some long routes: De Luxe, First Class, Tourist, and Economy. Pan Am—at that time exclusively an international airline—never went that far, but even for their trained personnel, the new pattern of service was a chal-lenge. Pan Am purser Sam Toaramina noted that for crews who were used to flying boats and jets, even though the first-class service was simplified, it took some getting used to.

> We had to go back to school because the service was entirely different. You set up a table, you put the condiments down first, and then you put your roll ups there. Then you bring up the food individually. The salads come out first, or soup service, then the entrées. Then you clean all that up and come out with a dessert. Later on, they started with a cheese cart. All different kinds of cheeses on it, and fruit. Then you come out with another dessert cart with gourmet pies, cakes, etc. and you went through that service. . . . It was a little more work because you had double the people or triple the people on there. You had to coordinate your flight, because the aircraft was so much faster. . . . I didn't want to be serving you lunch on your landing, going into London. I wanted that last hour for you to prepare for your arrival, not eating.

A Pan Am promotional film from 1958 showed a stewardess serving attrac-tively presented meals on a tray set with linens while a voiceover proclaimed, "Delicious food adds to the enjoyment. It is prepared in four simultaneously operating galleys, where dishes can be cooked in five-minute ovens."[12] Despite the visual presentation of highly individualized service, the meals shown were prepared by an industrial process and only reheated onboard.

The frozen inflight meals helped Pan Am maintain their American her-itage wherever they flew; for example, on Thanksgiving the airline served a full turkey dinner no matter where in the world their aircraft were. A purser named Diane White described a flight in 1967 inside Africa in which the shortest leg of the trip from Lagos to Accra . . . was the leg that we had to serve the full turkey meal. We had to dish up everything, but everything, separately. It went from soup to nuts and pumpkin pie with whipped cream for dessert and coffee. (Whipped cream had to be doled out separately.) Economy was full and there were 16 passengers in front and 1 person in the lounge. I was the Purser in front. My legs didn't touch the ground the entire day, we had to hurry so much. We sent a gal back to help in economy since they were not only full, but engulfed in boxes of food which had to be undone and set up and served somehow, somewhere. So there was only the galley girl and myself. There was a tall good-looking first class passenger, very friendly, whom I enlisted to carve the turkey and I would take it out, while the galley girl put all the other items on the cart and trays. He was delighted! He donned an apron and, as soon as we were ready, he sprang into action. Carved the turkey expertly; the potatoes, gravy, cranberry jelly, beans, etc., etc. were all on the plates and we were able to serve everyone rolls, seconds, etc., etc.[13]

The transatlantic rivalry between Pan Am and TWA became fierce, and the latter airline added a new gimmick—since they had the passport information for every passenger, they were able to find out whether someone had a birthday and would surprise them accordingly. Influential *Los Angeles Times* travel writer Jerry Hulse rhapsodized over this service aboard a flight from Los Angeles to Paris in 1962:

TWA found out it was my birthday and insisted on throwing a party (the reservations clerks check every passenger's passport for this very reason). The stewardess brought a vanilla-frosted two-layer cake that spelled out "Best Wishes." . . . As the movie ended the three stewardesses and steward in the first class section began serving a feast unseen since the Beverly Hills Food & Wine Society banded together last. Before leaving Los Angeles everyone was given a booklet which explained: "A Royal Ambassador meal is a series of impressions . . . the soft clink of cocktail glasses . . . the crisp, frosty tang of expertly mixed drinks . . . tasty snacks. . . ." There was a great deal of clinking all right; the beverage list alone contained 36 drinks. . . . This was merely the beginning—just a warm-up for dishes to come, such as Beluga caviar, smoked Nova Scotia salmon and fresh lobster medallion. Among other selections were just about anything you can name from chateaubriands to hot dogs and hamburgers. They even served malts to those who asked for them. The list contained so many selections this column would run overtime telling about them. But just to name a few: Le Canard a L'Orange Au Grand Mariner, or duckling with orange sauce; Les Filets de Sole Ambassadeur—meaning filet of sole with truffles and mushrooms. Sirloin steak, roast filet of beef, double thick lamb chops, etc. As for the salad, it was composed of hearts of palm imported from Argentina. Dawn was breaking as the meal ended. Through a rent in the clouds I caught a glimpse of the River Seine twisting through Paris. It was like coming home. Vive le TWA![14]

Since at that time TWA did not get the passengers' passport information prior to check-in, they must have had time to order a cake and have it decorated within the two hours between check-in and flight departure. This was presumably from one of the airport restaurants, and the incident illustrates one more advantage of having catering companies operating restaurants in the terminals.

All airlines that could afford to buy jets benefited from both the popularity of their fast flights and the economics of mass transport, and they plowed some of the profits into superior food service. This included some newcomers to the industry, carriers from former colonial nations that turned flights into celebrations of their culture. East African Airways flew the redesigned De Havilland Comets, neither the fastest nor most comfortable aircraft, but as early as 1960 they offered a choice of European or African vegetarian meals on all flights. With Air India, they were among the few carriers serving distinctively non-European meals, and in the decade to come others would follow their lead. They were behind most carriers in the United States in terms of the technology of their catering, which was still done with a motley assortment of vans, trucks, and the like, but culturally ahead of their time.

One carrier flouted all the standards of the industry; when non-IATA carrier Cathay Pacific introduced jet service from Hong Kong in 1964, they did something very unusual and offered contemporary cuisine instead of re-creating old favorites. This was remarkable because conventional wisdom held that in stressful conditions of travel, passengers would prefer comfort food that reminded them as much of safe, homelike meals as possible.[15] Cathay Pacific's multicultural menus included shark's fin or kangaroo tail soup, full smorgasbords of the type that were banned from SAS, and most surprisingly, flamed baked Alaska on their flights.[16]

European carriers also served luxurious meals, none more so than Alitalia, which benefited from some of the most lavish government subsidies in the world. Beginning in 1960 their DC-8s offered a continuous parade of food starting as soon as the aircraft achieved level flight. A steward named Silvio Depiante who later became a noted wine connoisseur reminisced that after cocktail service that featured extensive choices and a service of canapés,

> tables were laid for dinner with starched white linen, individual glass cruet sets, cutlery, butter on a china butter chip, wine and water glasses and a china side plate for bread. An antipasto service then followed of wonderful Parma ham with melon balls, sevruga caviar in an ice socle (plinth) with a torch

under the ice to shine through dramatically, or alternatively lobster medallions with lemon and truffle.

Specially selected Italian wines would be offered with each course and freshly baked bread from a basket. A choice of two soups would then be offered from the trolley in stainless steel tureens, one a Consommé with Sherry, the other a vegetable soup with croutons and garniture, served into white china soup bowls. A freshly tossed salad would then be presented from the trolley, with more wines, breads and water. The main course trolley would offer a fillet of beef carved to order with a typical Barolo wine sauce with other choices being Veal Piccata, Saltimbocca, or a fillet of fresh fish. Main courses would be accompanied by roast and boiled potatoes, semolina gnocchi, green beans and baby carrots. Desserts on the DC-8s would include the super Mimosa Torte, Cassata Ice Cream, Zuccotto and fresh fruit tarts, served after the cheese which could include up to five Italian cheeses such as Provolone, Bel Paese, Fontina, Taleggio and Parmesan which would be offered with fresh fruits.[17]

The coach passengers dined in less luxury but still were offered antipasti, salad, and a cheese course before their choice of two meals and dessert.

Other carriers did their best to match this type of service with their own ethnic touches; Lufthansa developed an ornamented beer keg on wheels that went up and down the aisle, which was appreciated by passengers but must have been dangerous if the aircraft entered turbulent air. An undated ad that shows what appears to be a crew member raising a glass with passengers must have appeared before 1968—until then, it was not illegal for crew to drink, only to be drunk.

Every carrier had their gimmick to try to compete for the transatlantic trade. In less competitive markets the food was generally not of the same standard, and in the 1960s the largest closed market was for flights within the Soviet bloc. Russian aircraft were used, of course, and these continued the long tradition of being built bigger than anything produced elsewhere in the world. The TU-104 jet went into service in 1956 carrying fifty passengers, more than the Comet that was its only competition in that era, and the larger TU-114 went into service two years later. This aircraft could hold as many as 224 passengers and was the first jet built with the galleys in the hold and an elevator to deliver meals—an innovation that American aircraft makers copied later. The service on board was luxurious by Russian standards but accomplished by primitive means—as Aeroflot historian Polina Kurovskaya explained,

Tea bags did not yet exist [inside Russia], and in order to avoid tea leaves getting into a glass, the flight attendants came up with brewing tea in cloth bags. A lot of canned food and food in glass containers was brought onboard: pickled cucumbers and tomatoes, apple juice (all in 3-liter jars); mineral water, lemonade in glass bottles. Sometimes the flight attendants had to open hundreds of bottles and cans per flight, breaking their nails and scratching their hands. Jars and bottles had to be brought back in Moscow for re-use (they were meticulously counted at the collecting point) so each plane hauled a lot of glass around the world. Black and red caviar was offered by spoons; the ration was 28 grams per passenger accompanied by vodka (which was not served on domestic flights). Most common hot meal was a chicken or a steak and a side dish: rice, peas, cucumber or tomato—the flight attendants had to put it on each plate.[18]

Aeroflot had a near monopoly on flights to Russia from the West in the early 1960s but started arranging reciprocal landing rights with other carriers as the decade went on. The airline faced direct competition across the Atlantic for the first time in 1968 when Aeroflot and Pan Am both started flying nonstop from New York to Moscow. The management there obviously recognized that their airline had a bad reputation to work off, and for the first flight of journalists and VIPs they mounted a full-scale charm offensive. Stewardesses sewed buttons on shirts for passengers, and the captain made an offer that any baby born aboard an Aeroflot transatlantic flight would get a lifetime pass. (Heaven knows why they would want to encourage this situation.) Their effort got them what was then some of the best press coverage the world could offer, including a cover story in *Life Magazine* that began

> It took the Soviets only one flying day to modify an image which seasoned travelers had expected would keep Aeroflot jets half empty on flights across the Atlantic. The image was of indifferent or nonexistent service. For the inaugural trip to the U.S., the Russians picked a crack crew which included Meritorious Flier of the U.S.S.R. Boris Yegorov as captain and Hero of Socialist Labor Aleksandr Vitkovsty as copilot. They also picked the prettiest and most efficient Aeroflot stewardesses—"the sort," one American reporter traveling on the plane wrote, "who have vanished from most U.S. airlines: smiling kids interested in passengers." The stewardesses poured tea for the queasy, vodka for the venturesome. The button-sewing was quick, and there was caviar and pressed chicken.[19]

The aircraft in this case was an Ilyushin 62 jet, the world's largest jet until the introduction of the 747. The next generation of two-aisle aircraft were cheaper to operate per passenger, safer, carried more people, and added new challenges to catering.

CHAPTER 13

~~~~~~~~~~~~~

Technology of Heat
in Flight, Part Two

The technologies of both heating and cooling were stimulated by the need to preserve and transport food during World War II, and the better systems found their way aboard aircraft almost immediately.

Refrigerators designed by Frederick McKinley Jones of the Thermo-King company for refrigerated trucks were smaller, lighter, and cheaper than anything that came before, all of which led to the end of dry ice boxes aboard aircraft. The most important patent, which Jones filed in 1943, was for a portable refrigerator that could be built into a box with very little venting. This enabled the development of a wheeled cart that could be filled at a flight kitchen, plugged into an outlet in a truck during transport, and plugged in again in the aircraft, all without ever opening the refrigerator door and exposing the contents to heat.[1] It was a revolution that improved hygiene and speed of loading and unloading, but the expensive units were another factor that priced small catering operations out of the market.

The new oven technologies followed an odder path. Visionary inventor William Maxson had pioneered the first efficient convection oven for the Air Force's frozen food experiments, and his company was steadily selling the units for military transports. By 1945 Maxson had turned his attention to the civilian market and had come up with the idea for the first multicompartment plate holding frozen food—the development that would later be reinvented as the TV dinner. Maxson called his invention the Sky Plate, and an article published in the July 1945 issue of *Yank Magazine*, a publication of the US Army, shows that he had things figured out well before his contemporaries:

> The oven used in Navy planes will take care of six Sky Plate meals at a time and weighs 33 pounds. It's not in production yet for retail sale, but tomorrow, or the day after, it will probably sell to housewives for from $15 to $25. Maxson can't quote any price yet on how much his packaged meals will sell for out of the icebox at the corner grocery store. Too much depends on how quickly the public takes to his idea, and what happens to food prices. The usual rule-of-thumb on prices for frozen foods is that they cost at retail about one and a half times as much as the same foods would set you back if you bought them fresh. Maxson thinks he will be able to sell his meals at about the same price as an average meal at a restaurant. The hard-eating inventor thinks that most of his customers will be people who want to whip up a quick dinner without much trouble. He seems justified in thinking that there are a lot of such people.
>
> Eventually, the Maxson Sky Plate will be available in 50 different menus. Just now there are only six. The main offerings of these meals are steak, meat loaf, beef stew, corned-beef hash, ham steak and breaded veal cutlets—meat courses of which most home-fronters have only the vaguest memory. Each plate comes with two vegetables, or one vegetable and hot bread. It all tastes good. Several commercial airlines are trying to get Maxson Sky Plates for meal service in the air, but so far the Navy and some Army planes have a monopoly on the product. Meanwhile, other manufacturers are beginning to work out all kinds of packaged meals. The ultimate aim of the manufacturers is to put out a meal in which there will be absolutely no waste. The next big development, obviously, will have to be a precooked, quick-frozen meal that you can eat plate and all. The plate, naturally, will be the dessert and conceivably better than the cake mother used to bake.[2]

The end of the war cut Maxson's military sales, and it took some time for civilian sales to pick up the slack, partly because most grocery stores in that era didn't have freezers. Pan Am served Sky Plates on a trial basis, and a few other airlines experimented with them. William Maxson developed his ideas with the zeal of a visionary, opening America's largest trout farm because he thought that trout would be an ideal frozen entrée.

The first Pan Am commercial flight to serve meals using Maxson's technology took off in January of 1949,[3] but William Maxson didn't live to see it—he died in July 1947. His heirs didn't share his enthusiasm for the business and sold the company, and development of the convection oven stalled for almost two decades. Ovens using Maxson's patents were manufactured by other companies, and as flight kitchens figured out how to make meals that were appropriate for the technology, the quality of food in flight gradually rose.

The strength of the Maxson convection ovens was that if food had been packaged appropriately, in thin trays that conducted heat, the hot air blowing past them could warm them to about two hundred degrees very quickly. The major disadvantage was that with the heating equipment and fans that were then available, they couldn't get any hotter. The circulating air also removed moisture from the food, desiccating it if left even a moment too long. Soups, stews, pastas, and meats in sauce were acceptable this way, though vegetables on those same trays tended to overcook. Unfortunately some of the most popular meals in the air, like steaks and lobster, were not well served by this treatment—cooking at low heat in a dry environment made them tough and unappetizing.

It wasn't until the mid-1960s that two different technologies offered a way to improve the inflight dining experience, and though they involved different teams and technologies, both were introduced within a year of each other. The first was an improved convection oven manufactured by

The De Havilland Comet was the first commercial airliner in service, and the first British-built aircraft to have a galley as sophisticated as those aboard American-built rivals. General Electric boasted their technological superiority in this 1959 ad.
According to General Electric UK, GEC was sold to Marconi, which went bankrupt with no successor

the Nordskog Company of Van Nuys, California, where engineers figured out a way to improve the motors for the circulating fans so they wouldn't be destroyed by high heat. This allowed temperatures as high as five hundred degrees—half what a high-end steakhouse would use for cooking a chunk of beef, but similar to what most restaurants could muster. The ovens were made of aluminum to reduce weight but still came in at a hefty sixty-five pounds due to the layers of insulation, and they cost $33,000 each, both of which were barriers to immediate adoption.

The first airline to do so was one whose management showed little regard for either finances or practicality. Northeast Airlines had been a successful New England regional carrier until the late 1950s, when they decided to drastically expand and start service to Florida. From that point onward they were in precarious financial health, and in 1965 the carrier was bought by a broadcasting company that sought a way to differentiate them in the market. Superior food seemed like a good bet, so the new ovens were added to their fleet of 727s, and a PR campaign like no other was used to launch the new service. This began by insulting their competitors before lauding their own improvements. A sample, printed in the *Montreal Gazette* in 1968, was headlined "Jan. 19, 1968—The Beginning of the All-Steak Airline to Florida. The End of Airline Food," and began,

> It always seemed sad to us that the first and last meals of your vacation, the meals served to you on an airplane, turned out to be the worst meals of your vacation. Sad because airlines don't start out with inferior food or bad cooks. Their meals just end up tasting that way. Because the meals that are served on planes aren't cooked on planes. Instead, they're cooked in big kitchens on the ground, loaded into planes and—one to three hours later—served. Which is why airline food tastes exactly like food that's been standing around from one to three hours. Your stomach deserves better. Northeast Airlines offers an alternative to airline food. Every one of our Yellowbird jets is now equipped with special broiling ovens. So we can now broil food at 30,000 feet, and the food we broil is steak. Northeast is serving nothing but steak on all our lunch and dinner flights to and from Florida. And not only in first class, but in economy class too. So instead of cutting into pre-cooked airline food, you can cut into freshly broiled steak—filet mignon or club steak in economy, filet mignon or filet of beef tenderloin in first class.[4]

The meals were evidently popular but didn't help the small airline compete with competitors with national route systems. Northeast lost money in every quarter except the one in which their major competitor was on strike, and was sold to Delta in 1972. The high-temperature convection ovens were adopted by other carriers and were often installed only in the first-class galley—economy-class passengers continued to have items reheated at low temperature until the price of the new ovens dropped.

The other new cooking technology had been under development almost continuously since World War II, but had hitherto been too heavy and unreliable for airline use. The Raytheon Company had started developing the microwave oven prior to 1950 and released the first usable model, the 1611 Radarange, in 1954. That model stood six feet tall and weighed 750 pounds, which made it obviously unsuited to the cramped spaces aboard an aircraft, and each unit was priced at about five thousand dollars.[5] Litton Industries was approached by airline companies as early as 1963 for a version that could be used in flight, and teams of engineers worked to reduce the size, weight, cost, and the fragility of the electronics. It wasn't until 1967 that a compact version suitable to a home countertop went on the market. That exact model might have been usable aboard aircraft, but was not approved by regulators for years due to fears that microwaves could leak out and disrupt the aircraft's navigational systems.[6] The version that was finally certified went into service in 1969, but not without difficulty; it had been loaded with sensors to detect leaking microwaves, and these frequently gave false positives that shut the ovens off. There was another sensor located below the tray where food was set to be cooked. This was designed to keep the oven from being turned on when it was empty, but it wasn't sensitive enough and couldn't detect light items like breakfast Danishes.

These problems, along with the inexperience of the crews, combined to give microwave cooking a very rocky rollout and made a lasting bad impression. Stewardesses who had never seen a microwave oven before weren't informed that it should only be used for foods with a high moisture index because the method involved heating water molecules. They tried using it for toast and other dry items, with unfortunate results. The combination of technical problems and insufficient training resulted in a disastrous rollout, but airlines continued to experiment with the new technology. The disadvantage of high power consumption was offset by the fact that heat was instantaneous and the unit itself remained cool, so there was less danger of the cabin crew burning themselves while working in the galley.

Unfortunately for anyone wanting to sell microwave ovens to airlines, the disadvantages of the technology were overwhelming. Convection ovens were excellent for heating many meals at once; microwaves weren't. Also, even after a generation of airline crews who grew up with microwave entered the workforce, people still used it inappropriately. Microwave ovens are still installed in aircraft to heat large volumes of water, a task they are ideal for, but these high-power ovens work differently than home versions. In 2007 a British Airways stewardess decided to heat a ready-made curry meal in one of these ovens and caused an inflight emergency and almost $40,000 dollars in damage to the aircraft—the headlines included "Exploding Curry Menaces 747."[7] Besides generating amusing news stories all over the world, the incident resulted in an airline rule that employees would no longer be allowed to heat up their own meals in aircraft kitchens. It's a problem that is much more unlikely to happen in the convection ovens, most of which have been specially designed to hold containers designed only for that purpose.

The next innovation in cooking in flight was introduced in 1995, when a company called B/E Aerospace fitted convection ovens with steam injectors so food could cook quickly without being dried out. The ability to cook at a variety of temperatures in either a dry or moist environment was hailed as the solution to a problem that had bedeviled airlines for decades.[8] The flying boat stewards who wrestled whole beef roasts and carved them in flight could have only wished they had such technologies.

CHAPTER 14

⊰⊱⊰⊱

Jumbo Jets, Excess, and Cultural Expression (1966–1975)

When the Boeing 747 was introduced in 1966, it was a revolutionary aircraft, two and a half times the size of the 707 that had been the standard for the world's long-haul fleets. Runways had to be lengthened so it could land, airport terminals expanded to hold the 342 passengers that could be flown in what was then the typical configuration. (Later variants would hold more than 400.) Development of the 747 had taxed the ingenuity of the designers and manufacturer and was going to do the same thing to the people who had to figure out how to serve meals aboard.

The aircraft was developed partly because of a pioneer of the industry—Juan Trippe, who had started Pan Am in 1927 and was still president of the company. Trippe saw the huge airliner as the answer to the problem of airport congestion, and he and Pan Am's engineers were involved in its design to an unprecedented degree. Pan Am ordered the first planes in April 1966, and the inaugural flight operated in January 1970 between New York and London.

The 747 utilized one feature that had only previously been seen on the Russian Ilyushin jets—a galley in the belly of the aircraft, with an elevator to carry food up to the passenger level. In these "lower lobe" galleys, trays could be prepared assembly line style in a purely functional space passengers would never see. It was a clever way to use undesirable space and increase the number of seats, and it was vital to serving food for the hundreds of people aboard. For that giant coach compartment, every decision came down to how to save labor. Pan Am, which had the giant aircraft first, had to work out how to allocate staff to feed what had once been a flying restaurant but was now more of a flying mess hall. Former flying boat purser Sam Toaramina found himself in a new position called flight director aboard a 747, overseeing the largest service crew ever assembled aboard one airplane.

> As flight director I think I had 16 or 17 stewardesses on that flight. There would be four people working in the back, another four for the business area, and then the other five or six in first class. . . . And you had the dining room upstairs. You had to put two people up there: you had someone to cook the food, then maybe a helper, because you had 12 people seated upstairs to feed.[1]

That upstairs dining room became a signature of Pan Am; though other carriers used the space for additional seating or bars and lounges, Pan Am tried to maintain the gentility of an earlier era. Flight director Jay Koren remembered that he found himself in the unusual position of trying to figure out which passengers would make the kind of interesting dinner party group that he was trying to assemble.

> Selecting those to be seated in the Dining Room was the responsibility of the flight director. After takeoff we passed through the cabin, seat chart in hand, discreetly studying the load to determine which passengers might best fit with which others. Pairs travelling together made the job easy; but, all too often, every passenger in first-class was flying alone. Sometimes during the early months, very few passengers could be persuaded to give our Dining Room a try. They were not in the mood for conversation, they had a good book to finish, or they simply preferred to eat in the privacy of their main deck seats. On one such flight the ever lustrous Julie Andrews and her husband Blake Edwards were among our guests. No one wanted to dine upstairs. Finally I cajoled the Edwards' into trying our new innovation, and we soon had a full Dining Room. As often happened, even well after the meal service was completed, the diners were having such a good time that we had to begin the movie downstairs without them! Word quickly spread among the travel agents and Pan Am's most sophisticated customers. Soon, advance reservations for the Dining Room became the custom when booking the flight. Flight Directors no longer needed to talk diners into climbing the stairs, though we continued to work out the seating and to print and position place cards. I did have my fun putting Arabs with Israelis, Dionne Warwick and a Liverpudlian rock star with Lord and Lady Lilywhite. We never heard any complaints. The Dining Room seemed to pull people together, to generate a spirit of camaraderie.[2]

The food served upstairs was the same as served to passengers who remained in their seats, and it was excellent—there was always carved roast beef, plus six choices that might include Sole Albert, Lobster Thermidor, Lamb Chops, and Chicken Maryland. Throughout the service, wine glasses were replenished frequently, including with Cristal or Dom Pérignon Champagne. The last three carts presented a selection of cheeses and fruits, desserts, liqueurs, and cognac. It was a magnificent meal that took two hours to serve and clear, deliberately as different as possible from what was being served on the other side of the curtain. There, as noted succinctly in *Flight Catering*, "Due to the large quantity of meals that needed to be produced, the food became simpler." All economy-class cold items were preloaded on one tray, a hot entrée was added as each plate came out of the convection oven, and it was served out as quickly as possible.

The pattern Pan Am set was duplicated as other carriers got their 747s, with minor differences in the utilization of the upper deck. Air Canada used it as a bar for first-class passengers, BOAC as a lounge with a microwave oven in the middle so passengers could heat meals at any time they wanted during the flight. (This was discontinued after a short time because the microwave ovens proved too unreliable.)[3] In 1970 Japan Airlines introduced an upper deck lounge called Teahouse in the Sky, where passengers were served hot or cold sake and their choice of elaborately crafted Japanese delicacies. The airline was already adept at this—a travel article the year before commented on pastries "made from a soft baked flour mixed with egg and containing excellent sweet red bean paste added with a little pulp of plums. The design on the pastry is of a 'Straw Thatched House In The Japanese Countryside'. [It is] . . . wrapped in an attractive simple packet. It tastes very good and it looks very good too."[4]

JAL's focus on creating a uniquely Japanese experience in the sky represented quite a turnaround in style, as not too long before this they had been serving almost exclusively European food even on their domestic routes. A menu from a 1966 flight between Tokyo and Okinawa offered a lunch of salad followed by marinated prawns, chicken galantine with glazed carrots, Brussels sprouts, braised potatoes, and a "bavarois panache"; although the prawns may have been made in Japanese style, the only certain element of that culture was the green tea served afterward.[5] By the mid-1970s JAL was serving authentic cuisine as one option, while maintaining the French-styled alternative for those who preferred it.

JAL was far from the only one to invest in 747s. Airlines around the world rushed to sign orders with Boeing, and most carriers got them just in time for a recession and huge increases in fuel prices. As they had already bought the aircraft and needed to fill them, preferably with high-paying passengers, all carriers entered into a scramble to see who could offer the most luxurious

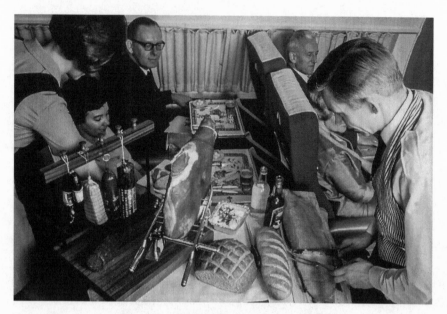

There was no question that you were among the elite when you were served custom-carved charcuterie and smoked salmon aboard SAS in the 1960s.
Image provided by SAS Museum, Oslo

experience for the thirty passengers in the front cabin. To go into details of all of these in this book would be tiresome and repetitive—most were minor variations of the standards set by Pan Am and described above, with the only interesting elements being the non-European dishes served in addition to the standard international menu. Those who are interested in information at this depth are advised to seek a copy of George Banks's wonderful *Gourmet and Glamour in the Sky,* listed along with other frequently cited books in the Recommended Reading list at the back of this book.

The enthusiasm for serving gourmet food and providing choices did not extend to noncompetitive routes, especially for passengers in the rear cabins. Passengers on BOAC's flights from London to Australia had no choice of main courses for the entire thirty-hour flight and had to pay for alcoholic drinks. On the same airline's flights to the Persian Gulf in 1971, then-catering coordinator George Banks remembered that in Bahrain BOAC loaded the same meal, a "turkey and asparagus mimosa," almost every day. They did this even though the catering operation at Bahrain had a wide selection and was well run by the standards of the era and region—at Abu Dhabi, sometimes it was difficult to even get water that could be loaded on board.

This is a reminder that the jet age arrived in some places that were barely out of the Stone Age, and it took heroic efforts to maintain reliable meals in places where roads deteriorated into muddy tracks outside the airport. European inspectors who made unannounced visits to inspect catering facilities sometimes came back with horror stories; Banks recalled a visit to the hotel restaurant in Banjul that catered first-class meals for British Caledonian flights in the 1970s. He was shocked to find that the cook preferred to work with his pet monkey sitting on his shoulder, a habit that would not be acceptable in a European catering operation.[6] Other African-owned catering kitchens were well run—Ghana Airways operated a flight kitchen in Accra that was clean, efficient, and turned out meals to high standards. That operation was something of an anomaly in the former British colonies in Africa. The former French colonies benefited from a chain of flight service kitchens operated by UTA that served Air Afrique and other carriers; these turned out meals of international standards and supplied African food options.

Many airports in the developing world had been converted from military airfields, and some were sited far from cities where there could be any choice of services. Local governments often operated these as monopolies, and some developed a reputation for dreadful or unreliable food. Sometimes the logistics departments of the international carriers found ways to bypass loading any meals at places were the food was poor or priced extravagantly because the local caterers figured that they had no competition. British Caledonian Airlines devised ingenious ways of compressing and stacking food in the refrigerated holds so they could carry two flight segments' worth of food in the space usually used for one.[7]

When meals were substandard, or didn't show up at all, whether because of strikes, road blockages, ordering mistakes, or other reasons, airline staff had to improvise. Experienced crews who flew routes that had a reputation for unreliability often packed a few loaves of bread, some cheeses, and cold cuts in a closet so that if food didn't arrive they could make sandwiches, arrange them prettily, and have something to serve. If too few meals were loaded, the crew could rearrange the food on the trays and add sandwiches on the side, and passengers might not even notice that lunch looked a bit different than usual. Occasionally food that was loaded for the crew was actually served to passengers; a South African Airways stewardess named Lynn McJarrow recalled that on a flight from Johannesburg to London, the fruit platters loaded for breakfast looked so bad that the crew refused to serve them. Several fruit baskets had been loaded for the crew to snack on, so while passengers were still asleep the crew cut up whatever they had and arranged it. As she recalled, "It took forever as our knives were not sharp veggie knives but the eating knives that don't cut that well. Nevertheless, the passengers got a great breakfast and one man even commented that the fruit looked better than what he has been accustomed to on previous flights. I just smiled."[8]

Carriers that flew to remote places with low hygiene standards had to consider another problem: getting their silverware clean in places where there was little water. In the late 1960s a company called Intercontinental Air Caterers in London had a solution: the first completely prepackaged meals using disposable utensils, called "Sky Diners." The plastic and paper utensils also saved weight, always a consideration aboard aircraft, and when a hot entrée was included, it was served in a lightweight foil tray. The meals in disposable containers with plastic utensils were then regarded as a novelty, and their ease of use and cheapness made them a favorite of British charter companies like Dan Air as well as safari charter operators. Since everything was made to cater to the tastes of British tourists, items like steak and kidney pie and shepherd's pie were staples as aircraft flew over African deserts and jungles.

Along with holiday charter operations, Dan Air operated scheduled flights to Ireland and short hops inside Europe, routes with such brief flight times that food service was difficult. The airline came up with one of the worst ideas in airline food history to deal with this problem, a plan called seat-back catering.[9] This involved stocking a meal for every passenger inside the seat in front of them, and giving each flyer a key that could be used to unlock the storage compartment for use when they got hungry. While this enabled food service without taking stewardess time, it was a failure on multiple levels. The meals for both the outbound and return flights had been locked in adjacent compartments, and hungry passengers quickly figured out that the same key unlocked both. This meant that passengers on the second leg of the flight often found that the previous person in their seat had eaten their lunch or dinner. Also, since Dan Air flew many routes of several hours' duration, whatever meal had been locked in that compartment for the second leg of the trip might have been unrefrigerated for six or seven hours. Even by the low standards of English budget-class tourists of the 1960s and '70s, this was unacceptable. Seat-back catering was one of the most spectacular failures of the era, and it only lasted about two years before being discontinued. It had taken some ingenuity, but someone had come up with a standard of economy-class airline catering so low that it prompted a revolt among passengers.

Savvy travelers who were looking for low fares and higher standards on international flights could still find them, often among the carriers that hadn't bought 747s and flew older and less fashionable aircraft. Finnair offered some of the most exotic cuisine aloft aboard their DC-8s, including various herring

Though the airline wasn't known for luxury in this era, Aeroflot did their best to project an image of stylish food and service in these ads from 1965.
Image provided by Aeroflot

dishes, reindeer soup, smoked lamb, and a selection of berry-infused aquavits. British Caledonian, which flew a wide network from London's Gatwick airport, maintained Scottish-style service wherever they went, with smoked salmon to start and Walker's shortbread to finish every meal. The airline was noted for publicity stunts like having a bagpiper escort a haggis on board a flight on the birthday of Robert Burns, Scotland's national poet. Other airlines, like Holland's Martinair, were less flamboyant but concentrated on bringing back passengers with steady, high-quality service.

In Asia, the differences in price and quality between globe-spanning and minor lines were even greater. Non-IATA carriers like Malaysia-Singapore Airlines, Thai International, and Cathay Pacific offered multicourse meals with a choice of entrée at a time when their competitors didn't. When Malaysia and Singapore dissolved their federation in 1965, there was doubt that the latter needed an airline at all—the tiny city-state obviously could have

Image provided by Aeroflot

no domestic routes. It was decided that if Singapore was going to survive as an international business hub an airline needed to exist, and it would only be viable if it offered a higher level of service than anybody else. Singapore Air debuted as the first carrier in Asia with hot meals and free alcoholic beverages, and their major competitors were forced to match them.[10]

Singapore Air bought brand-new planes, while Malaysian Airlines continued to operate the much older aircraft they already owned. They did the best they could, flying obsolete British Comet jets that had poorly designed galleys in which dishes and glassware went flying during rough weather. Even so, they served menus that included mulligatawny soup or consommé, fresh fish, beef rice noodles, and lamb curry. Though alcohol was served on board despite the fact that Malaysia is a Muslim country, pork products have never been served during the airline's history.

There was plenty of pork aboard China Airlines, which was particularly interested in establishing transit business through their Taipei hub. During the days of the two-China policy, the state-owned airline was seen as an instrument of diplomacy, and their emphasis was to show off Chinese hospitality. China Airlines' international advertising was almost exclusively centered on their food, which they marketed using the name "Dynasty Service" and the slogan "The World's First Flying Chinese Restaurant." A 1970 ad headlined "China Airlines to the Orient. You Can Taste The Difference" rhapsodized,

> Springrolls removed from the oven at the precise moment, sweet and sour pork you could write a sonnet about. Imagine bite size pieces, lightly breaded in a tasty sauce very few chefs know how to make perfectly. And then Mandarin chicken, seasoned flawlessly, served with shimmering gold noodles.[11]

Like almost everything in Chinese cuisine, all the food items listed in that ad require deep-frying or stir-frying in oil at high heat, techniques that are impossible in a passenger aircraft—the reference to removing spring rolls from the oven makes it obvious that despite the appeal to tradition, this wasn't the authentic experience. It was, however, better than what was offered by many of their competitors, and China Airlines became a major player in the transpacific market almost as soon as they entered it. These carriers and others that emphasized their heritage in their food were using the only weapon they had against entrenched Pan Am and the invasion of American carriers like United and Continental that brought the convenience of connections to and through the United States.

In the Pacific and around the world, there was probably never such a disparity of standards of service around the world than in the era between the introduction of wide-body aircraft and the beginning of deregulation in 1978. Though this was most pronounced in the international market, things changed inside the world's largest and most regulated system too. The big double-aisle aircraft took over the most traveled routes in the United States and were just as disruptive as they were elsewhere. Within two years of its introduction, the 747 was followed into service by Douglas's DC-10 and Lockheed's L-1011 widebodies, and aircraft prices plummeted as all three manufacturers offered easy terms in search of market share. The result was that any carrier that wanted widebodies could get them on credit, and airlines leaped to place orders. Even PSA, a California commuter carrier that had no conceivable use for a double-deck aircraft that could hold four hundred people, ordered L-1011s before discovering that they couldn't be operated profitably with their route structure, especially since fuel prices had recently risen.[12]

PSA returned the aircraft after a few months and kept doing what they did well, but other regional carriers that had ordered widebodies expanded their routes, both to get some use from the fleet they now owned and to compete with the "Big Three" network carriers—American, United, and TWA. Western Airlines, which had been a successful regional carrier centered in Los Angeles and Salt Lake City, started flying to Florida in 1976 and offered full meals even on flights that left near midnight and arrived at dawn. These "Midnite Suppers" had a Caribbean theme and were inspired by the late-night buffets aboard cruise ships. A typical menu included "chicken breast with stuffed egg moutarde and garnishes, accompanied by a delicate crab salad topped with asparagus spears and featuring a papaya boat filled with pineapple and strawberries."[13] Western had similarly over-the-top menu descriptions for meals aboard their "Islander" flights to Hawaii, which also featured the "Rolling Punch Volcano," a punch bowl on wheels with dry ice in the bottom so the liquid would bubble and smoke.

Western was a minnow compared to the Big Three, and those carriers deployed the big aircraft on medium and long-haul routes around the country. United started flying 747s to Hawaii with lavish Royal Hawaiian service in the front cabin, and a slightly modified version of the usual frozen meal in the back. On the rest of the carrier's domestic routes, meals were highly standardized. They were made by specialized airline kitchens according to that carrier's recipes, though some smaller lines ordered standardized meals created by food consultants. In chapter 6 of *Flight Catering* this system is described under the header "Food Production: The Manufacturing Process," which is entirely apt, as making meals on this scale is best treated as an industrial process rather than one requiring culinary skills and a chef's judgment.[14]

This didn't stop airlines from running ads claiming superior meal quality even as their food was being provided by fewer and fewer catering companies. Small, independent flight kitchens were no longer needed in the frozen meal era, and some airlines that had owned their own catering operations sold them and contracted with Marriott, Dobbs, Sky Chefs, and other operators.

In 1968 TWA decided to push the meal system to the limit and try the most ambitious promotion of the era. In order to promote the line's international flights, they decided to start what they called "Foreign Accent Service" inside the USA. English, French, or Italian themed meals were served by stewardesses wearing disposable paper costumes designed to look like a British pub server's dress, French gown, or Roman toga. Another design, a kind of gold lamé cocktail dress, was meant to represent New York. The meals were popular, and male passengers particularly appreciated that the

In this ad TWA did something fairly unusual—show both their first-class and coach meals alongside each other. Most carriers have always shown first-class meals even in ads that quoted coach airfares.
Rights held by American Airlines

dresses tore very easily and sometimes fell off. The promotion was abruptly ended when it was discovered that thanks to the inks that were used to make the paper dresses, they were extremely flammable. The airline could have kept serving the meals without the costumes, but instead reverted to serving typical fare.

Several carriers tried to lure businessmen aboard with on-board wine events, and United enlisted well-known winemakers to fly aboard their aircraft and give tastings. A sense of the party atmosphere they tried to create can be garnered from this snippet from the "Snoopin' Around" column in the *Argonaut*, a Los Angeles area weekly paper:

> United wants a bigger share of the LA to New York traffic and so has added live entertainment to its 8:45 AM flights, including a guitarist, a wine tasting party, and a caricaturist. The friendly skies have certainly gotten friendlier. As for you businessmen wondering whether an 8:45 AM wine party is the way to start a business trip, just consider it an educational effort. Paul Masson climbs aboard with a crew of experts who run through so many wine tips that even a gourmet wine man would be proud.[15]

At some point shortly after that article ran, someone at United must have wondered if carrying a guitarist, caricaturist, and team of wine experts could have possibly made any financial sense no matter how happy it made customers, given the number of seats these people used that could otherwise have been sold. The party was over as soon as those calculations were done.

By the mid-1970s, passengers had lowered their expectations about in-flight meals and service. Long-time stewardesses who remembered the old days of personal service mourned the change. Virginia Riley, who flew for United from 1946 to 1989, reminisced,

> In 1946, one stewardess flew on the 32-passenger DC-3, the 44-passenger DC-4 flew with two stewardesses, and we became fairly well acquainted with a passenger by the end of the flight. Nowadays the aircraft that carry two or three hundred passengers or more, like the B-747's and the B-767's, fly with eight or more flight attendants on duty. Flying has become another form of mass transportation with a lot of paper work.[16]

The most daunting paperwork was for liquor sales in flight, which in those days were handled entirely with cash and involved inventorying hundreds of little bottles of liquor and the associated mixers, as well as the prospect of making change throughout the cabin. Liquor service was complicated by the fact that at any time the cart was left unattended, passing passengers were tempted to steal a bottle or two. To deal with this a caterer invented a prepackaged liquor cart that was delivered inside a canvas cover that had a plastic window top. In this way inventory could be taken without even opening the case, and when the cart wasn't in use it was hard to steal from it. These carts, sometimes called "Speed Pacs," made one of the last elements of the flight where stewardesses had to interact with passengers much more efficient.

The one anomaly in the world of airline catering was the "aircraft of the future," the Concorde supersonic transport. Ironically, some aspects of the passenger experience were eerily reminiscent of flying just after World War II. The narrow aerodynamic fuselage allowed only two seats per side, just like a DC-3, and the rear galley area was tiny and cramped. Unfortunately for the crew, since the passengers had paid the highest airfare in the world, they expected food on par with the best first-class service—and it had to be served quickly, because the total time from New York to London or Paris was only three and a half hours. Since it took almost a quarter of that time to get to and descend from the fifty-six-thousand-foot cruising altitude, almost every free moment of level flight would be spent eating and drinking. The crew's job was complicated by the fact that the aircraft had an unusual nose-up flight position, so if a server let go of a serving cart without setting the brake firmly, it rolled toward the back of the aircraft at high speed.[17]

Everything about the Concorde was different because of the obsessive focus on weight; every pound of plates or cutlery was estimated to cost $400.00 over the course of a year, as opposed to about $25.00 aboard a 747. As a result, extra-lightweight crockery and silverware were used; in the years since the aircraft went out of service, these have become collector's items. The meals also had to be made differently because of the tremendous G forces during takeoff. For instance, cakes collapsed under their own weight or were smashed to the side of whatever container they were packed in.

Air France and British Airways were the prime users of the aircraft, though Singapore Air and the American carrier Braniff used it on short-term leases. All users began their service with caviar, and British Airways continued with any of four entrées—grilled lamb cutlets, veal steak, crepes with morel sauce, or a Mediterranean vegetable salad appear on one menu.[18] Afterward there was a passion fruit tart dessert, followed by a choice of three cheeses. On a representative flight on July 30, 1968, Air France served a surprising menu that was designed according to a theory called "sequences"—the idea was to reflect the speed of the flight with items that were cold, hot, then sweet.[19]

Unusually, this had three vegetable courses—salad cache, spinach subric, and buttered carrots—along with spiny lobster "Cote d'Emeraude," before serving petits fours and a fruit salad. Five wines and a selection of liqueurs were available, if there was time to serve them.

When orders were first accepted for the Concorde, sales of 747s and other wide-bodied aircraft fell because it was considered first of a new generation, and airlines wanted to wait until the promised supersonic widebodies were ready. Though over one hundred Concordes were ordered, only fourteen ever flew in commercial service, and the reign of the fast-flying needles was brief. The future would be slower, more crowded, and much more financially turbulent, because the era of deregulation was dawning.

CHAPTER 15

The Elusive History of Special Meals

For decades, many airlines have offered meals for people with dietary restrictions, whether these have been occasioned by religion, health, or otherwise. It is difficult to trace the earliest instances of these meals for a good reason—the airlines may have had them available, but have never really wanted people to order them. They cost more in terms of money and staff time and add to the complexity of catering, and as such they were offered but never promoted.

The earliest special meal that was based on a religious diet predates World War II. Practicing Catholics could be assured that some fish meals would be boarded on most aircraft on long-haul US routes, as well as on Pan Am, their South American subsidiary Panagra, and BOAC worldwide. Other carriers also offered seafood on Friday as an option, but I have been unable to conclusively document when they started. A TWA Flight Operations manual dated October 10, 1964, notes that "on fast days" a choice of fish or meat may be offered—making it obvious that on other days, there was no choice. A United Dining Service Checklist from the same year also shows no other options. Note that during this period seafood meals were not apparently an item that could be reserved in advance—some were boarded with the other meals on Fridays, and if you were Catholic or just preferred fish, you requested one and hoped they still had them.

The first meals available only by advance order were kosher platters, which were first mass-produced in response to the international services offered by El Al. Israel's national airline had a commitment from the beginning

to serve only kosher food, so when that airline started scheduled international services in 1950, caterers had to be found. This was no problem in the
United States, because kosher meals had been available on some US flights
at least as early as 1945 when Borenstein Caterers went into business. Prior
to this time, passengers who kept strict kosher aloft had to bring their own
food and utensils. Borenstein's market was small, but they had all of it—no
other US airline caterer was certified until 1962, when Siegel's of New York
entered the market.[1]

Borenstein's pioneered several patterns in kosher airline catering, including having separate washing machines for the meat and milk silverware that
is used on El Al. When Borenstein caters for other airlines, they provide
disposable silverware for coach flights and brand new silverware for first class.
After the kosher passenger uses it, it goes into general use.

Interviewed in February 2014, Borenstein's manager Chris Medina said
that the meals served in the early days are nothing like what is offered now.
"It has evolved as we have tried to keep up with the non-Kosher market.
Thirty years ago it was very simple—breakfast was a bagel, cheese, and lox,
and that was it."

The airlines were not eager to promote their kosher meal services for two
reasons. First, they are more labor intensive for flight attendants who have to
serve them. One of the problems with kosher meals inflight was impressing
on eager or busy airline staff the fact that these had to be treated differently
than other meals. Angela Waller, who wrote a book about her experiences
as a stewardess in Britain in the 1950s,[2] remembered, "Kosher meals were
delivered directly to the aircraft in a box, and we were told never to open
that box."[3] The rules of special handling and separate utensils were not well
understood outside the Jewish community at that time, and even with special
training, mistakes were made.

The second reason airlines didn't want to promote kosher meals was that
they always cost much more than standard meals.[4] As such, Pan Am was
concerned in the late 1960s when there was a sudden spike in the number of
passengers ordering kosher meals to and from Puerto Rico, despite the fact
that there was not, as far as they could tell, a larger number of traveling Jews.
Pan Am's vice president for catering services, James Kellites, explained in a
1974 interview,

> Passengers would see that the regular snack service was not equivalent to the
> quantity or quality with [sic] any of the kosher meals. At the time we didn't
> have Kosher snacks, so nonkosher meals would consist of a little sandwich
> while Kosher service was an entire meal. Mr. Rodriguez, let's say, eating a

sandwich, would be sitting next to Mr. Goldberg, who would be eating a steak or piece of chicken. The next time Mr. Rodriguez took a trip he would order kosher.[5]

Kellites also described a practice he called kosher roulette:

Out of New York City, Pan Am rotates its meals monthly in a three-month cycle. The veal is served for 30 days, beef for the next 30 days and then chicken, the least popular among travelers, for a month. . . . Seasoned travelers have gotten to have a pretty good idea of the schedule. A traveler will say to himself, this is chicken month, so I'll order a kosher meal. The passenger is gambling. If the kosher meal has steak and the regular meal is chicken, he'll own up to the stewardess that he's the one ordered a kosher meal. If it's the other way around, he'll tell the stewardess that there must be some mistake, he didn't order a kosher meal.[6]

Kellites estimated that the average economy-class airline meal at that time cost between $2.00 and $2.25, while kosher meals ran between $6 and $13. During the interview he was evidently trying to encourage people not to order kosher meals unless they were religiously required, but the reporter's enthusiasm for them gave the final article the opposite effect.

Internationally, kosher meals were available aboard a carrier that might not have been expected to serve them, since they were the airline of an officially atheist state. Aeroflot historian Polina Kurovskaya reported that

According to Aeroflot's veterans (former employees of the ground handling complex), special inflight meals appeared in the early 60s. A more precise date can not be established yet. The choice was between lean and kosher food. A special meal had to be ordered no later than 3 days before departure but such demands were very rare—a veteran we interviewed could only remember two such cases in ten years.[7]

When the kosher service was utilized, it was probably by tourists or foreign diplomats. It would have taken courage for anyone who was a Soviet citizen to identify themselves to the airline and their fellow passengers as observantly religious.

The strictness of kosher standards at airports around the world has occasionally been a matter of controversy among observant Jews. In 1982, El Al was embarrassed when the ultraorthodox Grand Rabbinate of Jerusalem charged that their inflight meals made in Israel were not sufficiently kosher because some employees of the catering firm worked on Saturdays.[8] El Al's management and the catering company angrily denied the claim. This is a reminder, in case any is needed, that even an astute flight attendant can't just look at a meal and be sure that it meets religious dietary standards.

Internationally, many airlines have offered other religious meals since 1945, or made them standard for all flights in the case of national airlines of countries with a state religion. Saudi Arabian Airlines, Kuwait Airways, Iran Air, Emirates, and Pakistan International are among the carriers that serve only meals that meet Muslim halal standards, and they also do not serve alcohol on board. On flights into Saudi Arabia, other carriers are not allowed to serve alcohol when actually in Saudi airspace. A posting from 2007 on the Airliners.net civil aviation discussion board mentioned that on an Air France flight from Riyadh to Paris, as soon as the announcement was made that they were no longer in Saudi airspace, "out comes the drinks trolley to the applause of the passengers, Saudis included (who have just been to the toilet to change out of their traditional gear into a western suit)."

Other aspects of Islamic law have caused religious disputes about food in flight, particularly issues regarding fast days. Fasts usually begin and end based on the local sunset, and someone aboard a high-flying aircraft may experience one that lasts for hours if going westbound. When questioned about when that person may break their fast, the modern Islamic scholar Ibn Abideen quoted several paragraphs of religious laws and commentary before delivering the following decision, which begins with a reference to an ancient question about when the sun goes down:

> the one who is in a high place, such as the lighthouse of Alexandria, should not break the fast as long as the sun has not set there (as witnessed from above the lighthouse), while the people down in the town are allowed to break the fast if the sun sets according to them before it sets according to him (the person on the lighthouse). . . . Accordingly, breaking the fast for those who travel by plane is due when they witness the sunset, according to the position where they themselves are. They are not allowed to break the fast according to the timing of the country over which the plane is flying, the country for which they are heading, or the country from which they departed. Rather, they should break the fast upon witnessing the setting of the full disc of the sun. Thus, if—in this way—the duration of their fasting is lengthened in a way that makes fasting difficult for the one capable of observing the fast in the usual cases, then they are allowed to break the fast due to the additional difficulty accompanying the travel and not due to the ending of the daytime, and they are required to make up later for such day/s in which they break the fast. Consequently, what is claimed by some pilots that the fasting persons aboard are allowed to break the fast according to the timing of the place of takeoff or the

place over which the plane is flying is incorrect. . . . Another case that is worthy of being explained is that in which the sun appears to have set and then resurfaces again in the west because of the high velocity of the plane. In this case, the fasting passengers are allowed to break the fast upon the "first sunset"; they are not required to consider the sun's resurfacing.[9]

There are other controversies regarding how Islamic law may best be observed inflight, and airlines that serve a large religious clientele face unusual challenges. For instance, some sects allow the eating of only fruit while fasting, and airlines like Emirates stock special plates at that time.[10] The same carrier also notes that during fasting periods, passengers who choose to eat may be served a cold meal rather than a hot one, so the scent of the warm food does not tempt those who wish to maintain their religious duty.

The dietary accommodations for Muslims are widely discussed, but it is much more difficult to get information about arrangements for observant Hindus. According to that religion's traditional practices, it is forbidden for members of high-ranking castes to eat food prepared or even touched by those of lower castes—to the degree that a thirsty Brahmin may not accept a glass of water from someone of lower caste. This system lost legal status in 1950, well after the foundation of Air India, which already served Hindu-compliant vegetarian meals on all flights. The carrier seems to have a policy of not answering any questions about whether caste restrictions on food handling or airline catering ever were in place, and if so when they were removed. All aspects of the caste system are controversial in the multifaith country that is modern India, and at this time it is not possible to discover much about how this was or is handled.

It can't even be said for certain exactly when Hindu and other special meals began to be available on flights to and through the United States, though it was some time in the late 1970s. Booking special meals required a call to the airline before 1976, when the first American travel agencies received computer systems. According to *Flight Catering*, "British Airways was a pioneer in introducing a vegetarian main course on Concorde in the nineteen seventies, which was then introduced in their first class, and later in WorldClass. Now it is also available in economy class."[11]

The first article I have found that addresses the availability of special meals in detail is from the *Post and Courier* of Charleston, South Carolina, in 1981. Headlined "Restricted Diets No Longer a Problem for Air Travelers," it treated the availability of special meals as a new and little-known phenomenon. After mentioning the availability of kosher, Hindu, and Moslem meals, the author went on to say,

The largest variety of special meals offered, however, are prepared for special health requirements. Air travelers now can special order such items as low-calorie, vegetarian, no-sugar, low-sodium and bland meals. Such esoteric selections as lacto-ovo (milk and eggs), gluten-free, low and high-fiber, and post-weaning infant meals are available on many airlines. Usually the larger the airline, the more varied the special meal service. However, often the smaller national flag carriers offer superior specialized meals associated with the cuisine of their countries. (Hindu meals on Air India, kosher on El Al, Japanese diet on Japan Airlines, etc.)[12]

He also noted the same tendency of savvy passengers to game the system:

some travelers order a special meal in the belief that they will get better food than those who are served the standard fare. However special meals are not automatically superior meals. Very often the special meal served in first class is identical to that offered in economy. The service may be different, but the food is the same.

The article finished with a list of the special meals aboard various carriers— American Airlines offered seven, Braniff thirteen, Pan Am nineteen. It was also noted that "some carriers can cross-reference to seat numbers, so announcements no longer need to be made at flight time." This points to automation as something that enabled the proliferation of meals—prior to the widespread adoption of computers by airlines, it was labor intensive for the carriers and caterers to figure out what meal needed to be where, especially if a passenger changed their flight. European carriers were much slower to automate their systems and install terminals in travel agencies, and also to offer extensive meal choices. An article in the London-based *Flight Magazine* dated 1985 treated the ability to select a vegetarian meal for a repeat customer based on their profile in the system as something that might be available in the far future.[13] It was available a year later to American travel agents.

By 1993 the major American carriers had the ability to book seventeen special meals—an edition of *United Times*, the airline's employee magazine, lists them as follows:

Asiatic/Indian
Baby Bland
Diabetic Friendly Skies
Gluten-free
High-fiber

Hindu
Kosher
Lacto-vegetarian
Light Choice
Low-calorie
Low-cholesterol
Low-protein
Low-purine
Low-sodium
Moslem
Non-lactose Special meal
Vegetarian (pure)[14]

Another meal that was first offered by United in this year was the antithesis of all the healthy selections—the first children's meals catered by McDonald's. The "McDonald's Friendly Sky meals" included "activities" (games and puzzles) and a toy and were offered on 80 percent of meal flights.

The long list of selections was a high-water mark for choice inflight, as the variety of meals would quickly shrink due to cost-cutting measures forced by deregulation of the industry.

CHAPTER 16

Years of Chaos and Change
(1975–1985)

The history of food in flight can not be decoupled from the economics of the airline industry, so when anything happened that fundamentally changed the way the system worked, the way airlines served passengers would change too. The changes in the 1960s and early '70s had mostly been technological, but the change of the late '70s was regulatory. A curious coincidence of timing led to most of the world's governments rejecting the way that airlines had been operating, with calamitous results for some venerable carriers and fortunate outcomes for others.

The airline market in the United Kingdom in the mid-1970s was more competitive and creative than the one in the United States thanks to the proliferation of independent carriers that operated from secondary airports. London-Heathrow, the main airport for international connections, was closed to the independents, but from Gatwick, Luton, Manchester, and other airports around the country a vibrant market served British tourists seeking budget flights. Many lines started their existence as charter carriers serving package tour operators but evolved into a curious hybrid that never developed in America—they operated seasonal charters while simultaneously developing scheduled services on routes too minor to interest the government champions BOAC and BEA, which merged in 1974 to form British Airways.

Dan Air, which had experimented with seat-back catering, was one of these hybrid carriers. In the 1960s that company faced increasing competition from British United Airways, which was the largest unsubsidized airline outside the United States. By 1970, when they were sold to a Scottish airline, BUA served Europe, Africa, and South America, and the combined carrier later became famous as British Caledonian Airways.

That carrier became increasingly respected in the industry, which couldn't be said of a former BUA managing director named Frederick Alfred Laker, who was later knighted as Sir Freddie Laker. Freddie, as everybody called him, was the single most disruptive person in the history of the European airline industry. He had a vision of a budget travel concept he called Skytrain that he was sure had the potential to draw hundreds of thousands of new passengers who had never been able to consider flying before.[1]

Laker took the well-worn path of starting a charter airline and applying for permission to operate scheduled services, all the while badgering regulators for permission to operate new routes at lower costs. He announced the Skytrain concept at a press conference in 1971, after he had formally applied for permission to fly regular scheduled London to New York service at the price of less than thirty-eight pounds per direction—far less than half the price charged by British Airways and Pan Am. Laker's application predictably went nowhere, but the British public adored the idea and started pressuring the government to consider the plan.

Laker didn't get what he wanted immediately, but the door opened a crack in April 1973 when the British government liberalized the rules on transatlantic charters. Previously these had been at least theoretically limited to so-called affinity groups like clubs and churches, but in practice many people paid a nominal fee to join a club for the sole purpose of going on a trip. (Some of these were deliberately given silly names to mock the system; the Birmingham Caged Bird Society, for instance, existed only as an excuse to take charter flights.)[2] The new rules ended the need for memberships and allowed airlines to operate an unlimited number of charter flights to create something that was almost regular scheduled service—the only restriction was that flights had to be booked in advance and couldn't be changed, restrictions designed to deter business passengers.

Laker launched services immediately and did heavy advertising on the theme "The End of Skyway Robbery," while lobbying the government to allow him to operate additional services to Hong Kong and Australia. He didn't get those, or much else that he asked for, but Skytrain services were up and running in 1974 and became wildly popular. Passengers could only buy their tickets on the day they wanted to travel—the polar opposite of the advance booking charters—and there were charges for everything—luggage, alcoholic drinks, and meals included. The payoff was the price, $245.00 round trip from New York to London.

Passengers swooned over the price and the cheerful service, though not the food. A travel article in the Norwalk, Connecticut, newspaper *The Hour* referred to a continental breakfast of "a stale roll, orange juice, butter and jelly, and a cup of coffee," while the cooked breakfast was "cold scrambled eggs, sausage, and a roll." Still, despite an article in which the author detailed the stress of lining up for tickets without knowing if she would get them and other inconveniences, she finished the article with "Would I go again? Take me, Freddie. I'm ready."[3]

A flood of new airlines leaped into the market for services from Britain to destinations on several continents, enabling connections to and from everywhere in Europe through London. The French government liberalized their airline market too, and a flood of new carriers sprung up. A few of these flew full-service flights, but most were emulating the high-capacity/low-service Laker. Almost all eventually went bankrupt, but they did their part to undermine the entrenched players in the market.

National carriers throughout and beyond the continent suddenly woke up to the fact that they faced something they had never dealt with before: price competition. Many were overstaffed and had deals with their governments that involved flying politicians and their families for free; faced with the inability to reform such systems, they were paralyzed. They could copy a few of the strategies from the discount carriers, such as eliminating meals on short flights and adding one extra seat to each row, and in short order they did. Australian travel writer John Pringle memorably mourned, "It is a curious fact that aeroplanes are the only form of transport which have got more uncomfortable with progress," and complained about the lines in airports with a song parody. Based on an old Fred Astaire number, it ran,

> We traveled Qantas to see the world,
> And what did we do?
> We stood in a queue.[4]

Pringle glumly admitted that millions of people would be able to travel in economy seats under the new airfare system, but he couldn't muster any enthusiasm for it. Neither could other sophisticated flyers, especially those who traveled for business, and it was here that the established airlines saw an opportunity. They would make a new overture to the only segment of the market they really understood: business travelers. Recognizing that many companies wouldn't pay for first-class seats anymore, in 1976 KLM pioneered the idea of special seating, then called "Full Fare Facilities" for passengers who bought nondiscounted tickets. Until that time, the only recognition that people paying the highest undiscounted economy fares received was a sticker on their luggage that theoretically meant it would be delivered first.

KLM's innovations were modest—the full-fare passengers were separated from those using discounted seats and given the area just behind first class, where they could board last and deplane first. It was left to British Air to actually differentiate the business-class experience in other ways. As columnist Richard Turen humorously put it in *Travel Weekly*, a magazine for the industry,

> The theory here was that passengers who were stupid enough to pay the list price for a coach seat ought to be separated from normal passengers. So they were allowed to sit in a special economy section between the really rich people in first class and the poor, unwashed wretches in the rear of the aircraft. Historians of commercial aviation will note that 1978 was the pivotal year in the development of the business-class concept. In the fall of that year, British Airways announced Club Class, for the express purpose of separating discount "tourists" from full-fare business clients. Soon afterward, Pan Am introduced Clipper Class. Qantas launched its business class, and Air France happily began providing better seats for its more sophisticated passengers. In 1981, SAS debuted EuroClass, which further separated business flyers from the population at large by employing separate check-in counters and lounges.[5]

The new class of service proved popular with business travelers and lured some away from the discount carriers, but not all airlines provided the same level of service. British Airways offered first-class-quality meals and free drinks in economy-class seats, while in 1979 Qantas became the first airline to refit their aircraft with seats that were wider and reclined further than economy, but not as much as first class. Even Laker Airways, the airline that had started the whole discount craze, started offering "Regency Service" in 1981 with leather seats, free drinks, Wedgwood china, real Champagne, and actual meals included, which caused some journalists to wonder if Laker had forgotten his roots.[6]

Other carriers were very slow to do anything that would discourage business travelers from flying anywhere but in first class. On Air India in 1979, according to author Rabindra Seth, "a seat just behind the first class and close to the exit plus free drinks was all the perks that went with a full fare."[7]

As business class became established as something more luxurious than coach and much cheaper than first, it created a situation both business travelers and airlines had been dreading. Companies that had been allowing first-class travel for executives started restricting them to business class. This cut the airlines' revenue from first-class seats and took away the glamour from businessmen's travel.

The state-owned airlines in Europe and Africa that were already losing money had no budget for refitting their aircraft with business-class seats and faced competition from other carriers that did. Many of them went with a canny strategy: rename their first-class cabin business class, so corporate travel departments would continue allowing executives to use it. This allowed the airlines to struggle on while still trying to formulate a strategy to deal with the discounters.

The state-owned carriers could go on for a while absorbing ever higher subsidies, so the first victims of liberalization in Europe were American. Pan Am went bankrupt in 1991; the carrier had no short-haul feeder system within the United States, a large pool of retirees with pensions, and a highly paid and aging workforce. Other American airlines would follow, because travel inside the United States was changing too.

In the US domestic market, where first a postmaster general and then the head of the Civil Aeronautics Board had upended the industry, it was the turn of a professor of economics to throw the system into chaos. In 1977 Alfred E. Kahn was appointed as the chairman of the Civil Aeronautics Board despite the fact that he admitted he knew nothing about the airline industry. Based on economic theories that stressed the virtue of competition, and with the European experience in which discounted seats had led to a flood of new carriers and lower fares for passengers, Kahn decided to throw the airline industry open to unlimited competition. The Airline Deregulation Act of 1978 eliminated the requirements that airlines serve some short and unprofitable routes in exchange for access to profitable longer routes, allowed market access for multiple carriers on routes which had previously been restricted to two, and abolished rules that said that airlines couldn't raise or lower fares without advance notice. The expectation was that whatever new paradigm emerged would be more robust and offer more passenger choice.

In the short term, he was right about the choice part. Freed of bureaucratic restrictions about where they could fly, regional airlines expanded and new carriers leaped into business. Southwest Airlines, once restricted to flying within Texas and the states bordering it, started the explosive growth that was to make them a national carrier—and they did it while serving only drinks and peanuts. They flew to secondary airports like Houston's Hobby Airport and Dallas's Love Field, which were as close or closer to the city centers of the respective cities but had landing fees that were a fraction of the major airports nearby. The lack of catering and low costs meant that Southwest could price their flights far lower than anybody else and still make a profit. It was a business model that airlines with established infrastructure at expensive airports couldn't imitate.

The major network carriers fought back with a brilliant plan: the frequent flyer program, introduced by American Airlines in 1981. The intention was to stop frequent travelers from considering each trip separately and booking the cheapest carrier for that journey, and instead book all flights with the same airline even if it wasn't the most convenient. The fact that the eventual benefits would probably be paid for by the travel budgets of the companies that business travelers worked for, but used for their own vacations, was an unstated but important factor. The major carriers began to claw back a little traffic from Southwest and the other upstarts, and for a while they kept their food service at current levels.

The carriers that were most endangered were the ones that didn't have the low cost structure of Southwest but lacked the nationwide coverage of United, American, and Delta. These had three choices: grow, merge, or die. Continental Airlines decided on aggressive growth, and in ten years of canny expansion went from a Denver-based regional airline to one that flew to Australia, Samoa, Japan, and a vast network throughout the United States, along with routes to the Caribbean and Mexico. Continental was able to keep a loyal following partly because their food service was well above the standards of most of their competitors; they owned a company called Chelsea Catering that employed Cordon Bleu chefs, and they regularly won awards as the best in the industry. At a time when other carriers were following Southwest's model and diminishing service, Continental introduced a pub concept with a bar, popcorn machine, and an electronic "Pong" game.[8] Continental's Hawaii flights included meals made according to the recipes from the famous Don The Beachcomber restaurant, with rum drinks to match.[9] The airline's "We Really Move Our Tail for You" ad campaign always included depictions of lavish food service, and the carrier successfully made the transition from minor to major carrier.

Western Airlines had always been one of the shakier carriers financially, partly because the CAB had blocked them from expanding substantially beyond their West Coast bases—and at many of those, they competed with low-fare carrier PSA. Deregulation gave the airline that chance to expand, but as one of their stewardesses named Teri Caroll observed, it was in a changed world.

> Overnight the whole industry changed. . . . The most notable difference was the passengers we were now flying. We were used to experienced business flyers. Deregulation seemed to create another group of travelers who didn't understand the nature of our business. We went from five flight attendants covering 120 passengers to four trying to serve 140 people—many of whom

had never flown before. The public's expectations just weren't realistic. I had women actually get upset that I wouldn't baby-sit their children or serve lunch on a 35 minute flight.[10]

Western's service to Alaska was particularly lucrative but involved competition with Alaska Air, a well-established carrier with a high reputation for service. Western rose to the occasion with "Pacific Horizon" service, featuring a fruit plate followed by two entrée choices at all meals and complimentary cocktails, wine, and beer. Western was successful for some time and flew some unusual routes like Honolulu to London with a stop in Anchorage. They continued as a viable carrier for almost a decade before being bought by Delta.

Many others were not so lucky. There hadn't been a single airline bankruptcy in the United States before deregulation was passed in 1979—within five years, twenty-four carriers had filed Chapter 11, and more had been acquired by other carriers at fire sale prices.[11] Faced with evidence that financial calamity was possible, regional airlines started merging, losing whatever distinctive personalities they had previously had.

Piedmont Airlines also tried the expansion route from their hub in North Carolina and eventually served both Los Angeles and London, bringing to those cities their unusually sophisticated menu. Though the main courses were the usual beef, chicken, or fish, they almost always finished with Southern pecan pie. Another signature was offering "Old Salem" Moravian ginger and sugar cookies, a North Carolina specialty.[12]

Another such example was Alaska Airlines, previously a small carrier that flew north from Seattle. The airline expanded as far south as Mexico and started service to several destinations in Siberia. To promote this they started "Golden Samovar" service featuring stewardesses in Cossack tunics serving borscht and beef stroganoff, along with a drink they called "Bolshoi Golden Troikas"—coffee, vodka, and coffee liqueur. Alaska became famous for the quality of their food and controversial for another element of their meal service: putting a small card with bible verses on every tray. Alaska Airlines continued doing this until January 2012, when they decided to stop "out of respect for its religiously diverse customer base."[13]

These were rare examples of airlines improving their service in an era when most were cutting back. The most famous example of a major carrier curtailing costs aggressively was the incident that became known as "Crandall's Olive." The president of American Airlines was reportedly aboard one of the airline's flights and began contemplating his dinner salad. As the *New York Times* put it in a business section article,

By now, it is the stuff of legend: in the 1980's, Robert L. Crandall, then the head of American Airlines, came up with the idea of removing just one olive from every dinner salad served to passengers. They would never notice, let alone squawk, he figured, and the airline could save some money. He was right, to the tune of $40,000 a year.[14]

It's one of the most famous decisions in the history of the airline, and cited in many studies of effective management, but there's some doubt that it actually happened. American Airlines has a corporate archive of Crandall's papers at the C. R. Smith Museum in Dallas and has been asked many times whether Crandall ever recounted that story, but the museum has never responded.[15] There is also a question about how much money might have been in question—the book *Corporate Creativity* claims $500,000. Many people have also questioned how removing one olive could save that much money, because olives aren't that expensive; the book explains that five-item salads from airline caterers cost substantially more than four-item salads, and that Crandall just looked at fellow passengers' meals to see what was left behind.[16] The same publication said that after the story became public, an association of olive growers threatened a boycott of the airline unless the olives were restored, and reports,

> After some negotiations, American agreed to stock every flight with olives and make them available to any passenger who requested them. This arrangement required no extra catering, since some olives were already put aboard every airplane for martinis.[17]

Whether it was really all about an olive, in 1981 Crandall did begin a program that cut the quality of airline meals, and other carriers followed. United removed beverage garnishes for an estimated savings of $50,000, Delta removed the strawberries from salads in first class for $210,000, and Continental even stopped serving pretzels and was said to have saved $2.5 million.[18] As *Flight Catering* expressed the situation,

> Deregulation of US airlines in 1978 changed nearly every aspect of airline operation, including catering services. In the drive to reduce costs, food service was cut back or even removed completely. The fewer flight attendants and greater number of feeder flights made it difficult or impossible to offer food service.[19]

The mania for cost cutting extended to every aspect of service. United and Delta started serving Taylor Cellars wine in aluminum cans in 1981, to widespread customer disdain. The airline stayed with it, because a case of canned wine weighs only half as much as the same volume of bottled wine, and weight was as much a consideration as ever.[20]

Airline meals had already disappeared from short flights aboard many carriers, and in 1981 a new airline took these trends to their logical conclusion. People Express started the American equivalent of Laker Airways and charged fees for everything—fifty cents each for a can of soda, bag of peanuts, or plastic-wrapped brownie, or two dollars for a "snak pak" containing cheeses, crackers, and salami. Charging for meals was a revival of the business model that had last been used in the 1950s, but no American airline had ever charged for nonalcoholic beverages before.

People Express began as a small regional carrier but quickly grew, charging rates that were actually cheaper than the bus fare to many destinations. They were sufficiently famous in their day that they were still a pop culture reference years later; in an episode of *The Simpsons*, Homer reminisces about a flight in 1985 and remarks, "People Express introduced a generation of hicks to air travel."[21]

After adding flights to London, Brussels, and Montreal, People Express's management decided to try their hand at buying another airline so they could feed their international routes. They made a giant mistake when they chose Frontier Airlines, which had previously offered premium service. A Frontier stewardess named Stephanie Knowles remembered,

All the food service disappeared and we had to sell a prepackaged snack box for $3.50 if a passenger wanted to eat. We sold coffee, tea, and soft drinks for 50 cents each, coffee refills were free. We had to keep track of the inventory, and flight attendants got a percentage of sales at the end of the flight. At the beginning inventory we got so many sleeves of cups, soft drinks, and snack boxes and at the end of the flight everything had to balance. It made a lot of paperwork, and we had to work more days to get our 85 hours of flying (monthly minimum). It was almost a relief when Frontier went out of business in 1986.[22]

The lost investment on Frontier had cost People Express so much money that the weakened company was sold for almost nothing to Continental the next year. It had been a case study of the perils of merging full-service carriers into no-frills carriers, and served as a cautionary tale for others.

The pressure from new entrants to the market weighed most heavily on the carriers that had high fixed costs like terminals in major airports, labor contracts negotiated during more optimistic times, and large numbers of retirees who were owed pensions. These carriers had to sell assets to survive, and one of the most valuable assets some carriers had was their flight catering operations. These were profitable and easily separable from the carrier in ways that other parts of the airline weren't, and so they went on the auction block. American Airlines, which operated flight kitchens exclusively for their own services under the name Sky Chefs, sold theirs in 1986 to a Canadian firm called Onex, who eventually sold the company to Lufthansa, which still owns it.

Airlines that had no large assets to sell resorted to a strategy that could best be called go big or go broke. Braniff Airways, which had operated successfully from the United States to South America, expanded recklessly to Europe and Asia and flamed out in 1982. Eastern Airlines, long the butt of jokes for their service, had some success in establishing themselves as a premium-quality airline. In 1985 they introduced Golden Wings service to London, featuring some of the best food in the air. When other carriers were cutting back even in first class, they served seven-course meals in the front cabin, including caviar, lobster, and standing rib roast. Business class was served on china with linens, and even in economy they offered all passengers hot towels, a choice of entrées, and other amenities. It wasn't enough, and the airline went bankrupt less than a year later, but they went out in style.

The deregulation years prompted many changes in airline service, unfortunately all toward service of lower-quality food, and less of it. For the first time since food started being served in flight, not a single technique to improve it was developed in over a decade. If one had even been discovered it probably wouldn't have been adopted unless it promised lower costs. There would be a brief resurgence of interest in providing a good experience before things got even worse.

CHAPTER 17

‒‒‒‒⟩⟨‒‒‒‒

Designing the Flying Meal

All airlines want to reinforce their branding with every aspect of their service, and in the era when carriers owned their own kitchens and handled their own catering, this was easily done. Major carriers could easily have their own branded china, glasses, and silverware because it all stayed within the same system—there was no concern that a United aircraft might accidentally have a meal delivered on TWA china because they had entirely separate operations.

Smaller carriers that outsourced all their catering to an outside service and couldn't afford the signature china had to be satisfied with using branded napkins and placemats and supplying the outside kitchens with signature recipes. This is far more cost effective but has had notorious failures when caterers prepared foods for palates very different from their own. Britannia Airways, an English airline that specialized in budget tour groups, found this out when they started running flights to Florida and provided recipes to their American caterer for the return flights. As related in *Gourmet and Glamour in the Sky,*

> The Catering Manager at the time, Ms. Jenny Groom, recalls having great difficulty in obtaining authentic dishes that would be acceptable to the very British clientele that they carried. At one point she visited sausage factories to make sure a suitable British style "banger" was produced in the English style. In the late eighties at Orlando in Florida the catering Manager at Dobbs catering confided to me that Ms. Groom had been back three times to ensure

the apple crumble was perfect and on the third occasion ". . . it was still not quite right!"[1]

If Brittania had this kind of problem when catering for a British working-class clientele, one can imagine what it is like for airlines whose national cuisine has a highly stylized presentation. A Japan Air Lines representative declined to provide details but stated that the carrier has had difficulty at times finding overseas chefs who can make sushi rolls and donburi rice bowls that come up to the standard of beauty that is suitable for their first-class cabin. Beauty is important because, as Michael Dick, international account manager for Marriott Inflight Services, observed in 1977, "You start to eat with your eyes." As the person who was interviewing him at the time, a reporter for the *Chicago Tribune*, noted,

> Unfortunately, though, it's your stomach, and not your eyes, that makes the final judgment. So who's to blame for that wilted salad, cold dinner roll, burnt peas, soggy dessert, or tough piece of mystery meat drenched in a sauce that resembles Gravy Train? The obvious answer would be the chef, of course. But with the airlines themselves "dictating" the menus and setting up very rigid guidelines the role of the chef in airline catering is quite different from that of his counterpart in the restaurant business."[2]

Airline catering has diverged further from restaurant cooking since that was written, and further from the airline business too. When Don Magarell started United's catering division in the 1930s, he was an airline employee and could get quick feedback from stewardesses who worked for the same company he did. Once centralized kitchens making frozen food became standard in the business, a meal might be consumed two thousand miles from where it was prepared and two months later. If airline passengers disliked that meal, the cabin crew that served it would have to fill out paperwork to send to managers who would contact the catering company. Fast and meaningful feedback is now impossible.

This points out an essential change in relationships: for the airline-owned caterers, the passenger was the customer who had to be pleased; for outside caterers, the airline is the customer. Passengers care most about quality, while airlines care most about price.

The only remaining link to fresh food aboard airlines is in first class, and it's natural that the food there will be more varied because airlines charge so much more and want to project a premium experience. There is another reason that the food in the economy section is so different from the food up front: the airlines assume that many coach passengers wouldn't like the food in first class if they tried it. In an article for *Delicious Magazine*, Danny Chapman, the development chef for Superior Foods, a UK-based caterer, said,

> For economy, it's basic flavours which the majority of consumers will like. The starter will either be a simple leaf salad or a simple dish like red pesto penne pasta with shaved Parmesan. The main meal will be predominately based around chicken (roast chicken, potatoes and vegetables), beef (beef lasagne) or vegetarian (roast Mediterranean ratatouille and for dessert a simple fruit salad with orange and passion fruit syrup). Most economy meals are served in a tray format.
>
> For Business and First Class passengers we study the current food trends and what new ingredients are in the market; a current dish is roasted vegetables on a bed of quinoa, and pomegranate salad topped with bar-marked goat's cheese.[3]

The British passengers from the 1970s who wanted their bangers and apple crumble just as they had it at home might nod their heads in agreement, but sophisticated airline passengers on a budget might wish it were otherwise. They're not likely to get their wish, because a meal that is bland or dull is still edible to someone who likes exotic food, while one that is highly spiced or original would be rejected by someone who has simple tastes.

So who makes the decision about what meals fit the flavor profile of the typical customer? In the same article, Chapman detailed the process:

> Once the meals have been developed, they will be presented to the airline for assessment. Some of the airlines choose to send their meals to a Food Jury made up of everyday people, who will taste and evaluate the choices. Depending on the feedback, the meals will be either tested for nutritional information and shelf life (both microbiologically and organoleptically) or reworked to meet the customers' and consumers' standards. Once all the technical information comes back and we have final customer approval the menu will then be launched with the airline.

For those who are about to head for a dictionary to look up organoleptically, it means "involving the use of the sense organs." Somehow it fits the stereotype of airline catering that the company's representative couldn't just say that the meal should be tasty.

Regardless, it appears that anyone who wishes to improve the variety of airline meals should get themselves into a "food jury." Even in a world that is increasingly multicultural, the definition of "everyday people" implies a fondness for the bland and familiar. Most of the airline food of earlier eras was based on the idea that airline passengers were dining on nothing much more adventurous than pot roast and fried chicken when at home. These days curries, Thai food, and Mexican cuisine are some of the most popular dining experiences in the world, but unless you're traveling on an airline from one of those countries, you won't be seeing those meals aloft anytime soon. Airline meals are stuck in an earlier era and are likely to keep serving your grandmother's comfort food.

CHAPTER 18

<div align="center">~~~~~~~~~~</div>

The Decline and Fall of Inflight
Dining (1985–Present)

The 1990s dawned in an environment in which food in economy class on
most major routes was being served less often, in smaller quantities, and by
fewer people. There was, however, a large section of the globe in which it
was becoming better: the former communist bloc. Aeroflot started operating
Ilyushin-96 aircraft in 1989, their first aircraft with a galley that was almost
as sophisticated as American and European airliners. And for the first
time, the food loaded into that galley in Russia was up to international
standards as well, since a Soviet-American consortium had started a catering
company called Aeromar at Moscow's airport.[1] The Soviet Union was in a
slow-motion disintegration, and for many Russian travelers, this was one
of the first benefits of opening to the West. In 1992 the airline received
Airbus planes, the first they ever owned with coffeemakers on board, so they
could finally ditch the awful instant coffee they had been serving since the
foundation of the airline.

Standards had already been rising among some other Eastern European
airlines, particularly Malev Hungarian Airlines, which had been using
American-built aircraft for some time. Others did not make improvements as
quickly—the author remembers a flight from Sofia to London aboard Balkan
Bulgarian Airlines in the early 1980s on which meals were served with such
rapidity that they were almost thrown on trays, after which the stewardesses
retired to the back of the cabin and were not seen again for some time. The
passengers had a lively debate about what kind of meat was beneath the

lumpy, tasteless gravy, and when the stewardesses returned to pick up the trays, they claimed they didn't know.

As standards rose in the east, they fell in the west. Most of the new European private carriers cut costs with fanatical zeal. Ireland's Ryanair has been the most famous at this, charging passengers for meals and almost everything else; at one time the airline even floated a proposal for installing pay toilets on board.[2] Most competing carriers didn't charge for meals but served a regimen known as "salads out and sandwiches home" regardless of the time or duration of the flight. One airline executive, Errol Cossey of fledgling carrier Air Europe, realized that there was a fundamental flaw in this strategy.

Back in 1979 the airports did not start to get busy until around 0900 hrs, so to get our slots and the sort of aircraft utilisation I was after without impinging on night slots, we had to start our day with departures at 0700–0730. This meant that if we were going to provide salads and sandwiches they would have to be prepared—and prepared fresh—which meant the caterers would have to pay premium rates (that they passed onto us) for getting the meals ready in the middle of the night in order to hit our departure times!

I looked at the situation and discovered that no matter what time the holidaymakers left home and travelled to their destination, they passed through a mealtime. I reasoned that the only time during that journey that they were worry-free was when they were sitting on the aeroplane—so that was the time when they would best appreciate food. I wanted to create a feeling that you were having a meal in a restaurant rather then being thrown a packet of sustenance. This way perhaps people's minds would be diverted from the high density seating.

. . . We could serve a hot English breakfast—sausage, bacon, scrambled egg, mushrooms and sautéed potatoes for less than roast lamb, so the order was to serve breakfast on all flights that vaguely touched breakfast time. . . . These meals costed out less than the labour intensive salads and sandwiches, due to them being factory produced well in advance during conventional working hours and then frozen. . . . It was also much easier to control quality. Due to the meals being frozen we could quite safely cater for the return sector by carrying the inbound food from the UK in the hold. This was far safer, and quality control was much easier, than relying on continental kitchens that had to gear up for high peak summer-only demand. When all the benefits were put together, we could provide a meal—starter, hot entree, pudding, cheese and biscuits and a chocolate—considerably cheaper than the limp "Spam Salad" that was being served by our competitors.[3]

The British carrier that rose to international prominence at this time based much of its appeal on the high quality of inflight food and service.

Virgin Atlantic was an outgrowth of record company entrepreneur Richard Branson's business empire, and from the carrier's founding in 1986 the airline used his credibility and the branding of his company to appeal to affluent younger travelers.[4] An ad from April 1988 explicitly aimed at college students compared flying other carriers to taking a trigonometry exam with a hangover, but boasted that aboard Virgin,

> How about a nice hot meal? In fact, a choice of three nice hot meals. That's right, it's airline food. With one major difference. It's actually edible. It's also followed by tea and pastries later on. So you can munch out while you do a little extra studying. (Yeah, right!)[5]

It was the first instance of an airline making a pitch to a hip demographic, and it was wildly successful. The airline served unusual snacks like Worcestershire sauce–flavored pretzels in economy class, and even there served meals with flair on their red and white china. Naturally, when Virgin Cola was introduced in 1994, that was served as well. Business class was more lavish and continued the deliberately quirky branding, most famously with the airplane-shaped salt and pepper shakers with the words "Nicked From Virgin Atlantic" embossed on each one. They were the first carrier to introduce meals-on-demand in business class, rather than serving when it was convenient for the crew.[6] The company won *Business Traveler Magazine*'s award for best business-class service in 1988, only two years after it was founded, and has won that award almost every year since, along with others for best food and inflight service.[7] Virgin Atlantic flew their millionth passenger only three years after the carrier was founded and has gone on to spawn a network that serves much of the world. It was a rare example of an airline betting on passengers appreciating quality service and winning.

There weren't many others. Asian carriers like Singapore Air, ANA, and Cathay Pacific kept standards high wherever they flew, but elsewhere cost-cutting was the mantra. The Gulf War of 1990–1991 caused tourists to cancel trips by the thousands, and even first-class business was affected as multinational companies restricted business travel.[8] Seats went empty at the same time that gas prices soared, and airlines all over the world suffered record losses. Air Europe, which had just expanded their fleet and was entirely devoted to recreational tourism, was one of the casualties.

European governments kept propping up national carriers with subsidies, but in 1994 the system was destroyed by a set of EU court decisions that limited government support to airlines and airports. Though the first rulings were limited, requiring Air France and Greece's Olympic Airlines to regard

The management at Virgin Atlantic obviously knew that passengers would steal the airplane-shaped salt and pepper shakers, which is why each was stamped "Pinched From Virgin Atlantic."
Image provided by Virgin Atlantic

previous state aid as loans instead of grants, they sent shock waves through the industry.[9] While private carriers complained that the decision didn't go all the way to demanding immediate repayment, the decision forced the French government to lift restrictions that stopped competing carriers from serving the most desirable airports, and forced Air France to sell the hotel chain they owned and to privatize the airline. It was the first of many court cases that would doom state-owned carriers to choose privatization, merger, or bankruptcy.

In the United States, where there had been no government control for decades, the heavily indebted major airlines had only two of those options. Those airlines that had assets to sell did so—United, which still owned the flight kitchens established by Don Magarell in 1936, sold them in 1993. The kitchens were highly profitable but the airline wasn't, and the 140 million dollars United's holding company received was needed to subsidize flight operations.[10] The only major airline that kept their flight kitchens was

Continental, which still treasured their reputation for high-quality food and wanted to retain control.

That airline stumbled badly when they tried to match the cost cutters at their own game. In 1993 Continental created what they hoped would be a competitor to Southwest called "Continental Lite." They removed the first-class seats, served only peanuts, and tried to emulate the fast airport turnarounds by rushing customers on and off the aircraft. It was a spectacular failure, alienating all their existing customers without bringing in many new ones, and it was dropped after only two years. It had been such a financial disaster that the airline brought in a new president, Gordon Bethune, who used a food metaphor when he told *Texas Monthly*, "You can make a pizza so cheap nobody will eat it, and you can make an airline so cheap nobody will fly it."[11] Bethune also shook up food service aboard Continental's regular flights, overturning the previous management's decision that food would not be served on flights of less than two hours, regardless of the flight time.

In an article for the *Harvard Business Review* called "Right Away and All At Once: How We Saved Continental," his partner in the strategy, chief operating officer Greg Brenneman wrote that they

> immediately started fixing our idiotic food policy. I don't know about you, but to me, a two-hour flight that leaves at 7:00 a.m. (after I have gotten up at 5:00 a.m. to get to the airport and haven't eaten breakfast) is a lot different from a two-hour flight at 2:00 p.m., which falls after lunch but before dinner. Customers told us they wanted and would pay for breakfast at 7:00 a.m. They may want food at 2:00 p.m., but they won't pay for it. We changed our meal service with an eye toward what our competitors were doing. Now our service reflects time of day, length of haul, and class of service.
>
> In addition to changing when we served food, we also changed the food itself. Gone are the days when Continental put the meat, potato, and vegetable in a little ceramic dish and heated it until they all tasted the same. Nowadays, Gordon and I personally select the food we serve on our planes, and we test it ourselves every three months. You will find items like fresh pasta, soup and sandwiches, and freshly baked cinnamon rolls in first class, and Subway sandwiches and jelly beans in coach. We try to give everyone some brand quality with gourmet coffees and microbrewery beers. We're not trying to be a four-star restaurant, just an airline that gives its customers something they'd be happy to pay for. And that's the whole point of asking the customer in seat 9C the right question. In a turnaround situation—or any business situation, for that matter—you can't afford to ask anything else.[12]

Abandoning the attempt to be a cost cutter did save the airline, and within two years Continental went from being ranked last in customer satisfaction by J. D. Power and Associates to first. Amazingly, despite the fact that Continental's "airline within an airline" strategy hadn't worked, United Airlines copied it to create a carrier they called "Shuttle By United."[13] They did execute it better and operations were marginally profitable, but customers disliked it and it was eventually folded back into the rest of the airline.

Other airlines tried to replicate the Southwest model and gained footholds in regional markets. ValuJet, Midway Airlines, Morris Air, and other carriers were briefly successful, but like so many others eventually failed or merged. One notable carrier bucked the trend. Midwest Express, an airline founded in 1984, became famous as an all-business-class airline serving high-quality meals and chocolate chip cookies baked on board. They almost immediately became the favorite corporate travel airline in America, and executives who had to fly to Chicago or New York were willing to make a change in Kansas City or Milwaukee to enjoy the 2 x 2 seating and full meals served on quality china. Though their services were wildly popular for over a decade, the airline was too small to survive as an independent and was eventually sold to Frontier, which gradually transitioned their services to standard economy.

Worries about terrorism and a sharp spike in fuel prices during the Gulf War caused a stream of bankruptcies after 1992, including venerable carrier TWA. The airlines that survived cut back severely on meals, selling only cold items even on transcontinental service. The process accelerated after the September 11, 2001, terrorist attacks and the massive losses that resulted from the subsequent two-week shutdown of the entire US airline system. Operations restarted with the carriers burdened with new and costly security procedures, with metal knives and forks even in first class replaced with plasticware, and passengers shunning flying in favor of other modes of transportation.[14]

To go into the whole long list of carriers that merged and shut down would be tiresome and repetitive. Suffice it to say that the same pattern was repeated everywhere: reduce the frequency and quality of meals. After 2003, when America West and Northwest introduced the practice, even major carriers started charging for them.[15] William McGee, author of the book *Attention All Passengers*, a critique of the industry, summarized the situation in an interview with the travel magazine *Roads and Kingdoms*:

> Buy-on-board meals are now the standard on domestic flights, turning what was once a major expense into a profit center for airlines. It's gone from hot meals to cold meals, cold meals to snacks. They conditioned us over time that our expectations should be lower and lower. What's happened conversely at the same time is the quality of food in airports has increased tremendously, which is why a lot more people these days are brown bagging.[16]

In a complete reversal from the days when airlines regarded their meals as part of their branding, Northwest started giving airline passengers discount coupons for Taco Bell, Pizza Hut, and KFC locations in airports, and United offered only McDonald's children's meals for young passengers on flights from Orlando. Many airlines allowed, and even encouraged, passengers to bring their own food. This caused problems for airline crews, who were suddenly faced with piles of randomly sized take-out boxes at the end of every flight instead of trays that fit neatly together. It also caused problems for passengers, because their fellow travelers did not make the calculation that airlines did regarding serving foods that smelled very strongly. *Bon Appétit* magazine ran a lengthy and hilarious rant by Jason Kessler called "I'm Sick of Stinky Food on Airplanes," that read in part,

> Have you ever been in this position? You're settling into a harrowing cross-country flight armed only with the in-flight magazine when someone sits down across the aisle from you holding a plastic take-out bag. It seems innocuous enough. Then, after you clear 10,000 feet, this stranger launches a full-on sensory attack. Turns out that plastic bag is filled with hazardous material: orange chicken from the fast food Chinese place in the terminal. Within 30 seconds, you're gagging on the sickly sweet smell of processed sodium-filled meat nuggets. After two minutes, you're thinking about an escape route. Ten minutes in, you've taken out your cell phone and are pretending to make calls just so the flight attendant will forcibly take you to the secret holding cell in the bottom of the airplane built expressly for people who attempt to make calls mid-flight. You didn't know that holding cell existed, did you? Now you do.
>
> This scenario happened to me (sans prison) a few weeks ago—and it wasn't the first time. Bringing and eating stinky food on board a plane is one of the most inconsiderate things you could possibly do to your fellow passengers. The air you breathe on that 747 is the same air that everyone else breathes because you're literally in a steel tube suspended in the sky (which, when you think about it, is disconcerting enough). Those orange chicken molecules are being recycled over and over again until your brain makes a deal with your nose that it's just going to ignore the problem.
>
> An airplane is not a mall. At the mall, you don't have to sit there and take it when somebody nearby digs into a foul-smelling lunch. You can move. On an airplane, you don't have that luxury. You're essentially trapped.[17]

Kessler was the magazine's professional curmudgeon, but his griping touched a chord. The message boards at Airliners.net and the Flyertalk.com forum, which cater to frequent airline travelers, were filled with complaints about the decline of the passenger experience and the nuisance of dealing with people who brought garlic-laden dishes on board aircraft. They also brimmed with complaints about the lack of food service aboard airlines that were still trying to brand themselves as superior to the discounters. United had set up yet another low-fare subsidiary called TED, and in 2007 they stopped serving even pretzels aboard flights. A passenger on the Flyertalk forum posted,

> Does UA think that they are going to save their airline or make them profitable by taking away a small bag with a few pretzels for each passenger? Is UA not trying to distinguish itself as a "Premium" airline and try to make it so that people are willing to pay a premium to fly UA? I would like to hear how much this saves UA a year, because this is simply shocking. Come on, two hours can actually be quite a long flight. With taxi, boarding, and everything, it can be well into three hours gate to gate and now we get absolutely nothing? Please UA, PLEASE tack twelve cents onto my ticket price you ba$tard$.[18]

Continental Airlines served up the industry's last free economy-class meal in October 2010, just before merging with United. That merger made United the owner of flight kitchens again, since Continental had owned Chelsea Food Services, based in downtown Houston. Those kitchens, which United still owns, turn out first-class meals and meals for purchase for United and other domestic and international carriers. Two decades before this, a company that size would have found it difficult if not impossible to cater for United alone, but times had changed. Far from using Chelsea to build United's brand and improve communication with their customers, United's CEO Jeff Smisek indicated in an interview that the airline would consider using other caterers. "How much volume we do through them will depend on cost," he explained in a 2010 interview with Bloomberg News.[19]

During the same period in Europe, carriers that had just begun to recover from the Gulf War slowdown were slammed again by the aftermath of the World Trade Center bombings. Traffic fell by almost 30 percent that year and did not recover fully for almost five years.[20] The slowdown and increased security costs hit established carriers at the same time that their long-opaque finances were scrutinized by increasingly activist EU authorities determined to prevent subsidies.[21] State-owned airline after airline declared bankruptcy—Sabena, Swissair, Olympic, Malev, and many others. National airlines merged in ways that would have been unthinkable in an earlier age—Air France and KLM, two of the world's oldest airlines that had been competitors since 1920, merged their management in 2004. They are now one carrier in all but name.

The situation in which state-owned carriers were seen as utterly reliable while their private competitors were chancy was inverted—suddenly passengers looked at an airline's balance sheet before paying for that advance booking. It was a boon for carriers that could boast that they were stable and profitable. Virgin Atlantic was one of these, and with founder Richard Branson's usual genius for publicity, he even managed to turn a complaint letter about his airline's food into a PR triumph. In 2008 a customer who had taken a flight from London to India sent a hilariously aggrieved letter to the airline's management about the quality of the Indian-style meal. It was lavishly illustrated with photos of the unappetizing dishes, and reads in part,

> by the end of the flight I would have gladly paid over a thousand rupees for a single biscuit following the culinary journey of hell I was subjected to at the hands of your corporation.
>
> "Look at this Richard. Just look at it: I imagine the same questions are racing through your brilliant mind as were racing through mine on that fateful day. What is this? Why have I been given it? What have I done to deserve this? And, which one is the starter, which one is the desert [sic?]? You don't get to a position like yours, Richard with anything less than a generous sprinkling of observational power so I KNOW you will have spotted the tomato next to the two yellow shafts of sponge on the left. Yes, it's next to the sponge shaft without the green paste. That's got to be the clue hasn't it. No sane person would serve a desert [sic?] with a tomato would they. Well answer me this Richard, what sort of animal would serve a desert [sic?] with peas in? I know it looks like a baaji but it's in custard Richard, custard. It must be the pudding. Well you'll be fascinated to hear that it wasn't custard. It was a sour gel with a clear oil on top. It's only redeeming feature was that it managed to be so alien to my palate that it took away the taste of the curry emanating from our miscellaneous central cuboid of beige matter. Perhaps the meal on the left might be the desert [sic?] after all."
>
> "The potato masher had obviously broken and so it was decided the next best thing would be to pass the potatoes through the digestive tract of a bird."[22]

This letter would have never made it to the desks of most airline presidents, but Sir Richard Branson not only saw it, he phoned the passenger and invited him to visit Virgin's London catering department to help select the food for future Virgin flights. The widely publicized letter, and Branson's response to it, gave the world's airline passengers a laugh at the same time as it bolstered the airline's reputation for customer service.

A few private carriers decided to see if the time was right for a higher level of passenger service than even Virgin, offering all-business-class long-haul flights. Silverjet flew from London to New York and Dubai, Maxjet from Las Vegas, Los Angeles, and New York to London, L'Avion from Paris to Newark, and Eos from New York to London. All won awards for the passenger experience, but Eos, which started in 2004 and went bankrupt

EOS CLASS MENU

WELCOME DRINK

Passionfruit Vodka Martini Cocktail

APERITIF

Cocktail or Beverage of your Choice

TASTING OF CANAPÉS

Marinated Brocconcini	Ham Wrap
Cray Fish	Goat Cheese
with avocado cream	*with olive and sun-dried tomato*
Roast Beef	Smoked Salmon
with sauce tartare	*with cream cheese*

MAIN COURSES

Osso Bucco
grilled zucchini, carrots, turned potatoes
served with fresh garden salad/balsamic dressing

Chicken Piccata with Lemon Pepper Rissotto
served with garden salad and scallop skewer
balsamic dressing

Mushroom Ravioli
served with fresh garden salad
balsamic dressing

DESSERTS

Cheese Plate
Brie, Butler's Secret, Blue Stilton

Mini Almond Pear Tart
served with yoghurt lime ice cream and hot chocolate sauce

Berry Ragout
served with vanilla crème fraiche

Chocolate Almonds – Taittinger Brut Champagne

———

AFTERNOON TEA
served 90 minutes before arrival

Assorted Tea Sandwiches

Scones/Clotted Cream

Preserves

Opera Chocolate Cake

Steven D. Green
Captain

Rob Buck
FIRST OFFICER

STN TeaSvc 3/15/08 part MMWC208

The last of the premium carriers was Eos Airlines, which flew between 2004 and 2008. This was the menu served on their final flight—the last supper for single-cabin luxury in the sky.
Menu in author's collection

in 2008, lasted the longest as an all-business-class carrier. Only one of this flock, Open Skies, continues to fly, though the airline was bought by British Airways. They now have three classes, and their service has degraded to the equivalent of other carriers.

As of early 2014, the only European airlines that have improved economy-class service are charging for it. In May 2013 Latvia's Air Baltic started allowing passengers to select from twenty different meal options at the time they book their tickets. The passenger's selection is relayed to LSG Sky Chefs, the caterer they contract with, and the charge for the meal is put on the passenger's credit card when the flight is booked.[23] Air France and Austrian airlines copied the idea later in the year, and other carriers are eyeing their experience. As this book goes to press, it looks like it may be the wave of the future.

The only region in the world where free economy-class airline service did not greatly deteriorate between 1985 and the present day was in Asia, the last bastion of state-owned carriers. As William McGee put it in *Roads and Kingdoms*,

> As a general preemptive measure, fly Asian airlines as often as possible. "The coach service in Asian and Middle Eastern airlines is comparable to the business-class service you get from American carriers," says William McGee. The Singapore girls will soak you in fruity Singapore Slings, All Nippon offers respectable soba and Japanese-style fried chicken to their coach passengers, and Korean Airlines boasts their own farm, which provides the building blocks for their legendary bibimbap.

While an increasing number of private airlines are serving Asia, these are generally forced by competitive pressures to maintain the same standard of service as their state-owned counterparts. There is no equivalent of the European Union's regulations against subsidies, so for now, at least, there are still routes where an economy passenger may enjoy a decent meal.

For the elite passengers in first and business class, the choices worldwide have actually expanded even as their number has declined. In 2012 a *Wall Street Journal* article stated that of the over five hundred aircraft flying to Europe, Asia, and South America, just 27 percent offered any first-class seats.[24] These are increasingly filled with passengers who are using frequent flyer miles to upgrade, but the airlines pile on the amenities anyway. A la carte dining (included in the fare, naturally), dining at the time of your choice, and meals designed by celebrity chefs have become standard amenities.

It is interesting to consider the ways in which airline meals have gone through a cycle: no food at all on the earliest flights, luxurious repasts in the late 1930s through mid-1950s for the elite that could afford to fly, democratized meals in the 1960s and early 1970s, a return to no food in the 1990s, and now abundance in one cabin while peanuts, pretzels, or nothing is served in the other. It is tempting to think that some future change in society might bring a return to abundance, if not luxury, for all passengers aboard aircraft, but it is hard to see how that might happen.

Rather than end this book on that depressing note, I'll turn to examining a related field in which even greater challenges were overcome: the journeys of humans into space.

CHAPTER 19

<del>~~~~~~</del>

Tubes and Cubes
Food in Space (1961–1965)

Unlike the first meal in flight, it's very easy to know precisely when the first meal was eaten in space. Cosmonaut Yuri Gagarin's food on April 12, 1961, was simple—beef and liver paste, followed by liquefied chocolate, both squeezed from metal tubes. The occasion might have merited something more festive, perhaps even popping a few Champagne corks as was done by the balloonists of a previous era, but this meal was practical rather than celebratory. It was a cautious start, using well-tested technologies in an environment that was unlike any other humans had ever experienced.

The challenges of providing food for humans traveling in space were fundamentally different from those for providing meals in flight, and accomplished by different entities. Though the first meals eaten in the air were aboard military transports in World War I, all the major advances in food in flight were made by civilian companies whose primary concern was the preferences of passengers. Those consumers were picky and could take another airline if they didn't enjoy the experience, which obviously wasn't the case for the race to travel beyond the atmosphere. Though the American space program always made use of private contractors, and the former Soviet program has been partially privatized, both began as military programs and remained that way for a long time.

The first thing the scientists at both programs had to figure out was whether it was even possible to eat and drink in space at all. There were concerns that food might be hard to swallow while in weightless conditions, and one of the tasks for John Glenn during his first orbit of Earth in 1962 was to drink water and see if he had trouble swallowing.[1] If America had finally gotten a man into space only to have him drown on a swallow of water, the reaction of the American public could only be guessed at, but Glenn disproved those who thought that a physiology evolved for gravity might not work without it. There was legitimate concern about this even though the Soviet cosmonaut German Titov had eaten twice during his twenty-five-hour mission the year before, because Titov had vomited it all back up after a bout of space sickness.

Glenn had no such problem. After that swallow of water, he ate applesauce that had been packaged in a tube similar to those used for toothpaste, then followed it with a pureed beef and vegetable mixture. (He had a tube of spaghetti available too, but apparently chose not to open it.)[2] It was not a gourmet delight, more like eating baby food sucked through a tube, but it was nutritious and convenient.

The tubes of food were not new inventions—they had originally been developed by the American Can Company in the late 1940s for fighter pilots who couldn't remove their gloves or helmets.[3] Both the Soviets and the Americans used this system for their early space flights, principally because of concerns that any solid food might produce crumbs that could float around the capsule, clog air vents, or gum up delicate instruments. The tubes were a well-tested technology, but they had several disadvantages, starting with the fact that the astronauts who used them all disliked both the flavor and the experience of squeezing food into their mouths.

Surprisingly, given the relative affluence of the two countries, the Soviets were much more concerned with giving their intrepid explorers a varied diet. They quickly diversified the number of items available in tubes to over thirty and provided bite-size bread rolls so their cosmonauts could enjoy a familiar pleasure without scattering crumbs.[4] (One might speculate that the heavy and moist dark bread favored by Russians might have been a better starting point for space food than the lighter white bread that was favored by Americans, since the lighter white bread would tend to crumble more easily.) Other earth-like foods enjoyed by the Vostok cosmonauts in 1961 were pieces of salami and fruit jelly. The Russians also gave their spacemen berry juices and beet juice, both beverages with a tangy, fruity bite that would be refreshing even under very dry conditions. These were already favorite non-alcoholic beverages of many Russians and helped replicate the taste of home even in space.

The Americans were obsessed with developing food as modern and groundbreaking as the program itself and deployed an arsenal of techniques to transform food so that it would be suitable for consumption in weightless conditions. They had a perfect example of what not to do during the flight that followed John Glenn's in 1962, when astronaut Scott Carpenter tried eating a cookie. As the *Los Angeles Times* reported it, " . . . the crumbs stayed behind to float in front of his face like so many large particles of dust."[5]

The next voyage, by astronaut Gordon Cooper, set the standard for the next several US space flights. Cooper's meal was powdered roast beef rehydrated into mush in a plastic bag of cold water, with water as the only beverage. After the sleep period in the middle of his thirty-four-hour flight he also had a dextroamphetamine pill, which would have both kept him alert and acted as an appetite suppressant, as if the prospect of eating more beef mush wasn't enough of one.[6]

That was the last American flight for three years, as the United States transitioned from the Mercury program to the Gemini flights, and during that time scientists experimented with ideas about how to create palatable meals in space. Their ideas ranged from conservative to zany; among the weirder ones was a concept that involved making parts of the capsule itself edible. According to *Newsweek* magazine, Sidney A. Schwartz, a psychologist who worked for Grumman Aircraft,

> worked out a recipe on paper and shopped in a Bethpage, N.Y. supermart for $5 worth of groceries—flour, corn starch, powdered milk, banana flakes, and hominy grits. After mixing the ingredients he baked them in a hydraulic press at 400 degrees Fahrenheit under 3,000-pound pressure. The result: a grainy brown slab as tough as tempered Masonite that could be cut on a bandsaw without splintering or drilled for bolts and screws. Aboard a spaceship, he says, it could be used as lightweight, inexpensive (10 cents a pound) cabinets, shelves, and panels. But how does it taste? Too hard to be eaten as is, the food has to be pulverized with a tiny grinder. After it is soaked for a few hours in water, says Schwartz, "it tastes like breakfast cereal topped with bananas. I rather like it."[7]

The idea of astronauts sawing pieces out of their spacecraft in order to pulverize, soak, and eat them was apparently not appealing to NASA, because there is no evidence that this was ever tried. Another idea that was conceived at this time would be revisited much later: growing food from leftovers. As a *Washington Post* article from 1963 reported it,

> A suburban research firm is working on tissue-culture techniques which it hopes might enable space travelers to grow one meal from the scraps of a preceding one, and so on and on. The ultimate result of the experiments conceivably could be production of food such as tomatoes without leaves,

stems or roots and steaks of controlled weight, shape and tenderness without growing an animal. Melpar, Inc., an aerospace firm in Falls Church, has been carrying on company-sponsored research for two years. The firm's president, Paul Ritt, said some 'very modest results' have been obtained in Melpar laboratories, but estimated it might be three or four years before the experiments succeed on a significant scale. The process requires a solution of nutrients containing the more than 90 substances that nature provides to growing organisms. A sample of the tissue—a piece of steak for example—is placed in this culture. Under strict conditions of light, temperature and sterility control, the tissue grows. The tissue culture first became known publicly in the late 1940s, when a Nobel Prize was awarded to a team growing monkey tissue culture for polio vaccine applications. Melpar scientists hope the equipment they are developing will make large scale production possible. They said the automatic culture of tissue could be applied to. . . . Space feeding—a never-ending compact supply of vegetables, fruit and meat. The space traveler would leave a small portion of his meal in the culture equipment so that it could grow back.[8]

As alluring as these technologies might be, NASA decided to stay with techniques they knew worked: dehydrating, freeze-drying, pureeing, and making food into gels. Dehydration and pureeing are ancient technologies that are practiced almost everywhere in the world, but freeze-drying is much more complex. As the European Union's Food Information Council defines it, this requires a special tool—the freeze-dryer.[9]

This machine consists of a large chamber for freezing and a vacuum pump for removing moisture. The treatment consists of four steps: 1) Freezing to provide conditions for low temperature drying, 2) Vacuum application to allow frozen water/solvent in the product to vaporize without passing through the liquid phase, i.e. sublimation, 3) Heat application to accelerate sublimation, and 4) Condensation to remove the vaporized solvent from the vacuum chamber by converting it back to a solid.

Surprisingly, freeze-drying is not a new technology; the Incas came up with a slow but effective way of freeze-drying potatoes in the cold and windy Andean highlands. It took thirty days rather than the few hours that can be achieved with a freeze-dryer, but produced the same effect. Though freeze-dried foods require more space for storage because they retain more of their original form, they are lighter than dehydrated foods and tend to bear a closer resemblance to their fresh state when rehydrated. They also tend to rehydrate more quickly and completely because the ice crystals that have sublimated out leave tiny pores, which makes meals easier and faster to prepare.

Making the food light is important because the weight of provisions is even more important than aboard aircraft, and dehydrated foods weigh very little. Most foods, even those we think of as not terribly moist, are between 50 and 90 percent water, so removing that weight makes them very light. Fully dehydrated food also doesn't spoil, because bacteria need moisture to thrive. It was the right solution for the problem, but at great cost in palatability, because when foods rehydrate, their texture tends to be mushy and unpleasant. This problem was increased by the fact that the early space capsules had no way of heating water, so everything was at the ambient temperature in the spacecraft.

Another technology that was tried was to take moist foods, cut them into cubes, and coat them with a glue-like edible protein so that there would be few crumbs. This was described in a *New York Times* article that appeared in 1965.[10]

Some of the foods, such as bacon-and-egg bites, red cubes, or cheese cubes, do not have to be reconstituted. But these have to be prevented from making crumbs that can float around the cockpit. The cubes are all bite-sized, so the astronaut can chew with his mouth closed. As a further safeguard against crumbs, which were a problem in some Project Mercury flights, all the cubes are coated with a starch called Amylomaize, which holds in the crumbs. The individual foods are packed in a four-ply plastic that performs a variety of functions. The innermost layer is a good-grade polyethylene that is compatible with food. The second layer is a nylon film to give the package burst and kneading strength. The third layer is a fluorocarbon film called Aclar, which prevents the passage of oxygen and water. And the outside layer is another polyethylene that gives heat-sealability to the envelope.

The cubes may have been nutritious, but as Jane Levi pointed out in an excellent article about the aesthetics of food in space,[11]

For the US Mercury missions in the early-1960s, bite-sized compressed foods were developed in flavours ranging from bacon, cheese and crackers, and toast, to peanut butter and fruitcake. Contrary to the Flavour Principle, which confirms that people not only respond to taste but also seek distinctions between the texture, appearance and sensations produced by different foods, they came in blocks of uniform size which rehydrated in the mouth as they were chewed. In contemporary photographs they are almost indistinguishable from one another: besides a slight variation in colour, the only real indication that they are, in fact, food with a choice of flavours comes from the label.

Groundside scientists kept tinkering with the cubes, but tubes remained the default and were already available in a variety of flavors—when Glenn traveled in 1962, he had a choice of "beef-vegetables, chicken-noodle, veal, applesauce, peaches, and a fruit concentrate." More flavors were added during the Gemini program, but the appeal was just as limited, partly because the way they were eaten totally bypasses the organs that transmit the sense of smell. Just as was the case in high-altitude aircraft with a dry atmosphere, food we can't smell may be nutritious but is unlikely to be appetizing. The problem was further complicated by the fact that anyone in weightless conditions tends to have fluids collect in their head, giving them a constant stuffy nose. If you imagine having a head cold and eating leftovers straight from the refrigerator, you get a sense of the experience.

The scientists and doctors who tried to figure out how human physiology would react to weightlessness had an immeasurably harder task than the ones who formulated food for high-altitude airline flights. A *Los Angeles Times* article in 1964 summarized the constraints as they were then understood:

> Rich desserts, spiced foods and many other "high residue" foods will be taboo because of the problems of getting rid of waste materials and the need to conserve storage space by use of the least bulky objects possible. Carbonated beverages and other gas producing foods and drinks will be left on earth. Gasses expand in the stomach at low pressure (and) high altitude, causing stomach pains. Instead, the astronaut's diet will be low residue combination of 17% protein, 51% carbohydrate and 32% fat.

The avoidance of spicy food must have contributed to the unpleasantness of meals, since things needed to be more highly seasoned in space to appeal to the traveler's dulled senses. There had been some advances in packaging, starting with ditching the metal toothpaste-type tubes. As the same article explained,

> Sausage patties, grapefruit juice and apricot pudding are some of the things future spacemen will eat. The form of space foods will be anything but traditional, however. Packaging now is done in polyethylene bags which contain dehydrated or freeze-dried products. These can be stored at room temperature for months without damage and a package the size of a small envelope provides a meal. Dehydrated foods will be reconstituted with water before being eaten . . .
>
> The technical problems of preparing and serving food in an atmosphere where all objects float is compounded by the normal earthly need for a balanced diet with a certain amount of bulk. . . . Food in pill form was suggested, but soon rejected because of the need for bulk and the psychological need to eat. Experiments with food in stress situations show that eating alleviates stress and that not being able to eat or eating unfamiliar foods compounds stress.

A squeeze tube apparatus inserted in the astronaut's mouth was used on early flights but discarded because of its bulkiness. The tubes couldn't be thrown out because they would travel right along with the ship, maintaining the same rate of speed. And garbage won't be rocketed back to earth because of the great expense. When the less bulky polyethylene bags were developed, problems of storing them became evident. Now they are made with a Velcro tab on the side which will attach to a matching piece of Velcro on the walls of the space ship. . . . To eat, astronauts will sit strapped in chairs side by side with a water source between them. After inserting the nozzle in one end of a dehydrated food package, they'll wait for the food to be reconstituted and then eat from the other end of the bag. Containers with only one opening were used on previous flights but astronauts had problems keeping the water in the bag after removing the nozzle.

. . . On the two-week Gemini flight astronauts will have a 2,500 calorie a day diet in four meals. Although the crew hasn't yet been chosen, astronauts know approximately what the crew will eat. The proposed menu for days 1, 5, 9, and 13 is:

Meal A: Sugar frosted flakes, sausage patties, toast squares and orange-grape-fruit juice

Meal B: Tuna salad, cheese sandwiches, apricot pudding and grape juice

Meal C: Beef pot roast, carrots in cream sauce, toasted bread cubes, pineapple cubes and tea

Meal D: Potato soup, chicken bits, toast squares, applesauce, brownies and grapefruit juice.

This Gemini menu is only the beginning. The field of space feeding is un-limited. When interplanetary travel is as pedestrian as freeway traffic, meals in space may be as common—and basic—as tonight's family dinner.[12]

A typical family dinner it might not be, but as these menus show, the Gemini astronauts did have foods with varied textures. In the case of the very first Gemini mission, Gemini 3, they had more variety than planned by Mission Control. A number of experimental foods had been packed for eval-uation—the first solid food provided by the American program, including in-dividually wrapped hot dogs and chicken legs, with brownies for dessert. This menu was augmented by astronaut John Young, who sneaked a corned beef sandwich aboard in a pocket of his spacesuit. Young, a notorious practical joker, offered the sandwich to fellow astronaut Gus Grissom in midflight, and when Grissom took a bite he inadvertently proved the wisdom of the ground-side engineers. Crumbs flew everywhere, and the sandwich was quickly stowed in the spacesuit pocket as the two astronauts tried to deal with the mess. The dialogue between the two, as recorded by NASA, is as follows:

Grissom: What is it?

Young: Corn beef sandwich.

Grissom: Where did that come from?

Young: I brought it with me. Let's see how it tastes. Smells, doesn't it?

Grissom: Yes, it's breaking up. I'm going to stick it in my pocket.

Young: Is it? It was a thought, anyway.

Grissom: Yep.

Young: Not a very good one. Pretty good, though, if it would just hold
together.

The flight directors at Mission Control were outraged by the frivolity,
and the press portrayed Young and Grissom as irresponsible with scathing
headlines like "Two Astronauts Team Up As Comics."[13] A congressional
committee even held a hearing on the matter, though it is notable that the
representatives who demanded it had been critics of the program for some
time and had been trying to cut its funding.

The corned beef sandwich incident was a debacle that resulted in strict
rules about what the astronauts could bring aboard—none had existed previously because it apparently didn't occur to NASA administrators that anybody might smuggle their favorite foods along. After weeks of hearings and
torrents of internal memos, the only ones who were happy with the incident
were the management at Wolfie's Deli, the restaurant in Miami Beach that
had supplied the sandwich.[14] For them every mention in the press was free
publicity of a kind they couldn't buy at any price, and tourists from around
the world stopped in to try the sandwich so good that it had been smuggled
into space. Wolfie's had accidentally profited from the mania for space, while
other food producers in the United States were doing so deliberately.

CHAPTER 20

Commercialization of
Space Food on Earth

Given that every astronaut ever interviewed about the taste of food in space complained about it, it's rather surprising that some items developed for, or associated with, the space program were popular hits. Or perhaps it's not—the surge in national pride when countries put people in space led to outbursts of enthusiasm for anything remotely related to the program.

By all accounts the Soviets had the most palatable food in the early days, but as might be expected in a country that officially spurned capitalism, there were few attempts to profit from cosmonaut mania. A type of cake—actually a thick biscuit, since there was no rising agent—called "Polyot," the Russian word for *flight*, became popular in the 1960s.[1] This was apparently occasionally decorated to look like a space capsule but was not a product ever actually eaten in space. It was also not mass-produced, and every bakery had its own recipe.

There were also various brands of candy like the "Kosmonavt" jelly beans, but these too were just standard items packaged to take advantage of space mania. It may be that Soviet planners considered the overwhelmingly negative reviews given to all space foods and decided that nobody would be enough of a fool to buy it.

A different calculation was made on the other side of the Atlantic. The great critic H. L. Mencken one said, "Nobody ever went broke underestimating the bad taste of the American public," and some American food companies decided to put this to the test.

The first product they marketed based on its association with the space program was Tang, which was actually created well before the first astronaut took flight. Tang was introduced in 1959, the invention of food scientist William Mitchell, whose other creations included Cool Whip, instant Jell-O, and Pop Rocks candy. It was a mix of sugar, fructose, citric acid, "orange juice solids," and vitamins that had a slightly metallic taste and lurid orange color. The crystallized instant drink was nutritious, easy to make, and initially, a sales disaster.

The turning point was when John Glenn was given some to try aboard his famous first flight—immediately the company could brand it as a drink "Chosen for the Gemini astronauts!" NASA used it instead of natural orange juice because dehydrated natural orange juice doesn't reconstitute well—it tends to turn into gritty particles suspended in liquid. Tang became a national best seller, and stores had trouble keeping it on the shelves. Recipes appeared that used Tang—among the most popular of these was Tang Pie, which used two of William Mitchell's creations, Tang and Cool Whip, in a creamy pie filling. For some reason, this is enduringly popular in Texas and parts of the South.

The irony was that Glenn, like several other early astronauts, apparently disliked the taste of Tang, though he drank it again when he returned to space aboard the shuttle in 1998. Glenn wasn't outspoken about his feelings about the drink, but later astronauts were—Buzz Aldrin bluntly said "Tang sucks!" during an interview with NPR in 1998.[2] It is not known whether Aldrin knows that there is a cocktail named the Buzz Aldrin, consisting of Tang and vodka with an orange slice for garnish. Given his feelings about the drink, he may not think this is a compliment.

The first item to be sold on Earth that used techniques unique to the space program was freeze-dried ice cream, a novelty developed by the Whirlpool Company that is best known for making washing machines and other appliances.[3] Most people who have tried freeze-dried ice cream wish they had stuck with a business they knew. The mix of coconut fat, sugar, milk solids, and flavorings looks very much like Neapolitan-style ice cream but has a unique gummy texture. It doesn't even work well as space food—on the only voyage into space where anyone tried to eat it, aboard Apollo 7 in 1968, it was discovered that its tendency to shatter and crumble made it impractical. It is still made and has retained a niche market among backpackers, who appreciate a sweet snack that is very light.[4]

The final fad food item to be associated with the space program was popular on Earth long before it was ever eaten in space. Unlike Tang, Space Food

The most commercially successful of the products designed for the space program but consumed on Earth was Space Food Sticks, the forerunner of the energy bar.
Source General Mills Company

Sticks actually were designed with the space program in mind. The Pillsbury Company's chief food technologist, Howard Bauman, was interested by the challenge of creating a high-energy food that would stay stable at room temperature and wouldn't create crumbs. Bauman found a stable formula and started producing the sticks in chocolate and peanut butter flavors, wrapping them in silver foil to give them a space-age look. The company started selling them in 1971, using packaging that featured pictures of astronauts and implied that they were already in orbit. The front of the box read, "Space Food Sticks—The energy food developed by Pillsbury under a government contract in support of the US aerospace program."

Space Food Sticks only actually went into orbit once, on the Skylab 3 mission in 1972, but they lived on in the United States for a few years;

production by Pillsbury ceased around 1980. They were more enduringly popular in Australia, where they continue to be popular to this day, and they are credited with spawning the market for energy bars. In an unlikely turn of events, in 2000 a website called retrofuture.com posted an article about Space Food Sticks and hundreds of people wrote in to bemoan that they were no longer available. The owner of that website, Eric Lefcowitz, eventually re-created them, and they are for sale in the twenty-first century both online and at places like Kennedy Space Center, the Smithsonian Air and Space Museum, and other places where people with space nostalgia congregate.[5]

CHAPTER 21

Apollo, Soyuz, and Variety
in Space (1966–1994)

Both the American and Russian space programs had a hiatus in 1966, one planned, one not. The American Mercury program had already scheduled its last manned flight for that year, in order to transition to more sophisticated and spacious Apollo spacecraft. The first Apollo launches would be unmanned to test equipment, and under the best of circumstances there would be a two-year lull in manned flight. The death of three astronauts in a fire aboard Apollo 1 during training set the program back more than a year.

The Soviet Union also had a planned transition, from the Vostok program to more sophisticated Soyuz capsules, but it was scheduled to be a brief one. The goal was to continue launches of manned craft, culminating with landing a man on the moon by 1967. The sudden death in 1966 of the great designer Sergey Korolov, who had headed the program, set off bureaucratic infighting and delays, and when the first manned Soyuz capsule was sent up in 1967, the cosmonaut was killed on reentry. This started more than a year of frantic redesigns, and the ambitious lunar program was scaled back so that the goal was now to orbit the moon by 1967. Even that was not attainable, and neither program launched a man into space again until October 1968.

The Apollo capsule that soared into orbit on October 11 was a marked improvement over its predecessors—there was room for three astronauts rather than two, and they had more space to work and move around. They also had a luxury that no previous space traveler had enjoyed: hot water. This enhanced the flavor and texture even of the type of rations that had previously been provided, especially the mashed potatoes that had previously been eaten cold.

Happily for the astronauts on that first mission, the variety and technology of food had both changed for the better. They not only had such items as bacon and eggs, tuna salad, hot dogs, beef pot roast, and spaghetti, they were able to eat them in a more natural way with the first utensils designed for use in space—the spoon bowl. This was a zippered plastic package of dry ingredients that was rehydrated with a water pistol—sticky items like the beef pot roast could be eaten with the spoon so astronauts could see, small, and taste their food.[1] The result was that for the first time there was something like the taste and texture of meals on Earth.

The astronauts had apparently been prepared for rations similar to those of Mercury and Gemini missions, and reacted with enthusiasm. An article in the *New York Times* was based on an interview with the crew, and read in part,

> Food on the Apollo 7 spacecraft still does not match home cooking, but it comes a lot closer than space food used to. Even at that, the astronauts reported, 'The beef stew tends to be very crumbly.' . . . Because Apollo has both hot and cold running water, packaged chunks of dried beef stew can be prepared and served hot. The Apollo 7 command pilot, Capt. Walter M. Schirra Jr., took some coffee on the flight and reported it was somewhat difficult to prepare but pleasing to the palate. Today's menu for Captain Schirra, who insisted on bringing the coffee on the flight, was spaghetti and meat sauce, tuna salad, banana and chocolate pudding. Walter Cunningham's menu consisted of beef sandwiches, beef and vegetable soup, and barbecued beef bites.[2]

The newfound enthusiasm for eating in space was gratifying to the administrators for more than aesthetic reasons; they had noticed that astronauts had lost weight and come back from previous missions weaker because they had so little enthusiasm for eating. These meals had been designed to give each astronaut about 2,300 calories per day, and sweet and rich items like cinnamon toast, gingerbread, instant cocoa, and butterscotch pudding were included. Astronaut Walter Cunningham complained that the meals were too sweet and too large, and said that all the astronauts were filled before they finished.[3]

Though tubes of food were still provided for emergencies, some meals were undehydrated and packaged in what were called wetpacks. As the *Encyclopedia of Kitchen History* describes these, "One type of wetpack was a flexible plastic or aluminum foil pouch; another was a can with pull-off lid. With this method, staff could pack a week's worth of rations per astronaut in a container no larger than three shoe boxes." It was a triumph of technology, food that occupied lower volume of storage but gave more satisfaction. On the next Apollo mission something unusual happened: the astronauts actually dined better than their counterparts on the ground.

> For Christmas 1968, Frank Borman, James A. "Jim" Lovell, Jr., and William "Bill" Anders, the pilots of Apollo 8 who looped the moon on a 150-hour flight, munched turkey chunks and spooned up gravy while envious Mission Control technicians staffed monitors and contented themselves with coffee and sandwiches.[4]

The Soviets managed to launch a pair of marginally successful missions the next year in their first spacecraft that carried three people, but their efforts were overshadowed by the landmark Apollo 11 mission. On July 16, 1969, that craft carried the first men to land on Earth's moon, and during the eight-day trip the voyagers enjoyed an option available to no previous crew: their choice of items from a pantry. All meals in space had been preplanned weeks or months in advance, but this time the astronauts were offered their choice at every course. The Whirlpool Corporation, last mentioned here in the context of their freeze-dried ice cream, proved that they could deliver variety and taste, and newspapers gushed about the change.

> When Apollo 11 astronauts land on the moon, they will be eating tasty, nutritious and varied meals supplied to NASA by the Life Support Division of the Twin Cities' Whirlpool Corporation. Neil Armstrong and Edwin Aldrin will spend about 24 hours on the moon and the rest periods, they will eat two meals there. Their first scheduled meal to be eaten on the moon will consist of bacon squares, peaches, sugar cookie cubes, pineapple grapefruit drink and coffee. The second meal will contain beef stew, cream of chicken soup, date fruitcake, grape punch and orange drink. In addition to the meals, other snack items such as dried fruit, candy, extra beverages, wet packs, sandwich spread, and bread will be included.
>
> Astronauts Armstrong, Aldrin and Collins will eat in the command module according to pre-planned menus and will also have pantry items which they can select at will. The meals are referred to as Meal A, B or C and are identified to each astronaut's predetermined menu by means of a colored tab of 'velcro' material. . . . Besides identifying the food, it acts as a holding device which keeps the food packs from floating in space. Unlike other missions, Apollo 11 will carry pre-planned menus for only the first five days of the flight. For the duration of the flight, the astronauts may select individual food items from a pantry. Pantry items are foods which are not assembled by menus but merely packaged in categories such as Desserts, Beverages, Breakfast Items, Bite-size

Cubes and Salads and Meats. The pantry system enables the astronauts to select at random whatever food item they desire. Other pantry items include: Rehydratable dessert items: banana pudding, butterscotch pudding, apple-sauce and chocolate pudding. Rehydratable beverages: orange drink, orange grapefruit drink, pineapple fruitcake, jellied fruitcake, jellied fruit candy and caramel candy. Breakfast items: peaches, fruit cocktail, Canadian bacon, bacon squares, sausage patties, sugar coated corn flakes, strawberry cubes, cinnamon toasted bread cubes, apricot cereal cubes and peanut cubes. Salads and meats: salmon salad, tuna salad, cream of chicken soup, shrimp cocktail, spaghetti and meat sauce, beef pot roast, beef and vegetables, chicken and rice, chicken stew, beef stew and pork and scalloped potatoes.[5]

Lost in the middle of all that was a mention of one of the oldest foods in human history that was included for the first time: bread. Nibbles and bites of bread had been included before, but the dry, oxygen-rich atmosphere of the capsule dried out sliced bread almost instantaneously. At some point before this mission, scientists figured out that packaging the bread in nitrogen could keep it fresh for two weeks, at little cost to flavor, and the moist bread would produce fewer crumbs.[6]

The Soviet program continued to launch spacecraft that were plagued by technical difficulties, such as the Soyuz 6, 7, and 8 that were supposed to dock together—though all three craft took off and landed safely, their highly publicized docking maneuver flopped. The program's first bright spot in years was Soyuz 9 in 1970, which broke a string of failures and also the record for duration in space at eighteen days. It was fortunate for people who were in space so long that their rations were the best yet and included many Russian traditional dishes formulated and packaged for orbit. For the first time on a Soviet-built craft they also had hot water, so could enjoy them to the fullest. An article by Vasily Dupik in the magazine *Space World* described in detail the ways that a truly Russian experience was created in zero gravity.

> The menu on the Soyuz-9 was highly appreciated by its crew. It was composed for Andryian Nikolayev and Vitaly Sevastyoanov with an eye to their tastes. There are tinned foods prepared the usual way, but with a decreased content of moisture. Their rations included milk and sweets, dried fruits, juices and dried fish. In was by their special request that Vobla (dried fish) was made a fixture in their daily menus. Here is the menu of one of the days during which the crew of Soyuz-10 was in outer space:
>
> **Breakfast:** Chopped bacon (or a choice of veal liver pate, or minced sausage), Borodinsky black bread, Coffee and milk, Candied fruit
> **Lunch:** Creme of cottage cheese and black current puree, Honey cookies

Dinner: Vobla (smoked fish), Kharcho (spiced meat and rice soup), Chicken (or ham or meat pate), Brown bread, Prunes and nuts
Supper: Meat puree, Borodinsky bread, Tinned Rossisky cheese.

. . . To this list should be added sorrel and cabbage soups, wieners, steak, pork, and puree of wild fowl, sweet meats and chocolate. The spacemen were also obliged to take polyvitamin pills containing vitamins A, B1, B2, B6, B12, C and E twice a day.

When composing these rations, Soviet specialists take into account the biological value of the foods, their taste and aesthetic appearance. Therefore, serious attention is paid to their wrappings. Part of the food is contained in metal boxes, and confectionary and some other foods in polymer film. Tinned meats . . . contain protein, little fat and an even smaller amount of other ingredients. They are sufficiently juicy, but have no brine which is dangerous in weightlessness, since it can form a 'raincloud' in the ship's cabin. The spacemen use cupronickel spoons and forks. True, they often have to violate etiquette and 'tame' the floating food with their hands.[7]

Unfortunately for the Soviets, their next two missions did not have the same success. Soyuz 10 took off and landed safely but did not accomplish its goals, but Soyuz 11 seemed to be going well and set a new endurance record of twenty-two days. One of the cosmonauts, Viktor Patsayev, celebrated a birthday during the mission, and his companions presented him with surprise gifts: a lemon and an onion.[8] Patsayev said he particularly enjoyed the onion, and as the craft headed back to Earth it looked like a perfect mission. Unfortunately, when the capsule was opened after landing, all three occupants were dead, suffocated by a ventilation system valve that had jarred open and expelled their oxygen.

The Soviets redesigned their spacecraft and kept launching Soyuz capsules on scientific missions, but by the second of these in 1973 the Americans had already been back to the moon five times. New foods were tested on each NASA mission, including one that became famous for all the wrong reasons: the strawberry cube. This was nutritionally balanced, but by all accounts tasted so nasty that none of the astronauts ever ate more than one. NASA acknowledged their complete failure as food, but found a use for them—they were encased in plastic and given to important visitors as souvenirs.[9]

Other foods were also tried with mixed success—NASA was trying to find the perfect meal for health in weightlessness, and on Apollo 16 in 1972 experimented with a diet high in potassium. Astronaut John Young, who had flown five years earlier, praised the taste of the meals, but in a memorable transmission from the moon to Earth stated his feelings about the diet unequivocally. He hadn't realized his microphone was turned on, and in a conversation he thought would only be heard by his companions in the cap-sule he complained that he was gassy, and went on about how much he hated belching the potassium-enriched orange drink. This was more than America wanted to know about its heroes on the moon, and Young stopped as soon as he realized that he had a larger audience than intended.

After the moon landings, America moved to the next milestone in space: the Skylab missions. The hundred-ton space station had more room than ever before for moving around, and the crew of nine had the first refriger-ator and freezer in orbit, allowing them to have real ice cream instead of the freeze-dried variety. As the *Encyclopedia of Kitchen History* noted, it was remarkably civilized compared to all that had come before.

> Meals came in rehydratable beverage dispensers and packages or aluminum cans. In the ship's circular workshop, ten water tanks held seventy-two gallons each. . . . In the wardroom below, food heating and service for the nine-man crew made use of a freezer and refrigerator, dining space, and table containing electronic heaters to warm meals. By anchoring their feet to footholds, the men were able to sit for meals and gaze out a circular window to Earth below. To assure their contentment and nutrition, space cooks had expanded the menu to include filet mignon, prime rib, lobster Newburg, chili, ham, mashed potatoes, steak, asparagus, and a dripless ice cream in the form of blue wafers that melt in the mouth.
>
> In microgravity, diners of all three 1973 manned Skylab missions consumed 2,800 calories per day to meet normal physiological needs for their age, weight, and exertions, particularly life science experiments. To ready food for the table, each of three three-man crews warmed packages by conduction on the heated tray, which engineers divided into recessed compartments. As a joke, during the second manned mission aboard Skylab 3 launched on July 28, 1973, electrical engineer Owen K. Garriott smuggled in a tape of his wife's voice saying, "This is Helen in Skylab. The boys hadn't had a home-cooked meal in so long, I thought I'd just bring one up."[10]

Skylab was occupied by three teams of astronauts in 1973 and 1974, all of whom enjoyed the experience of gathering around a table with a view of space. Food warmers had been built into the surface of the table so they didn't need to transport hot food, and the trays were locked into the warmers so that there was no danger they'd float away. Other aspects of the experi-ence were also more like dining on the world they'd left behind.

> Food containers for the Skylab astronauts consisted of aluminum cans with full panel pull-out lids. Cans containing thermostabilized food had a build-in

membrane to prevent spillage when removing the lid in the can and had a water valve for rehydration. Canned, ready-to-eat foods were held in the can with a slit plastic cover. Instead of plastic drinking bags, Skylab drinking containers were collapsible bottles that expanded accordion style when filled with hot or cold water.

Eating on Skylab was a fairly normal operation. Knife, fork, and spoon were held magnetically to the food tray until needed. A pair of scissors was added to the usual utensils for cutting open the plastic membranes. With careful use of the utensils, food would remain in the cans until needed. On occasion however, a too rapid motion with a fork or spoon would cause a piece of meat or other food to drift away from the tray.

Because of its relatively large storage space, Skylab was able to feature an extensive menu of 72 different food items. Unique to Skylab was a freezer for foods such as filet mignon and vanilla ice cream and a refrigerator for chilling fruits and beverages. Enough food was carried to provide each astronaut with 1.9 kilograms (4.2 pounds) of food per day. This weight also included the weight of the primary food packaging.[11]

After Skylab was abandoned in 1974 there was a last Apollo mission, one that was as much for symbolic purposes as it was for science. The Russians and Americans sent up Apollo and Soyuz capsules, which linked in space. As cosmonaut Alexi Leonov related in the book he coauthored with American astronaut Tom Scott, he had prepared a surprise for his American counterparts.

As the American crew spoke with their president, I pulled out the first of my surprises and watched carefully to see how they would react. Before we left Baikonur I had peeled the labels from several tubes of borscht and blackcurrant juice and replaced them with labels from famous brands of Russian vodka.

"Before we eat we must drink to our mission," I told Tom and Deke, handing them a tube each.

"There are many people watching everything we do," Tom said, looking a little concerned and referring to the television cameras we had spent so long repairing.

"Look, Tom, don't worry" I said. "I'll show you how it's done."

With that I took one of the tubes, squeezed its contents into my mouth and swallowed quickly. Tom gave me a broad smile, a wink and followed suit.

"Why it's borscht!" he said, eyes wide and slightly disappointed.[12]

Both the Russians and American program managers had packed much more luxurious items on this flight, each apparently determined to prove the superiority of their orbital cuisine. The Americans brought up fresh breads

The Russian sense of humor was nicely shown when their cosmonauts shared a toast with American astronauts. The vodka labels on the containers of fruit juice led to unmet expectations.

and cheese, the Russians pickled perch, a variety of meats, dried fruits, and cake. Over eighty different items were consumed during the nine-day mission, and in many ways it was a preview of missions to come aboard the International Space Station.

In 1974 the American space program entered another period of hiatus for the transition from the Apollo program to the Space Shuttle, and the Soviet program launched a series of military flights about which little information was ever released. They also sent several Salyut space stations into orbit, and crews spent increasing amounts of time aboard. After several failures, the Soviets managed the feat of sending unmanned supply ships to dock with the stations, and missions became longer—by 1979 a stay of 175 days was possible. The highly reliable Soyuz craft became a taxi for goods and scientists, including the first people in space who were neither Russian nor American. The Soviets used their space station as a tool of diplomacy, taking Vietnamese, Czech, Romanian, Mongolian, Hungarian, and Cuban scientists for trips aboard the world's only functioning space vessels. There is no record of special food for any of these orbital emissaries, but when French cosmonaut Jean-Loup Chretien visited in 1982, he insisted on bringing his country's cuisine with him. Cosmonaut Anatoli Berezovoi recorded in his diary that the Frenchman "broke the tedium" of Russian space food with "crab, cheese, hare, and lobster, followed by strawberries."[13] The Soviet space program was a rare bright spot in a period that came to be known as "The Era of Stagnation," and it was a source of national pride during the years when the Americans were working to develop the space shuttle. The Soviets could point to gourmet food aboard a station with the red star on the side and make an at least somewhat credible claim to be masters of the universe.

They continued this successful streak with the launch of Mir, the space station that lasted longer than all its predecessors combined. This station was launched in February 1986 and remained in orbit for fourteen years, setting an enviable standard for reliability. Even as the country that launched it fell apart, Mir grew from a single capsule to a maze of rooms as new modules were added.

The economic chaos following the end of communism extended even to the food supplies for the inhabitants of Mir—though supplies kept coming there was less variety, and at least once the ground crew stole luxuries intended for the cosmonauts. Nevertheless, the missions continued. Any questions about whether humans could survive in space for long periods was eliminated when cosmonaut Valeri Polyakov stayed aboard the station for 437 days. He was able to celebrate his milestone with a shot of vodka; one of the few improvements in rations since the fall of the Soviet Union was that the new administration allowed vodka and cognac to be shipped to the crew aboard Mir.[14]

In 1994, toward the end of Mir's life, supplies started arriving aboard a new type of spacecraft. The Americans were back in orbit again, and the space shuttle had been designed with docking ports that would match the aging Russian station. With the arrival on the scene of this craft, food in space would become more sophisticated and even more international.

CHAPTER 22

≈≈≈≈≈≈≈

The Difficulties of
Cooking in Space

Cooking is much more than just a means of producing food and has been recognized as a form of art and marker of culture since the days of the ancient Greeks. To make meals for a family or companions is an ancient signature of fellowship, one of the things that bonds people into a social group. For people living and working in space, it would seem to be an ideal pastime as well as a way of acquiring nutritious and appetizing meals.

Despite this, there have as yet been no actual kitchens aboard any space vehicle, no facility in which the most elementary cooking can take place. There is certainly enough space aboard—the tiny galleys of flying boats, and of submarines during World War II, both supplied gourmet food.[1] The problem lies in the nature of moving and working in microgravity, as well as the need to avoid contaminating the air supply.

The problems with performing even the simplest kitchen tasks are obvious—imagine trying to chop hard vegetables like carrots or onions when there is no gravity to hold them on a cutting board, or sautéing when things won't stay in the pan. There are convection ovens aboard modern space stations, but they can't heat anything above 180 degrees—like the ovens aboard DC-4s and other aircraft made just after World War II, they're fine for reheating but not hot enough for baking or broiling.

These problems aside, the major problem with cooking in space involves contaminating the environment. The most hygienically raised and completely washed natural ingredients have microbes as passengers, and airborne bacteria and fungi are major problems in space. The Salyut stations and Mir both had air filters that were designed to remove as much of these as possible, but both stations developed problems with mold and foul air as they aged.[2] Even thirty years later aboard the International Space Station, this remains a problem.[3] In as sterile a closed environment as humans have ever created, the bacteria and fungi that are on every human body find places to grow anywhere it is humid enough and there are nutrients. In 1998 a US astronaut aboard Mir opened a rarely accessed service panel and found a free-floating mass of dirty water "nearly the size of a basketball."[4] Humidity had been collecting over a period of months or years, and with no changes in temperature and no air currents, it was a perfect breeding place for microbes. The wiring nearby was covered with flecks of mold.

Now imagine the basic elements of cooking: heat, moisture, and usually some kind of oil or fat like butter that volatilizes when heated. Introducing these fat globules into the environment would add nutrients that those microorganisms would seize upon. Even with the best ventilation systems and filtration, bacteria and fungi would multiply in the air and be inhaled by the residents of the station.

The psychological advantages to cooking in space have been recognized for some time; in 1985 a New York Times article about food for US astronauts finished with,

> On the prolonged space flights expected in the future, NASA officials anticipate that some astronauts will want to cook as a form of recreation . . . administrators are considering cooking facilities in space vehicles so that a future space traveler, hit with the urge for a medium-rare steak and baked potato, could have just that.[5]

Almost thirty years later, that dream seems just as far off. Until spacecraft are developed that have a more earthlike environment with artificial gravity, a high volume of air treated so that microbes may be removed, and other features, humans in space are likely to be restricted to meals prepared on solid ground.

CHAPTER 23

Shuttles, the ISS, and Taikonauts
(1981–Present)

Much as airline food did during the same period, food in space reached a plateau in the 1980s—though there were minor improvements and greater variety, there have been no major technological breakthroughs since the Mir era. This isn't to say that subsequent spacecraft haven't had better food, but that the improvements were generally thanks to new cultural and psychological sensitivities.

When the first space shuttle launched in 1981, it was with a larger menu—there were seventy-four different foods and twenty beverages, including some fresh vegetables. Less than a day before each flight someone from NASA went to grocery stores to buy bananas, oranges, peaches, carrots, celery, and other fresh produce, then rushed it to be packed for orbit.[1] Since there was no refrigerator on the shuttle, all the fresh items had to be eaten within the first few days, but the fresh foods eased the transition from earth to space.

The rations included one treat that was to become an astronaut favorite: M&M'S. The chocolate candies might have been made for space travel—the hard candy shell kept the contents enclosed, and they were a literal taste of home for astronauts, food everyone had enjoyed since childhood in the exact same form. Astronauts developed games in which they did acrobatic tricks in zero gravity while catching M&Ms in their mouths, and the candies were major morale boosters. NASA never mentioned the candy's common name in their press releases due to an official policy of not endorsing products, but when news reports spoke of "candy coated chocolates" people figured out what they were.[2] The astronauts themselves were not so reticent—when astronaut Shannon Lucid was interviewed after 179 days aboard the Mir station and was asked what she missed most she immediately responded, "I would really like some M&Ms." She had just finished her last bag.[3]

The M&Ms weren't the only branded items in space, and using those packaged goods was more than just a cost-saving measure. The program managers at NASA had finally realized that the taste and style of regular meals was important. A *New York Times* article detailed the changes:

> 'We try to use as much commercially available food as we can,' said Rita Rapp, manager of the shuttle's food system, who has been with the National Aeronautics and Space Administration since 1961 and who worked on meals for the Apollo program in 1966. 'For years the crew have been saying they want to eat everyday things from the grocery store. It just shows that people like what they are familiar with. . . . The current crew might be eating breakfast rolls from Sara Lee, diced pineapple from Del Monte, chocolate instant breakfast from Carnation, or M&M peanuts from Mars, Inc. They can also spice things up with taco sauce, ketchup, barbecue sauce and other condiments, which come in the familiar cellophane packets offered by fast-food outlets.[4]

The shuttle's galley did have some minor improvements, including one that had been developed for airline use—a way of injecting steam while items were in the oven. This was different from the airline version in that each tray that needed steam had a valve built into it, rather than the oven being fitted with a baking chamber into which steam was introduced.[5] The *New York Times* article also gave details of the way that meals were cooked in the new galley:

> The galley, installed on the middeck of the shuttle cabin, resembles galleys aboard commercial airliners. The meal packages are removed from storage and those that require rehydration are placed in a rack. Crew members dial the proper number of ounces of water required and push in the rack, automatically puncturing the seals and injecting the water. Then items are placed in a convection oven above for heating to 180 degrees Fahrenheit. That is not enough to permit real cooking, not that shuttle crews have time for such diversions.[6]

It was a far cry from the old days of massaging dehydrated mashed potatoes with cold water, and the astronauts praised the meals, which they said were similar to homemade meals created with frozen vegetables. There was a minor upgrade of the shuttle's galley in 1994, but few changes to the methods of cooking—the principal aim was to reduce weight, not improve meals.

In 2001, Pizza Hut became the first company to deliver a pizza to space. Astronaut Yuri Usachov is shown giving the thumbs-up. Pizza Hut paid one million dollars to the Russian Space Agency for the promotional stunt.
Image provided by Pizza Hut

There were only slight improvements aboard the International Space Station, which launched in 2000. The best thing about dining aboard was that the menu was indeed international—Russian foods like tvorog (cottage cheese with nuts), smoked sturgeon, and beef-barley meatloaf were just as available as American standard items. Fresh foods were still sent up on the unmanned Progress supply ships, and after 2006 there were increasing cultural choices. In a 2006 interview, Vickie Kloeris, manager of NASA's Space Food Laboratory, detailed the cooperation between different countries as well as the ways in which earthbound chefs contributed to the program.

We have so much more variety. . . . You're going to have a fair number of meat-and-potatoes guys, but we've been incorporating more ethnic food. . . . It is the first time the European Union is contributing to a space menu jointly supplied by Russia and the United States. . . . The (Atlantis) shuttle, which is largely filled with construction material to expand the space station, will carry a limited cache of food for the station astronauts, including kiwis, oranges, and nectarines. And the shuttle astronauts might donate some of their flour tortillas, if they have any left over. Tortillas are useful in space because they can turn anything into a sandwich and do not produce crumbs or mold as easily as bread. When a crew had been stuck in space for six months, a fresh tortilla or the crunch of an apple can make all the difference in their mood . . .

One trick the NASA food scientists use to keep the astronauts happy is to add lots of tang and spice to the menu. (And that's not Tang, the powdered-drink mix.) . . . Eating out of the cans and plastic pouches stocked in the space station pantry also limits the olfactory pleasures that hot food brings. After a few months of that, a bottle of Tabasco or a raw garlic clove can be heaven.

"We crave anything with a nice, sharp flavor," Colonel McArthur said. He speaks with the precision of a restaurant critic when he describes his favorite space food dish, dehydrated shrimp cocktail. Medium shrimp coated in sauce are plumped with a spurt of water injected into a plastic pouch, which is massaged to mix the ingredients. . . . Salt and pepper can help . . . but they are in liquid form; Grains of salt and pepper in microgravity could clog equipment or become lodged in an astronaut's nose or eye. Even a fresh tomato, which the Russians often take when it is their turn to resupply the space station, can cause problems. Instead of biting right into one the crew has to slice it carefully . . .

Unlike many Americans, the astronauts eat almost all their meals together at a common table. Of course, they are not sitting. They are floating. They use a toehold to stay in place, and attach bottles of ketchup and utensils to the table with straps and Velcro. They use forks and spoons, but the food has to be moist enough to stick together. The astronauts use two heating systems for food, one Russian, one American. The American system is largely based on hot water and plastic pouches. The Russian one uses cans for food that are heated in compartments inset into the galley. But everyone shares food. Colonel McArthur developed a taste for the Russians' lamb stew, and he likes the pulp juice they supply. The Americans realized that the Russians want soup every day, so they included more soup in the communal pantry . . .

Sometimes, when the shuttles resupply the station, the astronauts get special treats. On the shuttle Discovery mission last month, it was food developed by Emeril Lagasse, the New Orleans chef and Food Network star. The NASA public affairs office contacted the chef 18 months ago to ask him to make a morale-boosting call to the astronauts. Mr. Lagasse's team . . . countered with the idea of creating a spicy culinary diversion. Mr. Lagasse developed five recipes that the NASA kitchen then turned into freeze-dried packets, each about the size of a deck of cards. . . . Fruit pan dowdy had to lose the crust (the crumb issue), and rum extract had to be used instead of real rum in the bread pudding because alcohol is not allowed in space. The three space station astronauts on Expedition 13—a Russian, a German and an American—tried the food this month, giving Mr. Lagasse their critiques directly in a live satellite chat. . . . The kicked-up mashed potatoes with bacon were a hit as was the jambalaya.

Back on earth, Ms. Kloeris, who manages the space station food system, said NASA was not seeking out more chefs to get into the space food business and was not likely to keep a steady supply of Mr. Lagasse's food shooting into space. But the green beans with garlic he helped develop may be adapted for future flights.

The parade of astronauts from various European countries accelerated aboard the ISS, and most brought some of their own cuisine to share. One odd incident pointed out the cultural collisions that were still possible— Swedish astronaut Christer Fuglesang was scheduled to fly on a mission in December of 2006, and decided to bring some reindeer jerky with him. The Americans pleaded with him not to do so, on the grounds that eating reindeer so close to Christmas would have broken the hearts of American children. Fuglesang inquired whether moose jerky would have the same effect, and when told it would not, he brought that instead.

There were no complaints when Italian astronaut Paolo Nespoli brought a meal that ranked with the finest meals that had been transported to the station—antipasti, lasagna, pesto risotto, tortellini, fettuccine, eggplants in

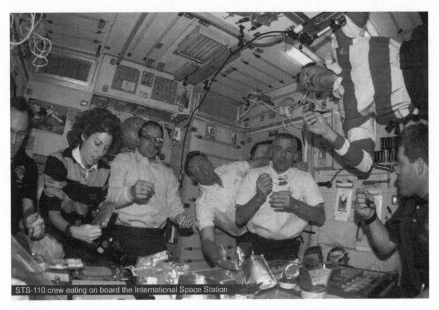

STS-110 crew eating on board the International Space Station

By the time the International Space Station was aloft, astronauts could share a meal much like any family—if you occasionally share holiday dinners while floating sideways.
Courtesy of AP Images

tomato sauce, and tiramisu were all included. The meal received worldwide coverage, which was exactly what the Italian Academy of Cuisine, which designed the menu, had in mind. They probably were been less thrilled with some news stories that appeared later that revealed that after that meal Signor Nespoli quietly rejected the Italian food items that were available and enjoyed exploring the other items in the station's pantry, like jambalaya, fajitas, and teriyaki chicken.[7]

The ISS received an upgrade in 2009—a recycling system that sanitized wastewater to drinking quality for the first time. Previously the water on board was generated by the fuel cells, but this was limited in supply and often had a harsh taste. Additional drinking water was brought up by Progress unmanned spacecraft, but the astronauts aboard the station were understandably nervous about the idea of something as vital as water being supplied by such a long lifeline. The system, known by the acronym ECLSS, eliminated the possibility that station residents might be without water due to some mechanical failure hundreds of miles below. In a television interview from space, astronaut Michael Barratt cracked jokes about the station's new equipment.

> "We have these highly attractive labels on our water bags that essentially say 'brought to you by ECLSS,' and 'drink when real water is over 200 miles away,'" Barratt said.
>
> . . . Astronaut Don Pettit spoke with the space station crew from Houston, as part of the STS-126 crew celebrating the overdue inauguration of the recycler . . . "We're getting ready to toast with some of yesterday's coffee with you guys," Pettit said. That prompted a tongue-in-cheek reply from the space station.
>
> "We're going to be drinking yesterday's coffee frequently up here, and happy to do it," Barratt replied.
>
> A round of "Cheers!" was followed by the astronauts "clinking" together giant water pouches, before each grabbed a sip from their straws . . .
>
> "Gennady's showing it's perfectly clear and worth chasing in zero-G," Barratt noted as the Russian cosmonaut closed in on an escaping water drop.[8]

The community that understood the magnitude of this achievement was delighted, while most earthside audiences were aghast that space explorers were celebrating drinking recycled urine. The people who watched the interview on TV or read about it later didn't understand something that would have been obvious to the pioneers who first went overland on the long trails from the East to West Coast—to any explorer, reliable water supplies are life itself.

The ISS has maintained predictable operations to this day, and launches and habitation of the station don't make the news anymore except when a charismatic astronaut who is a particularly good communicator does something to attract attention. The most interesting development related to food in space in the last decade involves the most recent arrivals in space—the Chinese. Taikonaut Yang Liwei, the sole man aboard Shenzhou V flight, China's first manned mission, ate cold space food much like that used in the Gemini program, but with Chinese seasonings. Steamed rice, which is elemental in most Chinese meals, was out of the question, and it says something for the ingenuity and cultural awareness of Chinese program managers that they found an elegant solution. There is only one area of central China where rice is often not served at banquets, the Sichuan region, which also has a tradition of cold, spicy appetizers. The food provided for Yang was therefore spiced in Sichuan style, which any sophisticated Chinese diner would recognize even if they were not from that region. Spaceman Yang had the taste of China, even if it was from the inland south rather than the northeastern coastal region where he was born.[9]

Things were better for subsequent taikonauts who visited the Tiangong space station that was launched in September of 2011. By this time over fifty different dishes were available, and they could be served hot—but rice still was not one of them. Cuttlefish with meatballs, beef with orange peel, and luxury dishes like Chinese hami melon could be had, but not the staple dish of the majority of Chinese people. Professor Bai, head of the Space Food and Nutrition Department at the Institute of Space Medico-Engineering, acknowledged in an interview that "the most difficult food to prepare in space is rice. We even have a research team working to get the texture and taste right. And as you know, we Chinese must have rice."[10]

It might seem like an inconsequential thing, having to substitute a foreign flavor that is easy to achieve for a familiar one that is difficult. This ignores the fact that for a Chinese taikonaut a different starch like mashed potatoes would be as alien and unpalatable as the cubes that so demoralized the Mercury and Vostok-era travelers who first journeyed to the void of space. It is safe to say that Chinese scientists will continue to work to replicate the taste of their region of the globe so that spacemen who will gaze at our entire planet from afar can do so while enjoying the flavors they enjoyed as children. In years to come, if Brazilian, Iranian, or Thais send missions beyond our atmosphere, they will do the same. Food is the most tangible and visceral cultural link to the nation and culture that launched them beyond the atmosphere, and like emigrants everywhere, the farther they get from their native land, the more they will cherish the taste of home.

CHAPTER 24

Recipes

To include recipes in a book on this topic invites some ridicule, because since people first started eating inflight the meals have replicated what was made on the ground. Comfort food is just that, whether made for a fussy child, stressed flyer, or space voyager. Perhaps airline passengers unconsciously fear that the people who take chances in the kitchen may have habits that rub off on those who are in the cockpit or performing maintenance. Cuisine in the air has almost always played it safe, evoking items with which most passengers would be familiar.

Since the food served most often in the early days of airliners was cold fried chicken, it would seem most appropriate to start with a recipe for it. I might have, if I had an early one that I knew had been served in flight. Unfortunately, most of the independent restaurants that used to supply airlines have changed hands or closed, and when the Marriott Corporation's historian tried to find any recipes from the pre-war Hot Shoppes for me, she was unable to do so. If you wish to replicate the fried chicken of this era, you can find a copy of the Fred Harvey Kitchen cookbook, make it as recommended, let it cool on a rack, and eat it an hour or so later. I don't think this would teach you anything about airline food, but if you'd like an excuse to eat cold fried chicken, go ahead.

What I will present here instead are recipes that the airlines collected and adapted for home use, rather than the saltier, fattier versions that taste better in flight. Airlines started publishing these in the 1950s, although some of the recipes they recommended seem more designed to impress and intimidate

home cooks than to actually be something any amateur might try to replicate. I have presented them as they were written with only the most minor
changes to put them all in the same format, with my additions or comments
in parentheses.

One of the easier items to make, and a very tasty dish, is the Chicago and
Southern Airways Creole Salad Remoulade that was published in the Memphis Commercial Appeal on October 1, 1950.

—⧫⧫⧫⧫— *Creole Salad Remoulade*

Vegetables:
½ head of lettuce, chopped (Use iceberg)
One diced tomato
¼ cup diced celery
½ cup cooked peas
½ cup cooked, diced carrots
Sauce:
One small jar mayonnaise (8 ounces)
One small jar Creole mustard (8 ounces)
¼ cup relish
¾ cup salad oil (Canola, safflower, or light olive oil)
¼ cup vinegar
Two teaspoons capers
Two tablespoons catsup
¼ medium onion—grated
½ teaspoon salt
Pinch black pepper
Diced shrimp (No quantity given in original—I recommend 1½ to 2 pounds cooked
    diced shrimp.)

1. Mix vegetables together lightly and put in individual salad bowls. Add diced shrimp.
2. Mix sauce ingredients and chill.
3. Cover with sauce before serving. Serves four.

(Preparation notes: The quantity made using this recipe is actually sufficient for an ap-
petizer for at least six people, or a light entrée for three or four. The recipe is shown as
printed—for best results, make the sauce an hour or so in advance and make the salad
and top with the shrimp and sauce just before serving. If you can't find Creole mustard,
use Dijon mustard with a teaspoon of horseradish. The peas and carrots can be the frozen
variety, lightly steamed.) ✈

The chicken pie recipe was originally published in *Woman's Home Companion* magazine sometime in the early 1950s.
Image from author's collections

Airline caterers knew that savory gravies work well inflight but don't have the eye appeal of dishes that are actually less tasty at high altitude. One way around this was to add a crust and call it something else.

⸻ Chicken Pie with Savory Topping

Filling:
4 to 4½ pounds chicken
few grains onion salt
4 tablespoons butter
few grains celery salt
4 tablespoons flour
1½ cups peas, cooked (canned, frozen, or fresh)
2½ cups chicken stock
¼ teaspoon salt
1½ cups carrots, cooked, cut in small dice
few grains pepper

1. Clean fowl, cook in salted water almost to cover for about 2 hours, adding a sprig of parsley, celery top, and sliced onion. When tender, remove from heat and allow to cool in its stock.
2. Remove skin and bones and cut meat in small pieces.
3. Make gravy as follows: Melt butter and continue to heat until brown; add flour, blend until smooth. Gradually add stock, continue to cook until thick and smooth; season with salt, pepper, onion salt, and celery salt.
4. In each of six individual casseroles place peas, carrots, and chicken. Pour on gravy to moisten well. Top with tiny savory biscuits.

⸻ Savory Biscuit Topping

2½ cups flour
1¼ teaspoons paprika
2½ teaspoons baking powder
2½ tablespoons parsley, minced
1¼ teaspoons salt
1 egg
2/3 cup shortening
about ½ cup milk

1. Sift flour, measure, add baking powder and salt; sift again.
2. Blend shortening into dry ingredients, add paprika and parsley.
3. Beat egg and add with milk to make stiff dough.
4. Roll out on floured board to ¼-inch thickness. Cut with small biscuit cutter about 1 inch in diameter and place biscuits close together on top of hot chicken mixture in casseroles.
5. Bake in hot oven (450 degrees F.) about 20 minutes.

(Note: The recipe above is as printed, and contains two errors: step 1 mentions adding a celery top, but there is no amount given for this in the ingredient list. ½ cup of chopped celery top seems about right and works. Most celery now sold in markets is trimmed, and if you can't get untrimmed celery, use very finely chopped celery hearts.) It also calls for sliced onion, but no quantity is given—use a whole large brown or yellow onion. ✈

The chicken pie recipe is for an American favorite—the next is for something more exotic, at least by the standards of the day. In 1963 Harold Lindbergh, the manager of food service for Northwest Orient Airlines, published what were said to be his most requested recipes in the company newsletter. The airline was then serving Americanized Chinese food on many routes, and along with walnut chicken and sweet and sour fish Lindbergh included these Cantonese-style meatballs:

⟶ Chan Far Yook Kun (Fried Meat Balls and Crab Meat)

1½ pounds pork, ground
½ pound cooked or canned crabmeat
½ cup chopped mushrooms
½ cup chopped canned water chestnuts (optional)
2 teaspoons salt
½ teaspoon pepper
1 teaspoon sugar
1 cup cornstarch
2 eggs, beaten
1 tablespoon water
Fat for deep fat frying

1. Combine the pork, crabmeat, mushrooms, water chestnuts, salt, pepper, and sugar in a chopping bowl. Chop until well blended and very fine in texture.
2. Shape into 1-inch balls.

3. Dip each ball into cornstarch and coat well. Combine the eggs and water and dip each ball in the mixture.
4. Heat the fat to 360 degrees and drop the balls into it. Fry for 15 minutes.
5. Drain well. Serve with sliced cucumbers.

(Note: You do not need to fry these for fifteen minutes unless you like them dry and leathery—ten should do. You might want to serve these with a dip of some sort—thick sweet and sour sauce if you prize authenticity, Sriracha if you prefer the flavor.) ✈

Given that the sandwich wars were such a notable incident in airline food history, it seems fitting to include a recipe for one of the inflight appetizers served aboard SAS. This recipe for a tangy anchovy salad is very easy to make and colorful, and it's a good party item—or as noted, it can be made into an interesting fish hash.

Fagelbo (Bird's Nest)

4 to 6 Scandinavian anchovy filets, chopped
3 tablespoons chopped onion
½ cup diced pickled beets
1 tablespoon capers
1 raw egg yolk

1. Arrange chopped ingredients in rings, using anchovies for inner circle. Place raw egg yolk in center.
2. The first person to serve from the dish should mix ingredients well.

If you are not fond of raw egg yolks, mix ingredients, fry lightly in butter, and serve on toast. Note: Scandinavian anchovies differ completely from the Mediterranean variety; special aromatic spices used with Scandinavian anchovies are necessary for this recipe.

(Preparation notes: Use only a very fresh egg if you are making the raw version, but consider poaching the yolk instead—it is every bit as good a presentation and flavor, and safer. Scandinavian anchovies are also called sprats, and the direction to not use Mediterranean anchovies is not mere national pride—Mediterranean anchovies are much saltier.) ✈

Once broiling steaks inflight became possible, Northeast Airlines served theirs with one of the classic midcentury salads—lettuce with Green Goddess dressing. This recipe was published in 1968 in the *Montreal Gazette* and is not exactly like any other I have seen. (Glenn Howe, *Dinner in the Clouds: Great International Airline Recipes* [Glendale, CA: Interurban/Pentrex Press, 1985].)

～～～ Green Goddess Dressing

1 tablespoon dried tarragon
1 tablespoon chopped fresh parsley
1 tablespoon chopped chives
2 tablespoons chopped watercress
2 tablespoons chopped spinach
1½ cups mayonnaise
1 teaspoon lemon juice

1. Combine herbs, spinach, and lemon juice.
2. Whirl in blender. Strain and push through very fine sieve into mayonnaise. Stir to blend well.
3. Refrigerate. Makes 1¾ cups.

(Unlike modern versions of Green Goddess that use avocado, this can be made in advance and will keep for at least a week. This is good, because the amount produced by his recipe is enough for a large party or three or four meals. The original probably used iceberg lettuce, but I got excellent results from a mix of romaine and red lettuces, which have a slightly bitter flavor and contrast well with the dressing.) ✈

Airline kitchens have always had to be creative with their desserts, trying to come up with items that have broad appeal but can stand some bouncing around both during loading and in flight. One of the popular items was TWA's Banana Brunch Cake, which was introduced in 1974. The recipe was printed in the *Los Angeles Times* "Kitchen SOS" column on August 1, 1994.

～～～ TWA Banana Brunch Cake

½ cup butter
1 cup sugar
2 eggs
1 cup mashed banana
½ teaspoon vanilla
½ cup sour cream
2 cups sifted flour
1 teaspoon baking powder
1 teaspoon baking soda
¼ teaspoon salt

Nut Topping:
½ cup finely chopped nuts
¼ cup sugar
½ teaspoon cinnamon

1. Cream butter until light, then gradually add sugar, beating constantly. Beat in eggs, 1 at time. Mix in banana, vanilla, and sour cream.
2. Sift together flour, baking powder, soda, and salt and fold into creamed mixture, stirring just enough to moisten.
3. Combine nuts, sugar, and cinnamon to make topping.
4. Sprinkle half of Topping over bottom of well-greased 9-inch square pan or 10-inch molded pan. Spoon half of batter over Topping. Sprinkle remaining Topping over batter, then cover with remaining batter.
5. Bake at 350 degrees 45 minutes or until cake springs back when lightly touched. Makes 10 servings.

Each serving contains about: 363 calories; 215 mg sodium; 72 mg cholesterol; 16 grams fat; 50 grams carbohydrates; 6 grams protein; 0.24 gram fiber.
(Note: The original recipe did not specify what kind of nuts to use—I tried both pecans and almonds, and slightly prefer the pecans. Both gave excellent results.) ✈

No airline recipe list would be without one that was first served on the ground in an airport terminal, but is the single most famous product of the flying boat era. One of the only overseas routes on which Pan Am continued to fly civilian passengers during World War II was their service to Shannon, Ireland, which stopped at the Foynes Harbor seaplane terminal. As the staff at the Foynes Flying Boat Museum explain it,

In 1943, Brendan O'Regan opened a restaurant and coffee shop in the Foynes terminal building. This restaurant had been considered to be one of the best restaurants in Ireland at that time. Chef Joe Sheridan, originally from Castlederg, County Tyrone, had been recruited by Brendan. Late one night in the winter of 1943 a flight departed Foynes for Botwood, Newfoundland. After flying for several hours in bad weather conditions, the Captain made the decision to return to Foynes and await better conditions. A Morse code message was sent to the control tower at Foynes to inform them of their return. Staff were contacted to return to work and when the flight landed they were brought to the Airport Restaurant for food and drink to warm them. When Joe was asked to prepare something warm for the passengers, he decided to put some good Irish Whiskey into their coffees. One of the passengers approached the Chef and thanked him for the wonderful coffee. He asked Joe did he use Brazilian Coffee? Joe jokingly answered, "No that was Irish Coffee!!"

Director Margaret O'Shaughnessey of the Foynes Flying Boat Museum pro-vided this recipe:

～～～ *Original Recipe Irish Coffee*

1. In your Foynes Irish Coffee Glass, place a teaspoon and fill with boiling water for five seconds.
2. In this pre-warmed glass, put one teaspoon of brown sugar and a good measure of Irish Whiskey.
3. Fill the glass to within 1cm of the brim with really hot, strong black coffee.
4. Stir well to melt all the sugar. Then carefully pour lightly whipped cream over the back of a spoon so that it floats on top of the coffee.
5. Do not stir after adding the cream, as the true flavour is obtained by drinking the hot coffee and Irish Whiskey through the cream.

Suggesting recipes from space is also problematic—you can get a vivid sense of early astronaut food by rehydrating dried mashed potatoes and sucking it through a tube, but you will have to figure out your own proportions for that one. My editor wants me to try the recipes I include, and I refuse to undergo that experience.

I was only slightly more enthusiastic about eating a Tang pie, but as it is a valid expression of the 1950s space craze, I have included it for your plea-sure, if not mine. The recipe was widely distributed by General Foods, for obvious reasons—it included their products Cool Whip and Tang. It's very easy to make, and since it's sweet, creamy, and a lurid orange, it's popular at children's parties and in some parts of the American South.

～～～ *Tang Pie*

1 9-inch graham cracker pie crust, baked
1 14-ounce can sweetened condensed milk
1 8-ounce carton of sour cream
¼ cup + 2 tablespoons Tang powder
1 8-ounce tub of Cool Whip

1. Mix milk, sour cream, and Tang together.
2. Fold in half of the Cool Whip.
3. Spoon into the pie shell.
4. Top with the rest of the Cool Whip.
5. Chill for at least half an hour before serving.

Another recipe from the early rush of enthusiasm for space is this fruitcake, which was published in the Eau Claire, Wisconsin, *Daily Telegram* in 1968. I can't resist including the original introduction, which has the breathless writing style of the era. Note that the original recipe called for "Bordo" dates—this was the name of an importing company, and any type of dates may be used.

Although the U.S. Army Natick Laboratories originally created this fruitcake recipe for space food for the astronauts, there is no reason why you can't prepare this simplified version for the youngsters at your house. Surely they will like the idea of eating the same delicious dessert the astronauts eat. Furthermore, you'll like all the energy power and nutrients packed into each scrumptious slice, right along with glace cherries, chopped pecans and Bordo imported dates. So bake this very special "Astronaut Fruitcake" for your children this week, and stand by to receive a hearty "A-OK!"

~~~~~ Astronaut Fruitcake

1 cup sifted all-purpose flour
½ cup granulated sugar
½ teaspoon salt
8 large eggs
½ teaspoon vanilla
1½ cups chopped pecans
3 cups imported diced dates or whole pitted dates, cut up
1 cup glace cherries, quartered

1. Sift together flour, sugar, and salt.
2. Place nuts, cherries, and quartered dates in a bowl and mix until pieces of fruit no longer stick together and nuts are well dispersed in the fruit mixture.
3. Sprinkle the flour mixture over the fruit mixture, while mixing by hand. Beat eggs and vanilla until frothy. Add to the fruit mixture and mix until all ingredients are completely moistened.
4. Generously grease bottoms of 4½ x 9½ inch loaf pans, and bake fruitcake in preheated 300 degree (F.) oven for two hours, or until firm. Store in airtight container.

(Unless you enjoy very sweet desserts, you probably should use half the specified amount of sugar. For the cherries, stay away for the bright pink cocktail cherries and get real glacé cherries—modern cocktail cherries are nothing like a real glacé cherry.)

APPENDIX

~~~~~~~~~~~~

Unsolved Questions

There were two questions I had hoped to address in this book but was not able to find authoritative enough information to cover properly.

One was the nutritional changes in airline food over the years. Though airline chefs mentioned the importance of balanced meals as early as Don Magarell's interviews the 1930s, not enough details were published to estimate calorie counts, fat levels, or vitamins. Detailed data doesn't become publicly available until the 1970s, and the information was too scanty and over too short of a period to come to any meaningful conclusions.

The other question was about when airlines began to recycle the waste from their trays, and how much is now recycled. No caterer or airline was willing or able to give any meaningful data, probably because they don't actually know. Recycling is handled by local waste companies, and though the airlines hand bags of recyclable material to them, they don't actually monitor what happens to it. There is no way to give a useful estimate of the current amount recycled by percentage, weight, or volume. It can only be said that it varies by the jurisdiction in which it is offloaded, but the percentage is probably increasing worldwide.

Notes

Chapter 1

1. According to T. L. C. Rolt, *The Aeronauts, A History of Ballooning 1783-1903* (Longman, 1966), 73.

2. According to Constance Hieatt and Robin Jones, "A Cuire Chaire Sans Feu," from "Two Anglo-Norman Culinary Collections," *Speculum* 61, no. 4 (1986): 874, note 6.

3. According to T. L. C. Rolt, *The Aeronauts, A History of Ballooning 1783-1903* (Longman, 1966), 125.

Chapter 2

1. *International Year Book*, Dodd, Mead, and Co., 1901.

2. *Politiken*, September 19, 1912.

3. *Sydney Morning Herald*, September 21, 1912.

4. *Nelson Evening Mail*, September 21, 1912.

5. Harry Vissering, *Zeppelin: The Story of a Great Achievement* (Chicago: Wells & Co., 1920), 18–22. Full text available on Gutenberg.com.

6. August Seim, "The Rigger Tells a Tale," in *The Zeppelin Reader*, ed. Robert Hedin (University of Iowa Press, 1998), 77–78.

7. Douglas Robinson, *The Zeppelin in Combat* (Schiffer, 1994).

8. The first practical oven thermostat came on the market in 1915, but zeppelins of this era did not have them.

9. Vissering, *Zeppelin*, 53.

10. "Zeppelin Books 18 for Passage Here," *New York Times*, October 7, 1928 (p. 1).

11. Hugo Eckener, "A Sentimental Journey to Egypt," in *The Zeppelin Reader*, ed. Robert Hedin (University of Iowa Press, 1998), 195.

12. "Zeppelin Takes Off on Trip to America . . . ," *New York Times*, August 1, 1929 (p. 1).

13. Sample lyric from "Graf Zeppelin" by Trinidadian musician Attila The Hun:

I gazed at the zeppelin contemplatively,
And marveled at man's ingenuity
The whirring of the engines was all I heard
As it floated in the air like a giant bird.

As for Tennessee, there is the deathless lyric,

I left Memphis on the Robert E. Lee
Going to go back home on the LZ-3

Unfortunately, there is still no zeppelin service to Memphis.

14. *Flight Magazine*, December 6, 1929, article bylined "F.A. de V.R."

15. "R-100 Sets Fast," *Los Angeles Times*, August 15, 1930 (p. 1).

16. Douglas H. Robinson, *LZ 129 "Hindenburg*, Famous Aircraft Series (Dallas, TX: Morgan Books, 1964).

17. Webb Miller, *I Found No Peace* (Simon & Schuster, 1936). Text republished on airships.net website.

18. Harold Dick and Douglas Robinson, *Golden Age of the Great Passenger Airships* (Smithsonian Press, 1985).

Chapter 3

1. Per e-mail from Peter Elliott, head of archives, Royal Air Force Museum, December 16, 2013.

2. Paul Jarvis, curator of British Airways Heritage Centre, interview with CNN, May 2, 2012.

3. Aeronautical News, Reuters/Lismore *Northern Star*, June 2, 1922.

4. Paul Van Weezepoel, Dutch Aviation History, http://www.dutch-aviation.nl/Index3/1919-1939.

5. "London's Amazing Express Aeroplane Liners a Hundred Miles an Hour—Modern Fulfillment of Dreams of Jules Verne's," *Reuters Aeronautical News*, October 20, 1923.

6. *Albany Advertiser* (Australia), April 14, 1928.

7. "Paris-London Airway Has First Aerial Cafe," *Daily Record* (Morris County, NJ), October 2, 1925 (p. 14).

8. E-mail of January 22, 2014.

9. Frank J. Taylor, *High Horizons* (McGraw-Hill, 1962), 41. Hereafter cited as *HH*.

10. George H. Foster and Peter C. Weiglan, *The Harvey House Cookbook* (Taylor Trade Publishing, 2006), p. 160.

11. T. J. C. Martyn, "Air Liner Provides Luxuries of Travel," *New York Times*, July 16, 1929 (p. 2).

12. Helen McLaughlin, *Footsteps in the Sky* (Aviation Book Company, 1994), 19. Hereafter cited as *FITS*.

13. *FITS*, 20.

14. *DailyNews* (Perth), January 30, 1928.

Chapter 4

1. Per Peter Elliott, head of archives, Royal Air Force Museum, 16 December 2013.

2. Article on backpacking stoves, "Zen and the Art of the Alcohol Stove," zenstoves.net/stoves. No author name given.

3. Patent #US2024259A, Halstead & Troeber.

Chapter 5

1. *HH*, 112.

2. Peter Jones and Michael Kips, "Introduction," in *Flight Catering* (London: Longman, 1995), 4, citing "Bruce 2001 and Wright 1985." Hereafter cited as *FC*.

3. George Banks, *Gourmet and Glamour in the Sky: A Life in Airline Catering* (UK: GMS Enterprises, 2006), 19. Hereafter cited as *GG*.

4. E-mail of January 14, 2014, from Gordon Pirie.

5. Ibid.

6. GGITA, p. 7.

7. Martin Staniland, *Government Birds: Air Transport and the State in Western Europe* (Rowman & Littlefield, 2003), 23.

8. *FITS*.

9. The British RAF had installed heaters in their flying boats five years before, but for military and government flights only.

10. Those flights left from a location called Dinner Key, which is occasionally misunderstood to have been named because Pan Am loaded meals there. This is incorrect, as the area had that name as early as 1914.

11. Martha Ellyn, "160-Mile Airline Meals Good to the Last Mile," *Washington Post*, July 25, 1941 (p. 12).

12. *FITS*, 8.

13. San Francisco Airport Commission Aviation library—Louis A. Turpen Aviation Museum Oral History Program interview transcription. Interview recorded February 26, 1999, by Maureen Jane Perry. As of the writing of this book, only a few copies have been made, but the museum was considering making them available. Hereafter cited as *Toaramina*.

14. Even when only cold food was available, it was rarely served shortly after take-off because seaplanes took off with a full load of fuel that was very heavy—it took as much as an hour for the aircraft to struggle to cruising altitude of seven thousand feet. By the time an hour had gone by the aircraft was usually in calmer skies and less likely to need to maneuver suddenly.

15. Lufthansa also briefly operated service to South America, but primarily carrying mail rather than passengers.

Chapter 6

1. *HH*, 27.

2. Testimony before the Black Committee, January 1934.

3. *FITS*, memoir of Trudy Pracny, 33.

4. *HH*, 116.

5. *HH*, 40.

6. Audrey C. McCool, *Inflight Catering Management* (New York: John Wiley & Sons, 1995), 26. This reference says this happened in 1937, but Jones in *Flight Catering* gives the date as 1933 (p. 4). The 1933 date is more consistent with other sources.

7. *FITS*, 11.

8. *FITS*, 22. Also, Velma Maul Tanzer Scrapbook, Item 2005-0036, Smithsonian Institution.

9. Per dryiceinfo.com, an industry website.

10. *GG*, 8.

11. United Airlines did not answer repeated e-mails requesting clarification on this and other questions. There was no mention of it in *High Horizons*, which is generally regarded as the best history of the airline.

12. *Inflight Catering Management*, 27.

13. *HH*, 111–12.

14. From the *Food Timeline* website, http://foodtimeline.org/restaurants.html#inflight. No author name provided in original article.

15. Menu dated March 16, 1940, New York Public Library collection, online at menus.nypl.org.

16. Program of May 8, 1940. The *Capital Times* of Madison, Wisconsin, described the program as follows: "Why it takes six minutes to boil a three minute egg when you're 10,000 feet in the air and other problems of cookery in the clouds will be discussed when Fred Allen interviews Donald F. Magarell of United Air Lines . . . "

17. *Salt Lake Tribune*, January 21, 1961 (p. 16).

18. It can't have been Marriott, because they didn't begin operations there until 1946, so it was probably an independent company.

19. Grace Turner, "Picking a Meal Out of the Air," *Los Angeles Times*, November 13, 1938 (p. J15).

20. Daniel Rust, *Flying Across America* (University of Oklahoma Press, 2009), 164.

21. Polina Kurovskaya, Aeroflot historian, e-mail message to author, December 30, 2013.

22. Rob Mulder and Gunther Ott, "Focke-Wulf Fw 200 Condor with Danish Air Lines in War and Peace," in *Focke-Wulf Condor with Danish Airlines in War and Peace* (European Airlines Publishing, 2013), 52–55.

23. Several books have stated that no land-based aircraft of this era had a galley significantly more sophisticated than the DC-3. They are wrong; the 307 Stratoliner at the Smithsonian Institute's Udvar-Hazy Air Museum has been restored by Boeing to factory specifications and has multiple electric hot plates. (Dr. Bob Van Der Linden, curator, e-mail message to author, February 22, 2014.)

Chapter 8

1. Eugene Dunning, ed., *Voices of My Peers* (Clipper Press, 1996), 93. Hereafter cited as VOMP.

2. *Toaramina*, 18.

3. GG, 27.

4. E-mail from Peter Elliott, December 16, 2013.

5. AAF Manual No. 49-1, dated December 30, 1944.

6. Andrew F. Smith, *Eating History* (Columbia University Press, 2013), 169.

7. Captain Thomas M. Davis, USAF liaison officer, "Food and Ration Problems of the U.S. Air Force," in *Activities Report of the Quartermaster Food and Container Institute for the Armed Forces*, 1949, 270–71.

8. HH, 117.

9. DeltaMuseum.org website, history/aircraft-by-type page.

10. FITS, 174.

11. R. Dixon Speas, *Airline Operations* (American Aviation Publications, 1948), 88.

12. "The Log of Logan Airport," *Christian Science Monitor*, September 8, 1948, 2.

13. Audrey McCool, *Inflight Catering Management* (Wiley, 1995), 32–37.

14. Mary Dixon Lebeau, "At 50, The TV Dinner Is Still Cookin,' *Christian Science Monitor*, November 10, 2004, viewed in online archive at http://www.csmonitor.com/2004/1110/p11s01-lifo.html.

15. Sir Hudson Fysh, *Wings of the World: Story of Qantas* (Angus & Robertson, 1965), 63.

16. TWA's operations were disrupted by a strike in 1946, and by an internal management conflict that paralyzed decision making for some time.

17. Frozen food evaluation and letters provided by David Crotty, archivist of Qantas Heritage Collection, October 2013.

18. GG, 34.

19. Despite repeated requests, Air India did not respond to requests for information about catering history. This information is from GG.

20. FC, 12.

21. GG, 28.

22. Article by former purser Harry Proia in VOMP, 227.

23. Article by Yvonne Oliver in VOMP, 184.

Chapter 9

1. FC, 3.

2. Unattributed, "Commercial Flight in the 1930's," Century of Flight, http://www.century-of-flight.net/new%20site/commercial/Flight%20in%20the%201930s.htm.

3. Daniel Michaels, "Test Flight: Lufthansa Searches for Savor in the Sky," *Wall Street Journal*, July 27, 2010, http://online.wsj.com/news/articles/SB10001424052748 703294904575384954227906006.

4. Guillaume de Syon, "Is It Really Better to Travel than Arrive?" in *Food for Thought: Essays on Eating and Culture*, ed. Lawrence Rubin (McFarland, 2008), 204.

5. Ibid.

6. "Airlines Early Woes with Food Described," *New York Times*, April 26, 1939 (p. 48).

7. Some airlines made peanuts a symbol of cheap tickets; Continental advertised that passengers could "fly for peanuts!" on their commuter flights that served only that legume. Concern about peanut allergies caused most airlines to stop serving them in 2010.

8. Scott McCartney, "The Fight against Bland Airline Food," *Wall Street Journal*, November 14, 2013, http://online.wsj.com/news/articles/SB10001424052702303789 604579195823006518910.

9. CNN Interview with Lauren Said-Moorhouse, September 20, 2012, http://www.cnn.com/2012/09/19/world/airlines-wine/.

10. Jad Mouawad, "Can Airline Food Be Tasty?" *New York Times*, March 10, 2012, http://www.nytimes.com/2012/03/11/business/airlines-studying-the-science-of-better-in-flight-meals.html?_r=1&.

11. Same reference as 8.

12. Woods et al., "Effect of Background Noise on Food Perception," *Journal of Food Quality and Preference* 22 (2011). Abstract at http://www.sciencedirect.com/science/article/pii/S0950329310001217.

Chapter 10

1. Martin P. Staniland, *Government Birds* (Rowman & Littlefield, 2003), 124.

2. *Toaramina*, 57–58.

3. FC, 5.

4. VOMP, 121–2.

5. Unattributed Regulation news article, *Flight Magazine*, December 28, 1951, 817.

6. Ibid.

7. From http://www.klmhouses.com/houses-history.html.

8. From http://thestewardist.blogspot.com/2011_11_01_archive.html.

9. Air France historian Marc Branchu on http://corporate.airfrance.com/airfrance lasaga/dossiers/premiere-a-history-of-first-class-travel/.

10. GG, 12.

11. AP News story, noted in the *Calgary Herald*, May 7, 1958.

12. For more on this, see Rigas Doganis, *Flying Off Course: The Economics of International Airlines* (Routledge UK, 2010).

13. Interview with Hillary Clinton, *Pressan*, Reykjavik, May 18, 2011.

14. Memoir of Malaysian Airways Captain Roland Thomas, menu pictured at rolandabrahamthomas@blogspot.com.

15. Philippine Airlines Inc. History, www.fundinguniverse.com/company-histories/philippine-airlines-inc-history/.

16. David Lewis, *Airline Executives and Federal Regulation: Case Studies in American Enterprise* (Ohio University Press, 2000), 134.

17. We would now call what they served "méthode Champenoise sparkling wine," because it was made in California, but labeling standards were more lax then. Most airlines inside the United States didn't start serving real French Champagne until the 1970s, and even then only in first class.

18. *FITS*, 236.

19. "Tight Planning Will Be Needed for Serving Meals on Supersonic Flights," *Chronicle-Telegram* (Elyria, OH), April 24, 1965 (p. 16).

20. *Beating the Odds: A History of Western Airlines*, company publication, unattributed, 1976. The hunt caps were misidentified as derbies in this article.

21. Ann Billingsley Kerr, *Fujiyama Trays and Oshibori Towels* (Lady Skywriter Publications, 2008), 61. See recommended reading list.

22. Ibid., 64

23. "Tasty Meals Served High in the Sky Await Travelers," unattributed, *Memphis Commercial Appeal*, October 1, 1950 (p. 8).

24. Daniel Rust, *Flying Across America* (University of Oklahoma Press, 2009), 163.

Chapter 11

1. "Easy Chair" article from 1952, as quoted in "Flying Across America" by Daniel Rust (University of Oklahoma Press, 2009), 165.

2. Seen on www.edsullivan.com/alan-king-on-the-ed-sullivan-show.

3. From the original score—lyrics provided by Laura Frankos, author of the *Broadway Musical Quiz Book* (Limelight NYC, 2010).

4. Quoted in *How to Walk in High Heels: The Girl's Guide to Everything* by Hamilla Morton (Hachette, 2009). Ebook, no page number.

5. Obituary in *The Economist*, back page, June 12, 2010.

6. YouTube video entitled "Ellen DeGeneres on Flight Attendants, Peanuts, and Airline Food," uploaded January 24, 2010.

Chapter 12

1. "Tight Planning Will Be Needed for Serving Meals on Supersonic Flights," *Chronicle-Telegram* (Elyria, OH), April 24, 1965 (p. 16).

2. Dobbs is given credit for first use in *FC*, but the exact date is not given. Marriott's historian stated via e-mail that the company developed this technology first. The successor company to Dobbs did not respond to requests for information.

3. FC, 8.

4. United Airlines Form #12i90, revised 2/64.

5. HH, 211.

6. HH, 186.

7. Ad in author's collection.

8. Audrey McCool, *Inflight Catering Management* (John Wiley & Sons, 1995), 36.

9. "National Adds Gourmet Touch to Flight Meal," unattributed, *Palm Beach Daily News*, April 27, 1963 (p. 6).

10. *Northwest Airlines Employee Newsletter*, no page number, January–February 1959.

11. Ibid.

12. "Boeing 707 Launch Commercial" on http://www.youtube.com/watch?v= XnSIZ2ljCzY.

13. VOMP, 225.

14. Jerry Hulse, "Travelines: Airline Cuisine? Plane and Fancy," *Los Angeles Times*, January 21, 1962 (p. G11).

15. Guillaume de Syon, "Is It Better to Travel Than Arrive?" in *Food For Thought: Essays in Eating and Culture*, ed. Lawrence J. Rubin (McFarland, 2005), which is worth reading in its entirety.

16. GG, 14.

17. GG, 29.

18. E-mail from Polina Kurovskaya, Aeroflot historian, January 2014.

19. "Aboard the First Flights," unattributed, *Life Magazine*, July 26, 1968 (p. 22).

Chapter 13

1. US Patent #2336735A.

2. Sgt. Georg N. Meyers, "What's Cooking?" *Yank Magazine* 4, no. 3 (July 1945): 11.

3. One source says this first happened in 1945, but this was probably a military flight rather than a commercial trip.

4. Advertisement in the *Montreal Gazette*, January 17, 1968, 5.

5. Southwest Museum of Engineering website at http://smecc.org/microwave _oven.htm, accessed March 22, 2014.

6. Hagberg and Graff, "Airborne Microwave Oven Development," in NASA publication #SP-202, "Aerospace Food Technology," undated.

7. *The Register* (London), online edition, dated September 30, 2008, www .theregister.co.uk/2007/05/21/exploding_curry/.

8. "Cabin Comforts," unattributed, *Flight Magazine*, September 13, 1995, http:// www.flightglobal.com/news/articles/cabin-comforts-24234/.

Chapter 14

1. *Toaramina*, 99.

2. Jay Koren, *The Company We Kept* (Paladwr Press, 2000), 202.

3. GG, 63.

4. Quoted in GG, 16.

5. Menu in author's collection.

6. GG, 83.

7. GG, 51–52.

8. E-mail to the author from retired SAA crew site, January 30, 2014.

9. Much more information and photos at http://www.danairremembered.com/ on-board-dan-air.html.

10. Market analysis of Singapore Airlines by Martin Roll dated March 2014 at www .martinroll.com/resources/articles/asia/singapore-airlines-an-excellent-asian-brand/.

11. Double-page ad in author's collection, publication unknown. Run date established by reference to new 707s, which the airline received in 1970.

12. History tab at http://www.psa-history.org/about_psa/aircraft/tristar.

13. Menu provided to the author by Delta Airlines Museum, Atlanta, GA.

14. FC, 69.

15. David Asper Johnson, Snoopin' Around column, *Argonaut*, August 10, 1972.

16. FITS, 218.

17. FC, 7.

18. Author's collection, undated.

19. Air France official historian Marc Branchu on airfrancelesaga.com website, article dated December 3, 2013, http://corporate.airfrance.com/airfrancelasaga/dossiers/ premiere-a-history-of-first-class-travel/.

Chapter 15

1. Per "Timeline of Kosher" on OK.org, website of the kosher food industry in the United States, http://www.ok.org/about/our-ongoing-story/a-timeline-of-kosher. Siegel's is listed as the first in some references, which are incorrect.

2. Angela Waller, *Before There Were Trolley Dollies* (Dales Books, 2011).

3. "Can the Tarnished Age of Flight Be Restored to Gold?" interview for blog.apex .aero, http://blog.apex.aero/inflight-services-2/tarnished-age-flight-restored-gold/.

4. Robert Dallos, "Everything's Kosher Up Above," *Pittsburgh Press*, January 12, 1974 (p. E-1).

5. Ibid.

6. Ibid.

7. E-mail of March 11, 2014.

8. "Food Kosher?" *Canberra Times*, August 7, 1982 (p. 4).

9. http://www.peaceinislam.com/shane2k/131/.

10. Emirates.com website, Dietary Requirements tab, http://www.emirates.com/ english/plan_book/essential_information/dietary_requirements.aspx.

11. *FC*, 82–83.

12. Christopher Lofting, "Focus on Travel" article "Restricted Diets No Longer a Problem for Air Travelers," *Charleston News and Courier*, February 22, 1981, 10.

13. David Learmount, "Airline Management by Wire," *Flight Magazine*, October 26, 1985.

14. *United Times, Corporate Communications* 6, no. 7, 4 (August 1993).

Chapter 16

1. Information about the history of Laker Airways from "Sir Freddie Laker: The Man Who Gave Us Skytrain" by Bob Blufeld in *Airliner Classics Magazine*, November 2009, 81–83.

2. Frank Barrett, "In Memory of Laker Airways and Skytrain, the Birth of Budget Travel," *Daily Mail*, February 10, 2012, http://travelblog.dailymail.co.uk/2012/02/ in-memory-of-laker-airways-and-skytrain-the-birth-of-budget-travel.html.

3. "Freddie Laker's Skytrain: A Good Deal?" unattributed article, *The Hour* (Norwalk, CT), March 9, 1978 (p. 34).

4. John Pringle, "Painful Progress in the Air," *Sydney Morning Herald*, February 27, 1978 (p. 7).

5. Richard Turen, "A Simple Explanation of Business Class," *Travel Weekly*, February 24, 2014. Available online at http://www.travelweekly.com/Richard-Turen/ A-simple-explanation-of-business-class/. This "historian of commercial aviation" recommends that you read it.

6. Elizabeth Bailey, "The Cloud over Laker Air," *New York Times*, October 25, 1981, http://www.nytimes.com/1981/10/25/business/the-cloud-over-laker-air.html.

7. From *Tourism in India: An Overview, Vol. 1* (Gyan Press, 2005), 135.

8. Airliners.net thread #2595075 about Continental's Pub flights, http://www .airliners.net/aviation-forums/general_aviation/read.main/2588992/.

9. Continental Airlines ad from May 1981, publication unknown.

10. Quoted in *Beating the Odds: The First Sixty Years of Western Airlines* (Company publication, 1976), 22.

11. There are plenty of books on this topic—a good one is *Rapid Descent: Deregulation and the Shakeout in the Airlines* by Barbara Sturken Peterson (Simon & Schuster, 1994).

12. Menu in author's collection, provided by Delta Airlines Museum.

13. Jeff Schapiro, "Prayer Cards to Be Removed from Alaska Airlines Flights," *Christian Post*, January 26, 2012, http://www.christianpost.com/news/prayer-cards-to-be-removed-from-alaska-airlines-flights-68031/.

14. Claudia Deutsch, " . . . And to Penny-Pinching Wizardry," *New York Times*, May 6, 2001, http://www.nytimes.com/2001/05/06/business/and-to-penny-pinching -wizardry.html.

15. And not just to me; other people have asked, including prestigious business publications, and they neither confirm nor deny.

16. Alan G. Robinson and Sam Stern, *Corporate Creativity* (Berret-Koehler, 1998), 107.

17. Ibid.

18. Matt Goulding, "The Fare Up There," *Roads And Kingdoms*, September 13, 2013, seen online at http://roadsandkingdoms.com/2013/the-fare-up-there/.

19. FC, 7.

20. Kyle Schlacter, "Can Packaging from Beer World Work with Wine Too?" *Palate Press Online Wine Magazine*, December 7, 2011, http://palatepress.com/2011/12/wine/can-packaging-from-beer-world-work-with-wine-too/.

21. "Homer's Barbershop Quartet," *The Simpsons*, season 5, episode 1.

22. FITS, 213.

Chapter 17

1. GG, 34.

2. Connie Coning, "O'Hare's Flight Caterers," *Chicago Tribune*, March 27, 1977 (p. C3).

3. "Plane Food," undated article seen online at www.deliciousmagazine.co.uk/articles/plane-food.

Chapter 18

1. E-mail from Polina Krovskaya, Aeroflot historian.

2. Paul Makisma, "Ryanair Moves ahead with Pay Toilet Plan," *Boston Globe*, April 7, 2010, http://www.boston.com/travel/blog/2010/04/ryanair_moves_a.html.

3. GG, 36.

4. London Times 100 Business Case Studies, http://businesscasestudies.co.uk/virgin-atlantic/building-an-airline-through-brand-values/customer-service.html #axzz37kTL3rq8.

5. Seen in *Columbia Daily Spectator* (Columbia, SC), April 25, 1988 (p. 4).

6. Martyn Gregory, *Dirty Tricks, British Airways' Secret War against Virgin Atlantic* (Random House, 2010), 38.

7. List of awards in Peter Doyle and Susan Bridgewater, *Innovation in Marketing* (Routledge, 2012), 53.

8. Judy Anderson, "Gulf War Is Having Bad Effect on Tourism in London," *Baltimore Sun*, February 3, 1991, http://articles.baltimoresun.com/1991-02-03/features/1991034148_1_gulf-war-london-ticket-office.

9. Alan Friedman, "Competitors Decry EU Approval of $3.7 Billion Subsidy: Air France Bailout Heads for Court," *New York Times*, July 28, 1994, http://www.nytimes.com/1994/07/28/news/28iht-af_1.html.

10. Stanley Ziemba, "United Decides to Sell Its Flight Kitchens," *Chicago Tribune*, Business section, http://articles.chicagotribune.com/1993-02-18/business/9303181454_1_flight-kitchens-united-airlines-dobbs-international-services.

11. Gordon Bethune interview by Evan Smith, *Texas Monthly*, December 2004, http://www.texasmonthly.com/content/gordon-bethune-0.

12. Greg Brenneman, "Right Away and All At Once: How We Saved Continental," *Harvard Business Review*, September–October 1998, http://hbr.org/1998/09/right-away-and-all-at-once-how-we-saved-continental/ar/4.

13. Company reports; "Continental Is Dropping Lite Service," *New York Times*, April 14, 1995, www.nytimes.com/1995/04/14/business/company-reports-continental-is-dropping-lite-service.html.

14. Mark Tran, "The Airline Industry Slump," *Guardian*, September 20, 2001, www.theguardian.com/world/2001/sep/20/qanda.theairlineindustry.

15. "Airlines Experiment with Selling Food," unattributed article, *Gainesville Sun*, January 19, 2003 (p. 6D).

16. Interview in *Roads and Kingdoms*, September 13, 2013, http://roadsandkingdoms.com/2013/the-fare-up-there/.

17. Jason Kessler, "I'm Sick of Stinky Food on Airplanes," *Bon Appetit*, August 13, 2012, www.bonappetit.com/columns/nitpicker-columns/article/i-m-sick-of-stinky-food-on-airplanes.

18. Posting on http://www.flyertalk.com/forum/united-mileage-plus-pre-merger-closed-posting/646075-no-pretzels-flights-less-than-2-hrs-merged-threads.html, dated January 10, 2007.

19. Robert Fenner, "United Continental CEO Smisek Sees 'Significant Progress' in Integration," Bloomberg News, December 13, 2010.

20. Jurgen Brauer and Paul Dunne, "Terrorism, War, and Global Air Traffic," in *Economics of Peace and Security Journal* 7, no. 1 (2012): 22.

21. Magnus Smauch, *EU Law on State Aid to Airlines: Law, Economics, and Policy* (Lexxion, 2012), 349–52.

22. Charles Starmer-Smith, "How to Complain to an Airline," *Daily Telegraph*, January 28, 2009, http://blogs.telegraph.co.uk/travel/charlesstarmer-smith/8208627/How_to_complain_to_an_airline/.

23. Gulliver column, bylined "M. R.," *Economist*, May 1, 2013, http://www.economist.com/blogs/gulliver/2013/05/flight-meals.

24. Jack Nicas, "The Long, Slow Death of the First Class Seat," *Wall Street Journal*, July 19, 2012, http://online.wsj.com/news/articles/SB10000872396390444409790457 7535280680475986.

Chapter 19

1. NASA Food History page, http://liftoff.msfc.nasa.gov/academy/astronauts/food-history.html.

2. Nanette Gallant, "Subsistence in Space," on US Army Quartermaster Foundation website at http://qmfound.com/subsistence_in_space.htm.

3. "Glenn Had Space Snack by Tube; Food Squeezed Via Helmet Hole," *New York Times*, February 21, 1962 (p. 24).

4. Lev Lebedev, "Soviet Space Research History," *Space World*, November 1974, p. 40.

5. "Out in Space Table Manners Up for Grabs," *Los Angeles Times*, December 21, 1964 (p. D18).

6. "Mercury MA-9" article in *Encyclopedia Astronautica*, http://astronautix.com/flights/merryma9.htm.

7. "Astronaut's Breakfast," *Newsweek*, April 15, 1963 (p. 63).

8. "Way Sought to Grow Food From Leftovers," Associated Press, *Washington Post*, January 29, 1963 (p. A9). Note: There was an error in the *WP* article—though the first attempt to regenerate cloned animal tissue was in the 1940s, the Nobel Prize for doing so was not awarded until 1954.

9. Seen at eufic.org section on food technology, http://www.eufic.org/article/en/food-technology/food-processing/artid/Freeze-drying-value-quality-products/.

10. Frederic C. Appel, "Food Is Problem for Astronauts," *New York Times*, June 6, 1965 (p. 70).

11. Jane Levi, "An Extraterrestrial Sandwich: The Perils of Food in Space," *Endeavour*, 34, no. 1 (March 2010), 7.

12. "Out in Space Table Manners Up for Grabs," *Los Angeles Times*, December 21, 1964 (p. D18).

13. *Washington Post*, March 26, 1965.

14. Wolfie's had some experience with food in flight—the restaurant had catered Northeast Airlines flights from Miami to New York in the 1960s.

Chapter 20

1. Per e-mail from Russian food historian Anya von Bremzen, April 8, 2014.

2. Mark Memmott, "Now He Tells Us: Tang Sucks, Says Apollo 11's Buzz Aldrin," article on NPR's "The Two Way," June 13, 2013, http://www.npr.org/blogs/thetwo-way/2013/06/13/191271824/now-he-tells-us-tang-sucks-says-apollo-11s-buzz-aldrin.

3. James Hagerty, *NASA Spinoff* (Diane Publishing, 1994), 83.

4. Review and short history is available at http://www.icecreamnation.org/2013/04/space-ice-cream/.

5. There is a very good history of Space Food Sticks and pictures of old ads and packaging at http://spacefoodsticks.com/pres.html.

Chapter 21

1. Mary Ellen Snodgrass, *Encyclopedia of Kitchen History* (Routledge, 2005), 929.

2. "No Place for Gourmets," *New York Times*, October 13, 1968 (p. 74).

3. "Astronauts Assert Their Food Is Too Plentiful and Too Sweet," *New York Times*, October 14, 1968 (p. 39).

4. Ibid.

5. "Whirlpool Announces Lunar Fare: Local Industry Prepared Food for Apollo 11," *News-Palladium* (Benton Harbor, MI), June 30, 1969 (p. 3).

6. Sandra Blakelee, "Real Sandwiches Please Spacemen," *New York Times*, May 21, 1969 (p. 20).

7. Vasily Dupik, "The Soviet Space Man's Menu," *Space World*, December 1971 (p. 42–43).

8. "Birthday Party Is Held in Space," *New York Times*, June 20, 1971 (p. 29).

9. Nicholas C. Chriss, "Young Finds Potassium Too Rich in Burps," *Los Angeles Times*, April 23, 1972 (p. J12).

10. Mary Ellen Snodgrass, *Encyclopedia of Kitchen History* (Routledge, 2005), 930.

11. From NASA Food History page at http://liftoff.msfc.nasa.gov/academy/astronauts/food-history.html.

12. From *Two Sides of the Moon—Our Story of the Cold War Space Race* by David Scott and Alexei Leonov (St. Martin's Press, 2004). Quote seen on the Food Timeline Library website at http://foodtimeline.org/spacefood.html.

13. Brian Harvey, *Europe's Space Programme* (Springer, 2003), 252.

14. Alan Boyle, "Alcohol in Space? Da!" NBC News, October 14, 2010, http://cosmiclog.nbcnews.com/_news/2010/10/14/5291711-alcohol-in-space-da.

Chapter 22

1. I have found no good pictures of cooking taking place in a flying boat galley, but for submarines see "Pig Boats, Fleet Boats, and Mystery Meat," by Philip Rutherford, originally in *Undersea Warfare* magazine, http://www.public.navy.mil/subfor/underseawarfaremagazine/Issues/Archives/issue_46/pig_boats.html.

2. Trudy Bell, "Preventing Sick Spaceships," http://science.nasa.gov/science-news/science-at-nasa/2007/11may_locad3/.

3. See *Stress Challenges and Immunity in Space*, by Alexander Chouker (Springer, 2011), 301–3.

4. Trudy Bell, "Preventing Sick Spaceships," Science.NASA.gov website.

5. Robert Reinhold, "Dining a la Carte in the Space Shuttle, with a Choice of Entrees," *New York Times*, January 16, 1985 (p. C1).

Chapter 23

1. Mary Ellen Snodgrass, *Encyclopedia of Kitchen History* (Routledge, 2005), 930.

2. NASA food education page at http://education.ssc.nasa.gov/fft_halloffame .asp.

3. Ibid.

4. Robert Reinhold, "Dining a la Carte in the Space Shuttle, with a Choice of Entrees," *New York Times*, January 16, 1985 (p. C1).

5. Mary Ellen Snodgrass, *Encyclopedia of Kitchen History* (Routledge, 2005), 930.

6. Robert Reinhold, "Dining a la Carte in the Space Shuttle, with a Choice of Entrees," *New York Times*, January 16, 1985 (p. C1).

7. "After Italian Feast, Italian Astronaut Skips Spaghetti," unattributed article, *Digital Journal* 31 (October 2007). Online at http://www.digitaljournal.com/article/244462.

8. "Astronauts Drink Recycled Urine, and Celebrate," unattributed story from SPACE.com, May 20, 2009. Online at http://www.space.com/6733-astronauts -drink-recycled-urine-celebrate.html.

9. Jane Levi, "Conviviality in Microgravity," *Moving Worlds: Food, Culture, and Community* 6, no. 2 (May 2007): 10.

10. Ibid.

Bibliography

Anderson, Judy, "Gulf War Is Having Bad Effect on Tourism in London," *Baltimore Sun*. February 3, 1991.

Appel, Frederic C., "Food Is Problem for Astronauts," *New York Times*, June 6, 1965.

Bailey, Elizabeth, "The Cloud over Laker Air," *New York Times*, October 25, 1981.

Banks, George, *Gourmet and Glamour in the Sky: A Life in Airline Catering*, GMS Enterprises, 2006. Cited in this book's footnotes as GG.

Barrett, Frank, "In Memory of Laker Airways and Skytrain, the Birth of Budget Travel," *Daily Mail*, February 10, 2012.

Bell, Trudy, "Preventing Sick Spaceships," Online at science.nasa.gov/science-news/science-at-nasa/2007/11may_locad3/.

Billingsley Kerr, Anne, *Fujiyama Trays and Oshibori Towels*, Lady Skywriter USA, 2009.

Blakelee, Sandra, "Real Sandwiches Please Spacemen," *New York Times*, May 21, 1969.

Blufeld, Bob, "Sir Freddie Laker: The Man Who Gave Us Skytrain," *Airliner Classics Magazine*, November 2009.

Branchu, Marc, Air France history article at *corporate.airfrance.com/airfrancelasaga/dossiers/premiere-a-history-of-first-class-travel/*.

Brauer, Jurghen, and Dunne, Paul, "Terrorism, War, and Global Air Traffic," in *Economics of Peace and Security Journal* 7, no. 1 (2012).

Brenneman, Greg, "Right Away and All At Once: How We Saved Continental," *Harvard Business Review*, September–October 1998.

Bryant, Adam, "Continental Is Dropping Lite Service," *New York Times*, April 14, 1995.

Chriss, Nicholas C., "Young Finds Potassium Too Rich in Burps," *Los Angeles Times*, April 23, 1972.

Coning, Connie, "O'Hare's Flight Caterers," *Chicago Tribune*, March 27, 1977.

Dallos, Robert, "Everything's Kosher Up Above," *Pittsburgh Press*, January 12, 1974.

Davis, Captain Thomas M., "Food and Ration Problems of the U.S. Air Force," in *Activities Report of the Quartermaster Food and Container Institute for the Armed Forces*, 1949.

Douganis, Rigas, *Flying Off Course: The Economics of International Airlines* (Routledge UK, 2010).

de Syon, Guillaume, "Is It Really Better to Travel than Arrive?" in *Food for Thought: Essays on Eating and Culture*, ed. Lawrence Rubin (McFarland USA, 2008).

Doyle, Peter, and Bridgewater, Susan, list of awards in *Innovation in Marketing* (Routledge, 2012).

Dunning, Eugene (ed.), *Voices of My Peers* (Clipper Press 1996).

Dupik, Vasily, "The Soviet Space Man's Menu," *Space World*, December 1971.

Eckener, Hugo, "A Sentimental Journey to Egypt," article in *The Zeppelin Reader*, ed. Hedin, Robert.

Ellyn, Martha, "160-Mile Airline Meals Good to the Last Mile," *Washington Post*, July 25, 1941.

Fenner, Robert, "United Continental CEO Smisek Sees 'Significant Progress' in Integration," *Bloomberg News*, December 13, 2010.

Foster, George H. and Weiglan, Peter C., *The Harvey House Cookbook* (Taylor Trade Publishing 2006).

Friedman, Alan, "Competitors Decry EU Approval of $3.7 Billion Subsidy: Air France Bailout Heads for Court," *New York Times*, July 28, 1994.

Fysh, Sir Hudson, *Wings of the World: Story of Qantas* (Angus & Robertson, 1965).

Gallant, Nanette, "Subsistence in Space," on US Army Quartermaster Foundation website at qmfound.com/subsistence_in_space.htm.

Goulding, Matt, "The Fare Up There," *Roads and Kingdoms*, September 13, 2013.

Gregory, Martyn, *Dirty Tricks, British Airways' Secret War against Virgin Atlantic* (Random House, 2010).

Guillaume de Syon, "Is It Really Better to Travel than Arrive?" in *Food for Thought: Essays on Eating and Culture*, ed. Lawrence Rubin (McFarland USA, 2008).

Hagberg, Calvin and Graff, David, "Airborne Microwave Oven Development," in NASA publication #SP-202 "Aerospace Food Technology," undated.

Haggerty, James, *NASA Spinoff*, (Diane Publishing, 1994).

Haines, Lester, "Exploding Curry Menaces 747," *The Register* (London), September 30, 2008.

Hieatt, Constance & Jones, Robin, "A Cuire Chaire Sans Feu," from "Two Anglo-Norman Culinary Collections" (*Speculum* 61/4, 1986).

Howe, Glenn, *Dinner in the Clouds: Great International Airline Recipes*, USA Zeta Press, 1975? (Undated), republished Interurban 1985, now available from Pentrex, Glendale, CA.

Hulse, Jerry, "Travelines: Airline Cuisine? Plane and Fancy," *Los Angeles Times*, January 21, 1962.

International Year Book, (Dodd, Mead, and Co.), 1901.

Johnson, David Asper, Snoopin' Around column, *Argonaut News*, August 10, 1972.

Jones, Peter and Kips, Michael, *Flight Catering*, (Longman, 1995), several editions. Cited in this book's footnotes as *FC*. The page numbers cited in footnotes are usually from the first edition, but the information about special meals cited in chapter 15 is only in the second edition.

Kessler, Jason, "I'm Sick of Stinky Food on Airplanes," *Bon Appetit*, August 13, 2012.

Koren, Jay, *The Company We Kept* (Paladwr Press, 2000).

Lebeau, Mary Dixon, "At 50, The TV Dinner Is Still Cookin'," *Christian Science Monitor*, November 10, 2004.

Lebedev, Lev, "Soviet Space Research History," *Space World*, November 1974.

Levi, Jane "Conviviality in Microgravity," *Moving Worlds: Food, Culture, and Community*, Vol 6, no. 2 (May 2007).

Levi, Jane, "An Extraterrestrial Sandwich: The Perils of Food in Space," *Endeavour* 34, no. 1 March 2010.

Lewis, David, *Airline Executives and Federal Regulation: Case Studies in American Enterprise* (Ohio University Press, 2000).

Learmount, David, "Airline Management by Wire," *Flight Magazine*, October 26, 1985.

Lofting, Christopher, "Focus on Travel" article "Restricted Diets No Longer a Problem for Air Travelers," *Charleston News and Courier*, February 22, 1981.

Makisma, Paul, "Ryanair Moves ahead with Pay Toilet Plan," *Boston Globe*, April 7, 2010.

Martyn, T. J. C., "Air Liner Provides Luxuries of Travel," *New York Times*, July 16, 1929.

McCartney, Scott, "The Fight against Bland Airline Food," *Wall Street Journal*, November 14, 2013.

McCool, Audrey C., *Inflight Catering Management* (New York: John Wiley & Sons, 1995).

McLaughlin, Helen, *Footsteps in the Sky* (Aviation Book Company, 1994). Cited in this book as *FITS*.

Memmott, Mark, "Now He Tells Us: Tang Sucks, Says Apollo 11's Buzz Aldrin," article on NPR's "The Two Way," June 13, 2013

Meyers, Sgt, George M., "What's Cooking?," *Yank Magazine* 4, no. 3, July 1945.

Michaels, Daniel, "Test Flight: Lufthansa Searches For Savor In The Sky," *Wall Street Journal, July 27, 2010.*

Miller, Webb, *I Found No Peace* (New York: Simon & Schuster 1936).

Morton, Hamilla, *How to Walk in High Heels: The Girl's Guide to Everything* (Hachette, 2009).

Mouawad, Jad, "Can Airline Food Be Tasty?" *New York Times*, March 10, 2012.

Mulder, Rob and Ott, Gunther, *Focke-Wulf Condor with Danish Airlines in War and Peace* (European Airlines Publishing, 2013).

Nicas, Jack, "The Long, Slow Death of the First Class Seat," *Wall Street Journal*, July 19, 2012.

Perry, Maureen J., *Oral History Program interview transcription, Subject Sam John Toaramina*, (Louis A. Turpen Aviation Museum 1999), cited throughout as *Toaramina*.

Petersen, Barbara Sturken, *Rapid Descent: Deregulation and the Shakeout in the Airlines* (New York: Simon & Schuster, 1994).

Pringle, John, "Painful Progress in the Air," *Sydney Morning Herald*, February 27, 1978.

Reinhold, Robert, "Dining a la Carte in the Space Shuttle, with a Choice of Entrees," *New York Times*, January 16, 1985.

Robinson, Douglas, *The Zeppelin in Combat* (Schiffer, 1994).

Robinson, Douglas H., *LZ 129 "Hindenburg,"* Famous Aircraft Series (Dallas, TX: Morgan Books, 1964).

Roll, Martin, "Market analysis of Singapore Airlines," dated March 2014 at www .martinroll.com/resources/articles/asia/singapore-airlines-an-excellent-asian-brand/.

Rolt, T. L. C, "The Aeronauts, A History of Ballooning 1783–1903" (Longman 1966).

Rubin, Lawrence J., ed., *Food For Thought: Essays in Eating and Culture* (McFarland, 2008).

Rust, Daniel, *Flying Across America* (University of Oklahoma Press, 2009).

Said-Moorhouse, Lauren, CNN World Business Traveler, 20 September 2012.

Seim, August, "The Rigger Tells a Tale," in *The Zeppelin Reader*, ed. Hedin, Robert (University of Iowa Press, 1998).

Seth, Rabindra, *Tourism in India: An Overview, Vol. 1* (Gyan Press, 2005).

Shane 2K, "Breaking Fast While On The Plane," online at peaceinislam.com/ shane2k/131/.

Smauch, Magnus, *EU Law on State Aid to Airlines: Law, Economics, and Policy* (Lexxion, 2012).

Smith, Andrew F., *Eating History* (Columbia University Press, 2013).

Smith, Evan, "Gordon Bethune interview," *Texas Monthly*, December 2004.

Snodgrass, Mary Ellen, *Encyclopedia of Kitchen History* (Routledge, 2005).

Sondheim, Steven and Rodgers, Richard, Original score to "Do I Hear A Waltz?" (Sony Broadway, originally published 1964).

Speas, R. Dixon, *Airline Operations* (American Aviation Publications, 1948).

Spooner, Stanley, Editorial Comment, *Flight Magazine*, December 6, 1929.

Staniland, Martin, *Government Birds: Air Transport and the State in Western Europe* (Lanham, MD: Rowman & Littlefield, 2003).

Starmer-Smith, Charles, "How to Complain to an Airline," *Daily Telegraph*, January 28, 2009.

Taylor, Frank J., *High Horizons: Daredevil Flying Postmen to Modern Magic Carpet* (McGraw-Hill USA, 1962). Cited in this book as *HH*.

Tran, Mark, "The Airline Industry Slump," *Guardian*, September 20, 2001.

Turen, Richard, "A Simple Explanation of Business Class," *Travel Weekly*, February 24, 2014.

Turner, Grace, "Picking a Meal Out of the Air," *Los Angeles Times*, November 13, 1938.

Unattributed, *Beating the Odds: A History of Western Airlines*, company publication, 1976.

Unattributed article, "Aboard the First Flights," *Life Magazine*, July 26, 1968.

Unattributed article, "Astronauts Assert Their Food Is Too Plentiful and Too Sweet," *New York Times*, October 14, 1968.

Unattributed article, "Cabin Comforts," *Flight Magazine*, September 13, 1995.

Unattributed article, "The DC-3," *Century Of Flight*, www.century-of-flight.net.

Unattributed article, "Freeze-drying adds value to high-quality products," *European Food Information Council* website at eufic.org, July 2009.

Unattributed article, "Space Food Hall of Fame," Stennis Space Center website at http://education.ssc.nasa.gov/fft_halloffame.asp.

Unattributed article, "No Place for Gourmets," *New York Times*, October 13, 1968.

Unattributed article, "Plane Food," *Delicious Magazine*, undated, http://www.deliciousmagazine.co.uk/articles/plane-food.

Unattributed AP News story, "Airline Pays Fine for Innuendo in Sandwich War," noted in the *Calgary Herald*, May 7, 1958.

Unattributed AP News story, "Food Kosher?" *Canberra Times*, August 7, 1982.

Unattributed AP News story, "Way Sought to Grow Food From Leftovers," *Washington Post*, January 29, 1963.

Unattributed business case study, "Building An Airline Through Brand Values: A Virgin Atlantic Case Study," online at businesscasestudies.co.uk/virgin-atlantic.

Unattributed news story, "After Italian Feast, Italian Astronaut Skips Spaghetti," *Digital Journal* 31, October 2007. Online at digitaljournal.com/article/244462.

Unattributed news story, "Airlines Early Woes with Food Described," *New York Times*, April 26, 1939.

Unattributed news story, "Astronauts Drink Recycled Urine, and Celebrate," *SPACE.com*, May 20, 2009.

Unattributed news story, "Airlines Experiment with Selling Food," *Gainesville Sun*, January 19, 2003.

Unattributed news story, "Astronaut's Breakfast," *Newsweek*, April 15, 1963.

Unattributed news story, "Freddie Laker's Skytrain: A Good Deal?," *The Hour* (Norwalk, CT), March 9, 1978.

Unattributed news story, "Glenn Had Space Snack by Tube; Food Squeezed Via Helmet Hole," *New York Times*, February 21, 1962.

Unattributed news story, "The Log of Logan Airport," *Christian Science Monitor*, September 8, 1948.

Unattributed news story, "London's Amazing Express Aeroplane Liners a Hundred Miles an Hour—Modern Fulfillment of Dreams of Jules Verne's," *Reuters Aeronautical News*, October 20, 1923.

Unattributed news story, "National Adds Gourmet Touch to Flight Meal," *Palm Beach Daily News*, April 27, 1963.

Unattributed news story, "Out in Space Table Manners Up for Grabs," *Los Angeles Times*, December 21, 1964.

Unattributed news story, "Paris-London Airway Has First Aerial Cafe," *Daily Record* (Morris County, NJ), October 2, 1925.

Unattributed story, "Tasty Meals Served High in the Sky Await Travelers," *Memphis Commercial Appeal*, October 1, 1950.

Unattributed news story, "Tight Planning Will Be Needed for Serving Meals on Supersonic Flights," *Chronicle-Telegram* (Elyria, OH). April 24, 1965.

Unattributed news story, "Whirlpool Announces Lunar Fare: Local Industry Prepared Food for Apollo 11," *News-Palladium* (Benton Harbor, MI), June 30, 1969.

Unattributed "Regulation News" article, *Flight Magazine*, December 28, 1951.

Van Weezepoel, Paul, *Dutch Aviation History*, www.dutch-aviation.nl.

Vissering, Harry, *Zeppelin: The Story of a Great Achievement* (Chicago: Wells & Co., 1920).

Waller, Angela, *Before There Were Trolley Dollies* (Dales Books, 2011).

Woods et al., "Effect of Background Noise on Food Perception," *Journal of Food Quality and Preference* 22 (2011).

Ziemba, Stanley, "United Decides to Sell Its Flight Kitchens," *Chicago Tribune*, 18 February 1993.

Index

About the Author

Richard Foss has been writing about food and drink since 1986, when he became the restaurant reviewer for the *Los Angeles Reader Newspaper*. Since then he has written for more than twenty different publications, both journalistic and academic, authored a book on the history of rum, and written scholarly articles for the *Encyclopedia of World Food Cultures* and the *Oxford Companion to Sweets*. He is currently on the board of the Culinary Historians of Southern California and is the California Curator for the Museum of the American Cocktail and the SoFAB Institute.